CONFRONTING LEVIATHAN

MARGARET HALL
TOM YOUNG

Confronting Leviathan

Mozambique since Independence

OHIO UNIVERSITY PRESS
ATHENS, OHIO

Published in the United States of America by
Ohio University Press,
Scott Quadrangle,
Athens, Ohio 45701
© 1997 by Margaret Hall and Tom Young
Printed in India by Thomson Press (India) Ltd.

Library of Congress Cataloging-in-Publication Data

Hall, Margaret.
    Confronting Leviathan : Mozambique since independence / Margaret
    Hall,0 Tom Young .
        p.   cm.
    Includes bibliographical references and index.
    ISBN 0-8214-1190-X (cloth : alk. paper). — ISBN 0-8214-1191-8
(pbk. : alk. paper)
    1. Mozambique — Politics and government — 1975- 2. Socialism-
-Mozambique—History—20th century. I. Young, Tom. — II. Title
DT3389.H35   1997
968.905—dc21   96-51952
                                                      CIP

PREFACE AND ACKNOWLEDGEMENTS

This book seeks to provide an interpretation of the main developments in Mozambique from independence till about 1994. Much remains unknown about that period and we have often had to rely on inadequate documentation. Extensive research remains to be done, although a new generation of active young scholars is now engaged in doing it.

In co-authored volumes it is often difficult to disentangle who contributed what. Broadly, Margaret Hall took responsibility for the chapters on the transition to independence and Renamo. Tom Young dealt with the internal politics and the political economy. The analysis of the regional and international dimensions is a joint effort. The theoretical perspectives of the final chapter are largely the work of Tom Young.

In the early stages the research assistance of Anthony Callan was invaluable. The School of Oriental and African Studies (SOAS) assisted financially and in other ways. Many people helped with materials: Alex Vines, Ken Wilson, James Sidaway. From these as well as others we learnt much about Mozambique: Americo Xavier, Agostinho Zacarias, Mateus Katupha, Polly Gaster, Lan White. Some others who provided useful information or insights would wish to remain anonymous.

A one-year leave of absence from the Research and Analysis Department of the Foreign and Commonwealth Office (FCO) during 1991 enabled Margaret Hall to draft much of her contribution. However, the results in no way reflect the position of the FCO, although its Library gave us permission to use the maps included in this book. Throughout the period of writing Tom Young was a member of the Department of Political Studies at SOAS. Two heads of that Department (Bob Taylor and David Taylor) proved indulgent in the best academic sense. The Departmental Secretary, Mrs Catherine Guest, selflessly provided assistance at crucial moments. A number of students – Anthony Callan, Donald Wilson and Eric Morier-Genoud – kept asking hard questions about Mozambique. The perspectives that inform chapter 9 were aired at departmental seminars as well as seminars or talks in Edinburgh (Centre for African Studies) and Amsterdam (Eduardo Mondlane Foundation). We would also like to note that, while patience is perhaps one of the first arts a publisher must master, Christopher Hurst and Michael Dwyer have been almost saint-like in the face of endless procrastinations and excuses. For that we are grateful.

Finally, because much of the modern history of Mozambique and southern Africa generally remains extremely controversial, it should perhaps be emphasised that the interpretation of events offered here is entirely our own, and is likely to be contested by many of those from whom we have learnt most.

London, January 1997   MARGARET HALL
                                                 TOM YOUNG

CONTENTS

MAPS

TABLES

ABBREVIATIONS

AAM	Associacão Académica de Moçambique
ANC	African National Congress
BOSS	Bureau of State Security (South Africa)
CAIL	Lower Limpopo Complex
CEA	Centro de Estudos Africanos
CIA	Central Intelligence Agency (USA)
CIO	Central Intelligence Organisation (Rhodesia)
CMEA	Council for Mutual Economic Assistance
CNP	Commissão Nacional do Plano/National Planning Commission
CONCP	Conferência das Organizações Nacionalistas das Colónias Portugueses
COREMO	Comité Revolucionário de Moçambique
CSU	Christian Socialist Union (West Germany)
DGS	Direcção Geral de Segurança
DMI	Department of Military Intelligence (South Africa)
FAM	Forças Armadas de Moçambique/Mozambique Armed Forces
FICO	Frente Independente de Convergência Ocidental
FPLM	Forças Populares de Libertação de Moçambique
Frelimo	Frente de Libertação de Moçambique/Mozambique Liberation Front
FUMO	Frente Unida de Moçambique
GDP	Gross domestic product
GDs	Grupos Dinamizadores
GEs	Grupos Especiais
GEPs	Grupos Especiais Pára-quedistas
GNP	Gross national product
GUMO	Grupo Unido de Moçambique
IMF	International Monetary Fund
JSN	Junta of National Salvation (Portugal)
JVC	Joint Verification Committee
MANU	Mozambique African National Union
MFA	Movimento das Forças Armadas
MIO	Mozambique Information Office

MNR	Mozambique National Resistance
MONAMO	Movimento Nacionalista de Moçambique
NATO	North Atlantic Treaty Organisation
NESAM	Nucleus of Mozambican Secondary Students
NGO	Non-governmental organisation
OAU	Organisation of African Unity
OECD	Organisation for Economic Cooperation and Development
OJM	Organização da Juventude Moçambicana/Organisation of Mozambican Youth
OMM	Organização das Mulheres Moçambicanas/Organisation of Mozambican Women
ONUMOZ	United Nations Operation in Mozambique
PAIGC	Partido Africano da Independência da Guiné e Cabo Verde
PCN	National Coalition Party
PIDE	Polícia Internacional e de Defesa do Estado
PPI	Plano Prospectivo Indicativo
PRE	Programme of Economic Rehabilitation
Renamo	Resistência Nacional Moçambicana
SAAVM	Sociedade Agrícola Algodoeira Voluntária dos Africanos de Moçambique
SADCC	Southern African Development Coordination Conference
SADF	South African Defence Forces
SAPs	Structural adjustment programmes
SAS	Special Air Service
SNASP	National Security Service
SSC	State Security Council (South Africa)
TANU	Tanganyika African National Union
TPDF	Tanzanian People's Defence Force
UDENAMO	National Democratic Union of Mozambique
UN	United Nations
UNAMI	National Union for Mozambican Independence
UNEMO	União Nacional dos Estudantes de Moçambique
ZANLA	Zimbabwe National Liberation Army
ZANU	Zimbabwe African National Union
ZNA	Zimbabwe National Army

1

THE CLOSE OF PORTUGUESE RULE

'In every Mozambican military base in Cabo Delgado, one comes across a huge heap of earth shaped in the form of Mozambique with the provinces and any other prominent features marked. The militants are constantly given lectures by the commanders using these earthern maps as visual aids so that the militant realises that he is fighting for the liberation of the whole of Mozambique up to the Limpopo and not just for Cabo Delgado.' [...]
There are quite a few who would be petty-bourgeois but who, instead, have merged with the people's struggle and are doing a lot to give the people a better vision concerning the struggle. Commander Notre, for instance, was leading his men in an exemplary way. We stayed in the camp he was commanding for more than 3 weeks. He never missed any opportunity to politicise the masses. A powerful orator, he would daily explain any phenomenon so that it linked up with the essence of liberation. It is Christmas Day, for instance, 1968. There is no church-service....Instead we have a military parade and a flag-raising ceremony'.[1]

Only a third as wide as it is long at the broadest point along its northern river boundary with Tanzania (following the river Rovuma), Mozambique is bordered by the Indian Ocean to the east and enclosed inland by Zambia, Malawi, Zimbabwe and, in the south, Swaziland and South Africa. Almost half the country is less than 200 metres above sea level, and it is crossed by some fifty rivers, the largest being the Zambezi, the Limpopo and the Save. These three great rivers divide the country laterally into three broad cultural and linguistic 'bands'. To the north of the Zambezi live matrilineal groups who have historic links with the Islamic influences of the East African coast. A diverse cultural border zone along the Zambezi valley itself divides the north from the patrilineal

[1] Y.T. Museveni, 'Fanon's Theory on Violence: its Verification in Liberated Mozambique' in N.M. Shamuyarira, (ed.), *Essays on the Liberation of Southern Africa*, University of Dar es Salaam Studies in Political Science, no. 3, 1972.

Shona-speakers (Manyika, Ndau, Teve), who are akin to the majority in neighbouring Zimbabwe. Below the Save river the Thonga and related peoples form part of a southern cultural world, linked to the Swazi and the peoples of South Africa.

From the arrival of the Portuguese navigator Vasco da Gama in 1498 till the late nineteenth century, the Portuguese presence was mainly limited to forts and trading posts along the coast or by the Zambezi river. The Portuguese took over Muslim trading posts established in the fifteenth century at Sena and Tete to deal with the gold-producing kingdom of the Monomotapa, centred on what is now Zimbabwe, and also installed themselves at Sofala. Settlement of the Zambezi area proceeded during the seventeenth century through a system of granting land concessions (*prazos*) to Portuguese subjects, who ran them as feudal landlords under the Portuguese Crown. Mozambique was administered by the Governor-General of Goa (India) until 1752, and throughout the age of sail communication (and therefore settlement) was easier to reach from Goa than from distant Portugal. Over time the *prazos* developed into virtually independent kingdoms sustained by slave armies, with ruling families of mixed Afro-Goan-Portuguese descent and thoroughly Africanised culture.[2]

In the middle decades of the nineteenth century, however, the *de facto* power over the entire area of what is now Mozambique south of the Zambezi was not the Portuguese, but rather the regiments of Soshangane, an Nguni warlord. Soshangane's Gaza empire, a product of the Nguni expansion northwards from Natal, was initially centred on the middle Save and grew in strength from the 1830s onwards. Other Bantu peoples were incorporated into a Zulu-type kingdom based on age regiments, whose authority extended a little to the south of the Limpopo. Existing Portuguese settlements were reduced to a position of tribute-paying vassalage. But assimilation operated fully only at the heart of the empire, which after Soshangane's death in 1856 was weakened by internal dissension. Imperfectly incorporated and subject peoples later broke away. In 1889 Gungunyana, the last Gaza king, also the last great independent Bantu monarch in southern Africa, shifted his capital to a site near the Limpopo. In 1895, under pressure from European competitors to show effective occupation of the land they claimed, the Portuguese found a pretext for war.[3]

Gungunyana, who died in 1906 in exile in the Azores, remained

---

[2] On the *prazos* see M.D.D. Newitt, *Portuguese Settlement on the Zambesi*, London, 1973.

[3] J.D. Omer-Cooper, *The Zulu Aftermath*, Harlow, 1966, pp. 57-61.

a powerful symbol of resistance in the south, particularly in Gaza province, the area from which many of the national leadership of the Mozambique Liberation Front (Frelimo) arose in the 1960s. (A grandfather of Samora Machel, independent Mozambique's first President, was one of the commanders of Gungunyana's army. Frelimo's first president, Eduardo Mondlane, was tightlipped about Gungunyana: his own people, the Chepe of Inhambane, suffered at his hands.) Although white cavalry were to the forefront in the final battle in the conquest of Gaza, the Portuguese increasingly relied on African allies who thereby profited from the opportunity to loot, and wreak revenge on, traditional enemies; this prolonged the bitterness of these campaigns and resistance to them.[4] The Gaza wars were over by 1887, but elsewhere Portuguese 'pacification' of the interior was long and bloody, entailing almost annual military campaigns from 1894 onwards. Other figures and centres of resistance have local resonance elsewhere, and resistance continued into the twentieth century, most seriously with the Barue revolt of 1917, coordinated by spirit mediums, which involved a wide coalition of forces centred on the Zambezi valley.[5]

The Portuguese colonial order

Once a degree of military control was established in an area, administrative functions were granted to concession companies. The Companhia de Moçambique (1891) covered the area of present-day Manica and Sofala provinces and a small part of northern Gaza, while the Companhia do Nyassa (1891) covered Niassa and Cabo Delgado. Other companies, of which the most important was the Companhia da Zambézia (1892), were granted rights over extensive areas of Zambézia and Tete. Only the Nampula area and most of the (now) southernmost provinces of Gaza, Inhambane and Maputo were retained within the direct administration of the colonial state. Portugal revoked the northernmost concessions in 1929, but the last of these charters south of the Zambezi did not lapse till 1941. Only subsequently was Mozambique brought under a single unified system of administration. A native forced labour system (*chibalo*) then operated on the Portuguese-run plantations, as well as in urban areas and for public works, and was avoidable

---

[4] R. Pélissier, 'Angola, Mozambique. Des guerres interminables et leurs facteurs internes', *Hérodote*, 46 (1987), pp. 83-107.

[5] See A. Isaacman, *The Tradition of Resistance in Mozambique: anti-colonial activity in the Zambesi Valley, 1850-1921*, London, 1976. For the earlier history of Mozambique see M. Newitt, *A History of Mozambique*, London, 1995.

only by attaining *assimilado* status, or by labour migration outside the colony.[6] Agricultural production on Portuguese-run plantations was subject to heavy bureaucratic direction from the 1930s onwards. Each of the major export crops was administered by an export board, while quotas guaranteed a share of the market in Portugal for colonial producers.[7] Over vast areas of the north, where settlers were few and small-scale peasant production predominated, a harsh regime of forced cotton cultivation was in operation from 1938 till 1961.[8] Within four years of its introduction, 700,000 peasants were compelled to grow cotton for export to Portugal.

However, most of the territory's revenue continued to derive from the export of labour and transit fees. Export of labour from southern Mozambique to the gold and diamond mines of the Rand started in the nineteenth century. In a series of contracts called the Mozambique Conventions, begun in 1875 and renewed till 1964, South Africa paid part of the wages of hired labour in the mines directly in gold to the Portuguese authorities. By 1897 more than half of the 180,000 workers on the Rand came from Mozambique, and from the beginning of the new century the number of Mozambicans who went to work in South Africa each year rose to 100,000-150,000. Working a contract on the Johannesburg mines became part and parcel of the household economy and the male culture for the southern districts – so much so that a period on the mines became both a necessary form of initiation into manhood, and a means of accumulating cash for *lobola*, (bridewealth payments).[9] But Mozambique also supplied labour to plantations in Tanganyika and Nyasaland, and in significant numbers to Southern Rhodesia. The rest of the country's income mostly derived from its railways and harbours. Under the Mozambique Conventions, South Africa agreed to send part of its railway traffic through Lourenço Marques, which also served Rhodesia. Rhodesian traffic travelled via the shortest route, to the port of Beira at the mouth of the Pungue river, although Beira (which required

---

[6] Under a law of 1927, an African could apply for *assimilado* status if he spoke Portuguese, could give references to his good character, and was regularly and gainfully employed.

[7] Malyn Newitt, *Portugal in Africa*, London, 1981, pp. 194-5.

[8] See Isaacman, 'Coercion, Paternalism and the Labour Process: The Mozambican Cotton Regime 1938-1961', *Journal of Southern African Studies*, 18, 3 (1992), pp. 487-526. See also M. Anne Pitcher, *Politics in the Portuguese Empire: The State, Industry and Cotton, 1926-1974*, Oxford, 1993.

[9] See Ruth First, *The Mozambican Miner: A study in the export of labour*, Maputo: Centro de Estudos Africanos, 1987.

constant dredging) was a poor rival to the natural harbour of Lourenço Marques. This economic structure shaped the colony's rail system: the Lourenço Marques/Transvaal rail link opened in 1895; that between Beira and Southern Rhodesia in 1897; and work on the Beira/Nysaland line began in 1888, but was not completed till 1922. By 1963 Mozambique had six separate railway systems, each operating inland from a coastal port.[10]

However violent and extractive the nature of Portuguese colonialism, Portugal's 'civilising mission' in Africa was a key ideological component of the Salazar dictatorship of 1932-68. Indeed, it can be argued that the fragility of the dictatorship's own political legitimacy, rather than economic weakness, underpinned the tenacity of its fight to retain its African empire against the forces of nationalism.[11] 'Lusotropicalism', the idea that Portugal was uniquely capable of making the races work together, entered official Portuguese propaganda late in the day in response to the threat of African nationalism.[12] Essentially a myth to sustain Portuguese self-esteem, this ideology of non-racial cultural assimilation nonetheless discouraged some of the cruder forms of white racism being imported from neighbouring Rhodesia and South Africa, which might otherwise have been expected to affect Mozambican urban society.[13] However, it did not prevent the development of a tacit system of job reservation for whites in minor government services in the cities and at the lowest levels of management.[14] Indeed, it has been suggested that the situation was worse here than in other Portuguese African colonies, so that racial antagonism and a sense of racial humiliation found greater expression in Mozambican literature than elsewhere, even in Angola.[15]

The assumption of African cultural inferiority in Mozambique was indeed explicit and deeply pervasive. Even the repeal in 1961 of the native statute of 1954, which led the regime to claim that

[10] C.F. Spence, *Moçambique*, Cape Town, 1963.

[11] Pitcher, *Politics,* pp. 278-9.

[12] On Lusotropicalism see Newitt, *Portugal in Africa*, pp. 183-4.

[13] Jeanne Penvenne, 'The Unmaking of an African Petite Bourgeoisie: Lourenço Marques, Mozambique', Mozambique Working Paper no. 57, African Studies Center, Boston University, 1982.

[14] Keith Middlemass, 'Twentieth Century White Society in Mozambique', *Tarikh,* 6, 2 (special edition on 'White Society in Africa') published for the Historical Society of Nigeria.

[15] R.G. Hamilton, *Voices from an Empire*, Minneapolis, 1975. See also David Birmingham, *Frontline Nationalism in Angola and Mozambique*, London, 1992, pp. 16-18, 20-2, and P. Chabal (ed.), *The Postcolonial Literature of Lusophone Africa*, London, 1996.

all the inhabitants of the empire now enjoyed equal status, was not quite what it seemed. Previously Africans in Angola and Mozambique who did not apply and qualify for classification as *civilizados* – as they were officially known until 1961 – were considered *indígenas*, part of a community ruled by a chief and subject in the first instance to African customary law. However, the Portuguese were in reality simply returning to the situation which had existed in the nineteenth century, and the population continued to be divided into two groups – those living under customary law and those subject to Portuguese civil law. The difference was that instead of being automatically subject to customary law until the basis for assimilation had been acquired, Africans could freely choose to adopt civil law, without going through the elaborate process of petitioning and being tested, and the decision was treated as irrevocable and binding on their descendants.[16] More significant was the removal of the obligation on the previously 'non-civilised' Africans to work for Europeans, which in Mozambique had enabled the authorities to employ forced labour on a massive scale.[17]

These assumptions and practices did much to shape the racial and status features of colonial society. The *civilizados* comprised the Portuguese and other Europeans, *mestiços*, Indians and Africans 'assimilated' to Portuguese culture. Of Mozambique's total population of some 8,234,000 at the 1970 census, the 220,000 whites, mestiços, Chinese and Indians constituted the large majority of the territory's educated, technical, and managerial cadres (together with those assimilated blacks who in 1965 were estimated to have numbered a bare 300,000). Of the 158,000 Europeans, all but 5,000 were Portuguese. Nearly three-quarters of them were concentrated in the main cities and urban centres of more than 2,000 people, especially Lourenço Marques (38%) and Beira (10.5%). About 60,000 lived dispersed in the rural areas as administrators, technicians and farmers.[18]

The Portuguese administrative network was in principle formidably centralised, with Lisbon's authority bureaucratically channelled down to the individual villager.[19] If an area contained a

---

[16] Gervase Clarence-Smith, *The Third Portuguese Empire ,1825-1975: A study in economic imperialism*, Manchester, 1985, pp. 214-15.

[17] Tom Gallagher, *Portugal: A twentieth century interpretation*, Manchester, 1983, p. 174.

[18] A. Rita-Ferreira, 'Moçambique post-25 de abril. Causas do êxodo da população de origem europeia e asiática', *Moçambique. Cultura e história de um país*, papers of the 5th seminar of African culture, Centre of African Studies, Institute of Anthropology, Coimbra University, 1988, pp. 121-69.

[19] James Duffy, *Portuguese Africa*, Cambridge, MA, 1959, p. 288.

number of *assimilados* or Portuguese colonists the territorial unit was the *concelho*, headed by an administrator who corresponded to the municipal magistrate in Portugal, whereas in largely African areas the primary unit was the *circunscrição* ('circumscription'). The intention was that as the task of 'civilising' the African people went forward, the number of *concelhos*, which implied a limited degree of local self-government, would increase. The line of authority ran down from Governor-General to the district governor (administrator of the *circunscrição*), to the administrator of its several subdivisions (*postos*). After the adoption of the Organic Law of 1963, many former *circunscrições* were elevated to concelhos with the eventual aim of replacing all with *concelhos*.[20] Yet despite the longevity of the Portuguese presence in Mozambique, modern colonial rule was not imposed till the 1940s. Moreover, though a highly centralised structure on paper, it almost certainly functioned only at the lower levels because officials were able to divert some tax revenue into their own pockets.

As the anti-colonial war intensified, the higher ranks of the administration gradually became militarised, so that by the late 1960s about half the district governors were military officers. The *administradores* were mainly products of the Instituto Superior de Estudos Ultramarinos in Lisbon. Lower ranks were often recruited locally, from the ranks of the '*civilizados*';[21] although in the later stages of the guerrilla war large numbers of civil servants were said to have been brought in on short-term contracts from Portugal itself to act as *chefes do posto*. Various African officials were integrated into the administrative hierarchy in auxiliary roles as interpreters, *sipaios* (police), and *régulos* (chiefs). Chiefs who might be traditional leaders or simply Portuguese appointees with no local legitimacy were subordinate to the administrator or *chefe do posto*. They were held directly responsible for everything which went on in their areas, including the collection of taxes, the provision of labour for the roads and elsewhere, and above all for ensuring the Portuguese presence.[22] The *régulos* presided over *regulados*, and provided the link between the local colonial administration and 'native political authority'. Within the *regulado* groups of villages were headed by their own chiefs. Once invested, *régulos* had the right to form defence militias, organised locally with simple arms,

---

[20] Norman A. Bailey, 'Government and Administration' in D.M. Abshire and M.A. Samuels (eds), *Portuguese Africa: A handbook*, London, 1969, pp. 133-45.

[21] Lord Hailey, *An African Survey*, Oxford, 1957, p. 357.

[22] James Duffy, *Portuguese Africa*, pp. 287-8.

but receiving some supplementary weaponry from the administration.

Beyond the formal administrative structures the Catholic church played an important role in the colonial order. Under the terms of the Concordat and Missionary Agreements of 1940 and 1941 the Roman Catholic Church was officially recognised as a 'civilising agency' in Africa, and its activities – especially in the sphere of education – were privileged by the Portuguese state. Diocesan bishops, for example, were officially on a par with district governors both in status and salary.[23] But Protestant mission schools – the main ones run by the Swiss, American Methodists and Anglicans had also been active in Mozambique since the late nineteenth century, particularly in the southern provinces. Though more or less tolerated by the authorities, they were regarded with considerable suspicion not merely for their Protestantism but for their leanings towards anthropology and the encouragement of literacy in Mozambican languages – regarded as subversive of the 'nationalising' project in which the Portuguese language and assimilation to Portuguese culture were central.[24] Indeed, Protestant missions were not without influence on the development of nationalist politics, especially the important Presbyterian Church of Switzerland active in the south. Of figures later prominent in Frelimo, Eduardo Mondlane, Daniel Mbanze and Graça Simbine were all educated at the mission of Cambine, and Mondlane received his university education through the good offices of the Presbyterian Church.

The Portuguese of course believed their very presence to be a 'civilising' influence. A Christian agrarian society was to be constructed through the settlement of Portuguese peasants in colonisation schemes, in some of which Africans would also participate. African agricultural colonies under the direction of Portuguese technical and administrative cadres would equally create conditions favourable for economic and spiritual assimilation. Thus in 1940 the Colonial Ministry devised plans for African villages jointly managed by the colonial administration and the Catholic Church; although these never progressed beyond the drawing board, mixed schemes and some African *colonatos* did get under way in the 1950s.[25]

---

[23] Art. 19 of the Missionary Statute Decree-Law no. 31, 207, 5 April 1941 (a law of the Portuguese Republic implementing the Agreement with the Vatican of the previous year).

[24] Judith Marshall, *Literacy, State Formation and People's Power*, Cape Town, 1990, p. 58.

[25] James Duffy, *Portuguese Africa*, pp. 308-9.

Most *colonatos* – or Government-sponsored settlements on state-owned land – were, however, populated by Portuguese immigrants and by 1974 they constituted about half Mozambique's commercial farms. Lisbon offered choice tracts of land, cash bonuses, long-term, low-interest credit, and substantial technical assistance to settlers. Colonial officials promoted in particular the Limpopo Valley Scheme in the south, and the 'white highland' area of Manica. The arrival of these settlers resulted in the expropriation of large areas of land, especially in the provinces of Gaza, Manica and Sofala, Lourenço Marques and Zambézia.[26] A large part of the investment in both the first and second Development Plans, which covered the years 1953-8 and 1959-64 respectively, was set aside for such white development schemes; in the second no less than 84% of all agricultural investment in Mozambique was linked to the *colonatos*.[27]

The immobilism of the Salazar years gave way after the dictator's incapacitation by a stroke in 1968 to a number of reforms, some significant and some less so. His successor, Marcello Caetano, made a serious attempt to delink the metropolitan economy from that of the African colonies – previously centrally directed as a single unit. In Mozambique's case, this involved the imposition of import substitution, conversion of territorial debts to a National Debt and the setting up of financial institutions ready to fulfil the functions of a Reserve Bank.[28] But the economy also experienced rapid growth, attaining a 10% annual increase in gross national product (GNP) during the period 1971-3.[29] This was in part directly stimulated by the war, and its related infrastructural expenditure on tarred roads, airfields, hospitals and the programme of fortified villages (*aldeamentos*), which was often counted as part of the civilian rather than the military budget. The country was also seriously opened up for the first time to external investment, by far the largest slice of which came from South Africa. Portugal itself gave a major injection of capital with the completion of the massive Cahora Bassa hydro-electric scheme in Tete province, which apart from selling electricity to South Africa was designed to form part of an accelerated regional development project: indeed, Portuguese

[26] See Irene S. van Dongen, 'Agriculture and other primary production' in D.M. Abshire and M.A. Samuels (eds), *Portuguese Africa*, pp. 253-93.

[27] Newitt, *Portugal in Africa*, pp. 194-6.

[28] Keith Middlemass, 'Mozambique: Two years of independence', Proceedings of a Seminar on Mozambique, University of Edinburgh, 1-2 December 1978, pp. 100-21.

[29] Keith Middlemass, 'Twentieth Century White Society in Mozambique'.

expenditure in Mozambique in the early 1970s has been described as perhaps the largest proportionate injection of capital ever undertaken by a colonial power.[30] By 1975 Mozambique ranked eighth among the most industrialised countries in Africa, but only 2% of the economically active population were engaged in manufacturing, and 80% of manufactures were consumer goods aimed at the local *colon* market.[31]

Significant efforts were also made to meet black grievances with a crash education programme which brought the numbers receiving schooling to 800,000, so that in 1973 some 40% of Mozambique's school-age population was receiving primary education of some sort. There were similar improvements in health facilities.[32] Black enrolment in the *lycées* (traditionally a white preserve) grew from 2,800 in 1960 to 7,400 in 1970, while in the technical secondary schools it went from 3,200 to 27,000 over the same period: yet on the eve of independence in 1975, the University had only a dozen blacks out of a total student membership of 3,000.[33] Under Caetano's constitutional reforms promulgated in December 1972 both Mozambique and Angola – henceforth to be known as 'states' and not provinces – gained a greater degree of autonomy. While Lisbon controlled defence and foreign affairs, each 'state' was to determine local legislation, budget and taxes. Government councils were created under the chairmanship of the Governor-General, who was also a member of the Cabinet in Portugal. Angola and Mozambique each gained an extra twenty seats in the National Assembly in Lisbon. Finally, the legislative council was enlarged to comprise thirty-two directly elected members, with a further twenty-one elected by interest groups.

Since, as part of this limited devolution of power to the African colonies, voting qualifications had been drastically lowered to admit anyone who could read or speak simple Portuguese, more than 1 million in Mozambique could have registered for the 1973 legislative election.[34] In practice only 111,559 did so, and only a quarter

---

[30] Keith Middlemass, 'Independent Mozambique and Its Regional Policy' in J. Seiler (ed.), *Southern Africa since the Portuguese*, Boulder, CO, 1980, pp. 213-33. See also Middlemass' important study, *Cabora Bassa: Politics and Engineering in Southern Africa*, London, 1975.

[31] Luis de Brito, 'Le Frelimo et la Construction de l'Etat National au Mozambique', Ph.D. thesis, Université de Paris VIII, 1991, pp. 31-2.

[32] Gervase Clarence-Smith, *The Third Portuguese empire, 1825-1975*, pp. 217-18.

[33] De Brito, 'Le Frelimo', pp. 50-1.

[34] Middlemass, 'Twentieth Century White Society in Mozambique'. Others estimated the number of eligible voters at about 500,000. *Financial Times*, 5 April 1973.

of those actually voting in the election were estimated to have been black.[35] But no opposition candidates stood, and although the Legislative Assembly's powers had been increased somewhat *vis-à-vis* the Governor-General, it was all too little and too late. (However, to keep voter apathy in perspective, only about 18 per cent of Portugal's 9.5 million people were eligible to vote in the metropolitan Assembly's last elections in October 1969, and since there was an abstention rate of around 60 per cent, only 10 per cent of the population went anywhere near the voting booths.[36]) There was no local excitement over the multiracial composition of this largely symbolic body.[37]

Frelimo: armed struggle and internal crisis

The opposition to colonialism drew on both political and ideological discontent among an educated stratum of Africans and on the grievances of the peasantry, although, as elsewhere in the Portuguese-speaking world, the development of nationalist politics was inhibited by the gulf between these two groups as much as by official repression. Certainly the early nationalists from the Portuguese colonies found sympathisers among the dissident democrats both in the colonies and in Lisbon.[38] The organisations formed in exile, in Paris and in Lisbon (for example, the Movimento Anti-colonial formed by Marcelino dos Santos in Paris in 1957, and the Casa dos Estudentes do Império) tended to be umbrella associations of lusophone African students abroad. The União Nacional dos Estudentes de Moçambique (UNEMO), created in 1961 by Mozambican students who had fled from Portugal to France, was later to become the student wing of Frelimo. NESAM – the Nucleus of Mozambican Secondary Students – established in Mozambique by Eduardo Mondlane on his return from South Africa in 1949, counted among its prominent members other future Frelimo leaders including Armando Guebuza, Joaquim Chissano, Marianho Matsinha and Pascoal Mocumbi.[39]

Rural discontent was allowed no legal form of expression. The massacre at Mueda in Cabo Delgado on 16 June 1960 undoubtedly radicalised opinion in that area and, when the time came, en-

---

[35] *The Times,* 30 April 1973; *Financial Times,* 5 April 1973.

[36] Gallagher, *Portugal,* p. 168.

[37] *The Times,* 30 April 1973.

[38] Birmingham, *Frontline Nationalism,* p. 3.

[39] See Munslow, *Mozambique: the revolution and its origins,* Harlow, 1983, pp. 64-7.

couraged willingness to take up arms, even if the number of fatalities (more than 600, according to some accounts) has possibly been exaggerated.[40] The peaceful protest which occasioned it was organised by the Makonde African National Union. The Makonde, a small group in northern Mozambique but more numerous in southern Tanzania, later came to form the backbone of Frelimo's fighting force. In his reports of 1958 and 1959 the anthropologist Jorge Dias had already warned of the strength of Makonde discontent. Those who were working, or had worked, contracts on the sisal plantations across the Rovuma compared conditions under British and Portuguese colonialism to the detriment of the latter, and were additionally subject to the influence of Tanganyikan political nationalism, and acquainted through the Tanganyikan African National Union, or TANU (founded 1954) with the model of modern political parties. The numbers open to such influences were large: as many as 25% of the estimated 100,000 Mozambican Makonde may have been labour migrants in Tanganyika at the time of Dias's study.[41]

The first Mozambican nationalist parties in a modern sense were all formed in exile in the early 1960s among such communities as these, and all patterned themselves on parties in their host countries. The National Democratic Union of Mozambique (UDENAMO), headed by Adelino Gwambe and the Reverend Uria T. Simango, was formed in Southern Rhodesia in 1960 with a membership drawn mainly from workers from central and southern Mozambique; the Mozambique African National Union (MANU) was set up in 1961, from a coalition of smaller groups in Mombasa, Kenya, the most important of which was the Makonde African National Union; finally, the National Union for Mozambican Independence (UNAMI), based in Malawi, drew its support mainly from the people of Tete Province. All three moved their headquarters to Tanganyika when it became independent in December 1961 (a politically stirring month, which also saw the Indian invasion of Portuguese Goa).[42] Julius Nyerere, the TANU activist who became independent Tanganyika's first leader, was instrumental in the formation of a nationalist front of these separate organisations, but Eduardo Mondlane was a critical figure in this process. Born in Gaza and educated first in South Africa and then in the United

---

[40] De Brito, p. 73; Pitcher, *Politics*, p. 252.

[41] Rui Pereira, 'Antropologia aplicada na política colonial portuguesa do Estado Novo', *Revista Internacional de Estudos Africanos*, 4 and 5 (January-December 1985), pp. 191-234.

[42] See Munslow, *Revolution*, pp. 79-81.

States, where he became a university lecturer, Mondlane had acquired a grasp of international politics as an official at the United Nations. He had the firm support of Nyerere. In addition, he had good international contacts and could raise funds for educational purposes (Frelimo's Mozambique Institute in Dar es Salaam received money from a variety of Western religious and other bodies). Finally, his high educational achievements symbolised for many of the *assimilado* stratum the triumph over colonial discrimination. When news reached Lourenço Marques of the creation of Frelimo under his leadership, many left clandestinely to join him.[43]

The Frente de Libertação de Moçambique, – Frelimo – was formed in 1962, with the military option apparently a foregone conclusion. Not only Nyerere but also the umbrella organisation for the Portuguese colonies, the Conferência das Organizações Nacionalistas das Colónias Portugueses (CONCP), facilitated military training.[44] Frelimo's first batch of 250 recruits went to Algeria in 1963. The lessons of abortive risings in Angola and Guinea, Algerian training and the study of such writers as Mao Tse-tung in China and General Giap in Vietnam all influenced the military choice of protracted guerrilla struggle accompanied by popular mobilisation.[45] Frelimo's main training camp was eventually established at Nachingwea, inside Mozambique, where with the cooperation of Chinese instructors military training became associated with political training from 1969 onwards.[46] In cooperation with Chinese-trained Tanzanian army officers, some 100 Chinese advisers offered instruction in small arms, explosives and tactics. But although guerrilla skills were imparted by the Chinese, Frelimo recruits were increasingly schooled in specialised skills by the Soviet Union or its allies.[47] Unusually at this period of intense Sino-Soviet rivalry in Africa, Frelimo was able to count on assistance from both Russia and China. Mondlane, the ex-UN official, used his diplomatic skills to good effect, also managing to avoid alienating American goodwill. But the use of Tanzania as a rear-base was decisive since Chinese military instructors were attached to the

[43] For Mondlane see de Brito, 'Le Frelimo', pp. 57-62.

[44] William Minter, *Portuguese Africa and the West*, Harmondsworth, 1972, p. 64. See also de Brito, 'Le Frelimo', pp. 92-3.

[45] Munslow, *Revolution*, p. 85.

[46] De Brito, 'Le Frelimo', p. 97.

[47] Thomas H. Henriksen, *Revolution and Counterrevolution: Mozambique's war of independence 1964-1974*, Westport, CT, 1983, pp. 187-9. See also P. Abbott and M.R. Rodrigues, *Modern African Wars, 2: Angola and Mozambique, 1961-1974*, London, 1988.

Tanzanian People's Defence Force (TPDF), and it would not have been possible for the Soviet Union to oust them from this position. Clandestine political agitation inside rural Mozambique preceded hostilities, launched on 24 September 1964 with Frelimo's original 250 trained guerrillas. However, Frelimo's plan to open fronts simultaneously in southern and central Mozambique, as well as in the northern provinces of Niassa and Cabo Delgado near Tanzania, was thwarted by a police clampdown in South Africa, Southern Rhodesia, and Swaziland. Penetrated by the Direcção Geral de Segurança (DGS – previously known as Polícia Internacional e de Defesa do Estado or PIDE), most of Frelimo's southern underground based in Swaziland and Lourenço Marques was dismantled only three months after the start of hostilities with the arrest of 1,500 Frelimo sympathisers (including many workers and students).[48] The plan also failed in central Mozambique since the guerrillas were denied access from newly-independent Malawi or Zambia, and it soon became clear that it would not be possible to resupply the units in Tete and Zambezia, which were then withdrawn. By 1965, the war was continuing only in Cabo Delgado and Niassa, and Frelimo relied completely on Tanzania as its rear-base and sanctuary.[49] Clearly Tanzanian support was of crucial importance in the early stages of the war. Portugal, sensitive to international condemnation, and especially to opinion at the UN and among its NATO allies, never mounted substantial pre-emptive or retaliatory strikes against the many thousands of armed guerrillas in sanctuary camps or the more than 45,000 Mozambican refugees there. That support was therefore never disrupted.[50]

Frelimo's political mobilisation concentrated on the need to overcome the Portuguese colonial system, and focused on such tangible grievances as the alienation of fertile land. This preceded guerrilla action and the establishment of bases in sparsely populated rural areas in the north, where the colonial presence and administrative network were thinnest and where an early effort was made by Frelimo to win over traditional chiefs. Reconnaissance was carried out by Forças Populares de Libertação de Moçambique (FPLM) members out of uniform. As time wore on, politicisation and intelligence work fell increasingly to members of the Women's Detachment, formed in 1967, who were better able to operate

---

[48] See Teresa Cruz e Silva, 'A "IV Região" da Frelimo no sul de Moçambique. Lourenço Marques, 1964-65'. *Estudos Africanos*, 8 (1990), pp. 127-41.

[49] Munslow, *Revolution*, p. 87.

[50] Henriksen, *Revolution and Counterrevolution*, pp. 199-202.

among the local population without attracting the attention of the authorities. Guerrilla operations, once launched, aimed to cut communications and to isolate and concentrate enemy troops; Initially infantry and sabotage groups blew up bridges and mined roads in order to create a climate of insecurity which would make troops reluctant to leave their bases.[51]

For four years after Frelimo's initial débâcle, operations remained confined to Niassa and Cabo Delgado provinces because of the Portuguese defensive strategy of constructing protected villages. This was the remotest, most sparsely populated and least economically important part of the country. Temporary success in blocking Frelimo's advance southwards was built upon the relative cooperation of the Macua-Lomwe, Mozambique's largest ethnic group. This cooperation was understood by the Portuguese in terms of historically ingrained enmity between the Macua and their northern neighbours, the Makonde. Indeed, the pattern of Frelimo – and therefore Makonde – attacks in Macua territory did suggest a degree of ethnic antagonism not evident elsewhere. In Niassa, initial attacks on Portuguese positions in September 1964 concentrated on the area of the lakeshore, but the Portuguese response was severe. The Anglican missionary John Paul has described how by mid-1965 the scorched earth policy of the Portuguese and the brutality of the marine commandos from the lakeshore had caused almost the entire population to the north of Messumba mission to flee to Tanzania, to Likoma island or into the hills where they sought Frelimo protection.[52] Frelimo was therefore forced to open a new front in arid and poor eastern Niassa. In the province overall population density was a mere 2.2 people per square km., and displacement of population and disruption of agricultural production brought serious and widespread famine, causing much of the local peasant population to flee, either to Tanzania or to areas under Portuguese control. Frelimo guerrillas suffered, since distance precluded supply trails from Tanzania or the establishment of a trading network. A short-lived front in southern Niassa closed in 1968, and thereafter Frelimo largely confined itself to operations from small, mobile bases in the remote empty lands north of Lichinga where the remaining civilians cultivated scattered fields and hid their granaries in the forest. Frelimo was able to move

[51] Munslow, *Revolution*, pp. 90, 123 and 119.

[52] See John Paul, *Mozambique: Memoirs of a revolution*, Harmondsworth, 1975, pp. 146-7, for an account of a visit to Frelimo's Matenje base in September 1965, following a Portuguese bombing raid.

back into southern Niassa in 1970, but made little further progress before 1974.[53]

Northern Cabo Delgado, however, threw itself into the war. Although sparsely populated, unlike Niassa it produced a tradeable agricultural surplus. Clandestine political organisers prepared the ground by utilising a network provided by the independent cotton cooperative movement established by Lazaro Nkavandame, the Sociedade Agrícola Algodoeira Voluntária dos Africanos de Moçambique (SAAVM), which at the time of its official recognition in 1959 (it was later suppressed) boasted 1,000 members.[54] Under Nkavandame's leadership, Frelimo's Department of Internal Organisation assumed great importance in the two years preceding the launch of the armed struggle. The Department had responsibility for such organising not only in Nkavandame's own area, but also in Niassa to the west, although it is doubtful that this authority had much substance.[55]

At the grassroots level two types of civilian committee existed in Cabo Delgado: committees of six ('sita'), which organised the transport of war matériel south from Tanzania, and also the local food contributions from the peasants for the guerrillas; and committees of ten ('kumi'), which dealt with social problems and disputes.[56] Run by the 'Chairmen' – Makonde headmen associated previously with the SAAVM – they had an undefined, uneasy and conflictual relationship with the young guerrillas on whom the peasants were reliant for defence, but who in turn depended on the Chairmen for supplies, including the provision of food to the base. Initially trade was entirely in the hands of the Chairmen by virtue of the flight of the *cantineiros*, or rural traders, from the war zones, and this allowed them to exercise control over the movement southwards of external donations to Frelimo warehoused in Tanzania. Ultimately all Frelimo commercial activity in Cabo Delgado fell to them, including its trade with Tanzania and the transport of war matériel and supplies, as well as the

[53] De Brito, Le Frelimo, pp. 102-4.

[54] See Anna Maria Gentili, 'Les Origines Rurales du Nationalisme Mozambicain: Les Cooperatives Linguilanilu du Plateau du Mueda 1957-63' in *Histoire Sociale de l'Afrique de l'Est. Actes du Colloque de Bujumbura*, 17-24 October 1989, Dept. of History, Université de Burundi, Paris, 1991.

[55] *Não Vamos Esquecer!*, 2, 4 (July 1987), Bulletin of the History Workshop, Centro de Estudos Africanos, Universidade Eduardo Mondlane, special issue on the liberated zones.

[56] *Poder Popular e desagregação nas aldeias comunais do planalto de Mueda*, Centro de Estudos Africanos, Maputo, 1986, pp. 9-10.

chain of posts along the Rovuma river, where surplus produce collected from the peasants was exchanged for consumer items.

Disputes between Lazaro Nkavandame and the Chairmen on the one hand and the younger, more radical guerrilla commanders led by Samora Machel on the other eventually polarised the movement in the late 1960s. Until 1969 Frelimo's military and civilian structures in Cabo Delgado remained separate (and increasingly at odds). Machel, a southerner at the head of the army, opposed the retention of chiefs and elders as the principal organisers of the liberated zones and accused Nkavandame of profiteering. But the dispute extended to other questions too with implications for the Chairmen's authority; these included the role of women, the use and allocation of land and the scope of hereditary authority. It was in Cabo Delgado, where Nkavandame was also the secretary of the province, that the conflicts developed most clearly. The quarrel eventually extended to military strategy, probably exacerbated (though the relevant Frelimo texts do not touch on this) by the decision in 1967 to carry Frelimo's campaign westwards into Tete province rather than concentrating first and foremost on liberating Cabo Delgado, as the Chairmen would have wished. Disagreements arose over the definition of the enemy, and whether this was a matter of class interests or of race; and over whether the correct strategy was one of gradually extending guerrilla war throughout the country or first concentrating on liberating the north of the Portuguese military presence and setting up a new state authority there.[57]

The eventual, and perhaps inevitable, outcome saw a progressive assertion of control by the military in alliance with a younger generation of more radical politicians, many of them educated southerners. The whole process entailed a rationalisation of Frelimo structures and a centralisation of power affecting administration of the liberated zones. It began with Frelimo's Second Congress, held against the Chairmen's wishes, and in their absence, in late July 1968 in northern Niassa. The Congress was dominated by military cadres and sympathetic delegates from the liberated zones. It officially adopted the strategy of 'prolonged people's war', thereby subordinating all spheres of activity to the war effort. It also created

---

[57] Ian Christie, *Machel of Mozambique*, Harare, 1988, pp. 54-5. Nkavandame appealed to the Tanzanians against Machel's strategy of circumventing rather than attacking Portuguese garrisons in Cabo Delgado. According to Col. Ali Mafudh, who was responsible for liaison with Frelimo, Nkavandame tried to manipulate Tanzanian politicians from the south, drawing on kinship links with people in northern Mozambique.

an Executive Committee which, apart from the president and vice-president, contained the nucleus of Mozambique's post-independence leadership: Samora Machel, Joaquim Chissano, Armando Guebuza, Jorge Rebelo, Marcelino dos Santos, and Mariano Matsinhe. A new Central committee, expanded from twenty to forty members, now included the frontline commanders.[58] Mondlane, who appears to have striven but ultimately failed to maintain unity between the opposing factions, was killed by a parcel bomb in February 1969, an event in which the DGS may be assumed to have had a guiding hand. Nkavandame's defection to the Portuguese followed. A triumvirate Frelimo presidency of Machel, dos Santos and Uria Simango (a Protestant pastor from central Mozambique) was short-lived with Simango expelled from Frelimo after he had accused other leaders of plotting against him and declared that the organisation was being taken over by southerners.[59]

Portuguese propaganda of course sought to play up ethnic divisions but in fact failed to make much of Nkavandame's defection. There was no simple ethnic factor in play. Makonde guerrillas did not desert the movement *en masse*, but on the contrary continued to fight within a military force which betrayed no signs of fragmenting. The young guerrillas, Makonde and non-Makonde, were clearly content to follow Machel's leadership, not that of the Chairmen. Indeed, the attempt at regional secession, after the pattern of Biafra, failed utterly, receiving no encouragement from Nyerere. The internal crisis of the late 1960s represented, above all, a takeover and centralisation of all power into the hands of the guerrilla commanders led by Samora Machel and like-minded civilian allies. It was the outcome of a convergence of interests between the fighters and young military commanders, many of them Makonde peasants from the north, and the mainly southern *assimilados* grouped around Mondlane and External Affairs Secretary Marcelino dos Santos. The young educated southern *assimilados* staffed the bureaucracy and controlled the upper echelons of the military apparatus. This allowed them to establish an alliance with the soldiers against the Chairmen and to impose their 'politico-military' notion of the struggle, formulated by dos Santos, which subsumed political and military organisations into one giving primacy to the war effort.[60]

---

[58] See Munslow, *Revolution*, pp. 110-11.

[59] See especially Munslow, *Revolution*, and *O Processo Revolucionário da Guerra Popular de Libertação. Artigos coligidos do orgão de informação da Frelimo 'A Voz da Revolução', desde 1963 até 1974*, Colecção textos e documentos da Frelimo, Maputo (undated).

[60] De Brito, 'Le Frelimo', p. 109.

A meeting of the Frelimo Central Committee gave the FPLM full charge of reorganisation in April 1969. The appointment of political commissars, answerable to the Department of Defence, with responsibility for overseeing the various organs created for the local or regional administration, was justified as preventing a resurgence and reconstitution of 'traditional power', and was clearly targeted at Nkavandame's supporters in Cabo Delgado. It represented the culmination of a process which had been under way for some time.[61] By the early 1970s the guerrillas were in effective control, supported by the decision to send all internal Frelimo cadres for military training. With the removal of the Chairmen and the Department of Internal Organisation, the guerrilla command and especially Machel himself assumed full control over the war effort at the time when the Portuguese were unleashing 'Operation Gordian Knot', their most concerted attempt to destroy the nationalist movement. Cash cropping and wage labour were abolished and a new Department of Production and Commerce was established under the control of the army. At the same time, Frelimo propaganda began to emphasise and laud collective production, although family production had always predominated in the liberated zones and continued to do so.[62]

The final phase, 1968-1974

The plan to carry the struggle into the economically significant central region was made in 1967. Both Mondlane and Machel envisaged Tete province in the west as the obvious bridge for expansion southwards into Manica and Sofala, where the 'vertebral column' of the enemy was located. Tete shared 1,150 km. of largely unpoliced frontier with independent Zambia and Malawi, and migrant workers from Tete travelled to both these countries as well as to the estates and farms of adjacent Southern Rhodesia. The administration was aware that the diverse and scattered population of this vast, empty province, with many links across ill-defined borders, was vulnerable to 'subversion'.[63] Frelimo for its part had indeed been carrying out a determined clandestine political

---

[61] See Luis de Brito, 'Une rélecture nécessaire. La genèse du parti-État FRELIMO', *Politique Africaine* 29 (1988), pp. 15-27.

[62] On this issue see especially *Não Vamos Esquecer!*, special issue, 1987.

[63] J.P. Borges Coelho, *O Início da Luta Armada em Tete, 1968-1969*, Estudos 7, Arquivo Histórico de Moçambique, Maputo, 1989. During 1966-7 the Serviços de Centralização e Coordenação de Informações de Moçambique (SCCIM) ordered numerous anthropological surveys.

mobilisation, especially in Moatize *concelho*, and in the whole strategically significant Mutarara area between the Malawi border and the north bank of the Zambezi. This natural route down into central Mozambique was traversed east-west by the rail line destined to carry supplies to the site of the planned Cahora Bassa dam. Frelimo's Tete campaign, launched in March 1968, did not, however, reopen in those areas, on account of both Malawian hostility and the strong local presence of Portuguese troops (Mutarara was a garrison town). Rather, the guerrillas installed themselves in a remote part of the Maravia plateau, far from administrative and population centres. Deep local economic discontents were shared by the peasants and by their headmen and *régulos*, whose collaboration Frelimo actively sought. They were ripe for political agitation, so that between the second half of 1967 and the start of 1968 the colonial order in the area, which rested on the *régulos*, 'began to collapse like a stack of cards'. In this vast area devoid of roads Frelimo established an interdependent network of mobile camps. The initial line of penetration south was along the Capoche river. From base camps in the Capoche valley Frelimo mounted ambushes of Portuguese troops and mined roads, pausing in mid-1968, as its supply-lines were becoming over-extended, to undertake some military training of the local peasantry.

Frelimo had the advantage of surprise and mobility, so that for several months the Portuguese army in Tete was attacking already deserted encampments. In September 1968 the army reorganised and mounted a counter-offensive using smaller heliborne units. Yet although they did manage to disrupt Frelimo's supply-lines, the army rarely encountered guerrillas. Civilians, however, experienced very harsh treatment in the course of these special operations. By burning *machambas* (plantations) and razing grain stores the Portuguese succeeded in temporarily checking the Frelimo advance. But driving the guerrillas back over the Zambian border proved impossible, since they were able to hide, disperse, move temporarily elsewhere and return in the next rainy season. The long frontier with Zambia was impossible to seal or police, and intelligence on infiltrations reached Portuguese ears long after the event. A new line of Frelimo bases was thus established along the Zambian border in early 1969. This time the Frelimo advance flanked the Capoche valley on either side, converging to the south of it very near the Zambezi and the Cahora Bassa dam construction site. Late in the day the army threw itself into the construction of *aldeamentos* – not, as originally planned, as a preventive measure but to impede contact between guerrillas and the people. This very brutal process caused a large-scale flight of refugees, especially from northern Tete, leaving large areas depopulated. By mid-1969 practically all of Tete north of the Zambezi was a guerrilla war zone, and the Portuguese were unable to reverse this during the dry season as they had in the previous year.[64]

By 1970 Portugal had more than 150,000 men in Africa – a deployment, relative to population, five times greater than that of the United States in Vietnam in the same year. The cost of this effort rose from approximately 25% of the national budget in 1960 to a peak of 42% in 1968, representing some 6% of GNP, while Mozambique's contribution in 1971 towards the cost of its defence was a mere 20% (in contrast with the Angolan provision of 50%).[65] While official Portuguese figures admitted a total of only 3,265 men killed in action in their African campaigns between 1961 and 1974, more realistic calculations suggest a loss of some 13,000 dead and 65,000 casualties from all causes by 1973.[66] As the military presence became greater, so also did the repressive power of the DGS. Decrees of 18 July and 1 October 1972 greatly increased its right to imprison and try people without judicial appeal or control of any kind.[67] According to figures released in 1974, 865 political prisoners died in Mozambique during the last three years of the Caetano dictatorship alone, directly or indirectly at DGS hands, while more than 3,000 political prisoners were released after 25 April 1974 from five major jails and some smaller ones run by it.[68] It was the density and ruthlessness of the DGS presence which kept the urban areas free of opposition activity, save for some political organising in the deepest clandestinity, and thus confined the war to rural areas.[69]

The Portuguese counterinsurgency strategy was primarily one of containment, based on a network of static garrison or holding units, and backed by mobile reaction forces.[70] They initially sought

[64] Borges Coelho, *O Início.*

[65] I. Beckett, 'The Portuguese Army: The Campaign in Mozambique' in I. Beckett and J. Pimlott (eds), *Armed Forces and Modern Counter-insurgency*, London, 1977.

[66] Cited by Beckett, 'The Portuguese Army', p. 151.

[67] Adrian Hastings, *Wiriyamu*, London, 1974, p. 110.

[68] *Observer*, 7 July 1974.

[69] According to Lourenço Marques radio of 12 June 1974, there were then more than 500 DGS in detention, and eleven were known to have escaped the country, all to Rhodesia. However, H. Ellert in *The Rhodesian Front War: Counter-Insurgency and guerrilla warfare, 1962-1980*, Gweru, 1989, records that following the Lisbon coup 'hundreds of Portuguese DGS officers, professional soldiers and Portuguese settlers poured into Rhodesia at Umtali' (pp. 64-65).

[70] As in Angola. See W.S. van der Waals, *Portugal's War in Angola, 1961-1974*,

to hold the Rovuma river line separating the colony from Tanzania, but as time went on increasing emphasis was laid on small unit operations against guerrilla infiltrators, since larger efforts only tended to force the guerrillas to operate elsewhere. All military equipment was supplied by NATO allies. By the early 1970s Mozambique had been divided into three theatre commands, each having élite units available in an intervention role, although they were also available at local level for mobile tasks such as convoy escort or immediate reinforcement. Tactical responsibility below theatre level was subordinated to sector commands, further subdivided into battalion and company areas. But the main danger came from Frelimo landmines, responsible for perhaps 50% of Portuguese casualties. One response was an extensive programme of road-tarring (an annual rate of 1,400 km or 870 miles, in Mozambique by 1972). A simple device, the *pica* or pointed stick, was used to probe the ground ahead of patrols, and convoys were preceeded by Berliet trucks with sandbagged floors and tyres filled with water to absorb the blast. From 1970 onwards defoliants were used to clear roadside vegetation which might conceal ambushes. By 1973-4 the air force in Mozambique had grown to comprise twelve Fiat G-92s, fifteen Harvard T6 converted trainers, fourteen Alouette and two Puma helicopters, and five Nord-Atlas and seven DC-3 transport aircraft. Naval craft patrolled Lake Malawi and sixteen 50-ton patrol boats undertook anti-infiltration duties along the coast.[71]

Outside the main towns the Portuguese presence in the northern districts of Cabo Delgado and Niassa was confined to isolated garrisons and frontier outposts. The civilian administration had collapsed, the Portuguese planters had fled and the rural shops abandoned years earlier by the *cantineiros* had been taken over by Frelimo and renamed *lojas do povo*. Yet Frelimo had only the thinly populated and remote far north under its effective control. The balance began to tilt after Frelimo shifted its main effort to Tete. The giant, prestige Cahora Bassa scheme, construction of which began in 1968, proved a most effective centrepoint for an international campaign to isolate Portugal ('Stop the Dam'), and tied down perhaps as many as 20,000 Portuguese troops in its defence which had become for Portugal a matter of national honour.[72] The

Rivonia, 1993, pp. 112-21.

[71] See Beckett, 'The Portuguese Army', and Abbott and Rodrigues, *Modern African Wars*, for details on the organisation and equipment of the Portuguese armed forces.

[72] *Guardian*, 7 January 1972.

defence was indeed successful, inasmuch as Frelimo never managed to break through, but the strategic cost was great. From 1971 onwards Frelimo mined access roads and the Beira-Moatize railway carrying supplies to the site, but circumvented the dam itself to infiltrate south towards the white settler farms and plantations of Manica and Sofala. It was aided by a shift in Malawi's stance, which after 1971 sensed that the Portuguese position was weakening so that it no longer impeded – and even aided – Frelimo transit and infiltration from southern Malawi.[73]

According to General Kaúlza de Arriaga, Frelimo had then about 8,000 trained guerrillas operating inside Mozambique, of whom about 1,300 a year were killed, but the numbers were continually replenished by recruitment and infiltration from Tanzania.[74] Although Arriaga would argue otherwise, Operation Gordian Knot had failed hopelessly in its ultimate objectives. This massive operation of encirclement and advance on Frelimo's Makonde bastion of the Mueda plateau during the 1970 dry season employed more than 10,000 Portuguese troops and continued for seven months. Despite the war matériel captured, and the (mainly deserted) Frelimo bases overrun, it accelerated the eventual Portuguese collapse. In early 1971 Arriaga claimed the following results from the operation:[75]

Bases destroyed	61
Sanctuaries and camps destroyed	294
Enemy caught or captured	1,842
Guerrillas killed	819
Arms captured	48 tons

But the initial destruction of bases just pushed men elsewhere. The coordination of heliborne assault after initial artillery and air bombardment, followed by mine clearance and consolidation on foot, caused Frelimo's northern infrastructure severe damage, but did not destroy its capacity for infiltration. It was criticised as achieving little at great cost and effort, and further operations were needed in the north during 1971.[76] At the same time the heavy concentration of Portuguese troops in Cabo Delgado and in Tete to guard the dam site denuded other areas in the north,

---

[73] See Henriksen, *Revolution*, p. 198.

[74] Report in the *Rhodesia Herald*, 9 April 1973.

[75] *Coragem, Tenacidade e Fé*, Lourenço Marques, 1973.

[76] Beckett, 'Portuguese Army', p. 155.

where the rebels could circulate freely, establishing new bases in the interior. Although Frelimo was hurt by Gordian Knot, Portuguese casualties were also high (132 killed and twice as many seriously wounded), and no other offensive was ever attempted on the same scale in Mozambique. Rather, the Portuguese relied on convoys and air power, constructing 8,000 miles of asphalt roads as landmine defence, despite the expense and the difficulties of the terrain. They fought a cautious, defensive war, tying up nearly five out of every seven of their line troops in convoy duty or in fixed positions.[77] Arguably this form of containment was the most viable option available to Portuguese commanders on the ground in an ultimately unwinnable war, where more Gordian Knots would have quickly depleted their resources.

Following Gordian Knot, Frelimo split into smaller and more mobile units and pushed increasingly through into Tete via Zambia, and (clandestinely) also Malawi. These westward and southern advances kept the Portuguese not only off-balance but also logistically over-extended from their command centre in Nampula. After 25 July 1972, when the Manica and Sofala campaign opened in central Mozambique, the Portuguese resorted ever more to forced resettlements and reprisals against civilians. Re-supplied by trails from the northern bases, and from the food-surplus district of Zambézia (to which access for Frelimo from Malawi was now possible), the guerrillas advanced into the vicinity of Vila Manica and Vila Pery, and even towards Beira, despite the Portuguese troop dispositions concentrated there, spreading panic among the European community at the end of 1972 and throughout the following year.[78] Although Frelimo's main activity remained mine-laying and hit-and-run attacks, it was becoming increasingly well armed (the 122-mm. rocket made its appearance in January 1973) and able to mount long-range bombardments of Portuguese positions.

Arriaga's response to the worsening situation was to threaten resignation unless he was made overall commander of both the Angolan and the Mozambican theatres, so that troops could be diverted from the former to the latter, where he argued that defence of the Cahora Bassa site tied down too many men to cope with the increasing Frelimo infiltration south. He was forced to carry out this threat in May 1973, returning to Portugal unhonoured,

---

[77] Henriksen, *Revolution and Counter- revolution*, pp. 51, 63 and 65.

[78] Joaquim Vieira, 'Moçambique: a 'guerra global' in João de Melo (ed.) *Os anos de guerra: 1961- 1975: Os Portugueses em Africa: Crónica, ficção e história*, vol. 2, pp. 7-26, Lisbon, 1988.

Caetano having tired of his optimistic claims about the war.[79] He had presided over a significant Africanisation of the 60,000-man defence forces, raising black participation to 60%, with plans to go to at least 75% by mid-1974.[80] His innovation was to introduce the special black paramilitary units: the GEs and GEPs. Grupos Especiais (GEs) were recruited from the militia in the fortified villages, or *aldeamentos*, for the defence of the tribes to which they belong and the places in which they normally live. Familiar with the environment and the war history of the areas in which they operate, they have exceptional qualities for carrying out localised operations aimed at the detection and annihilation of enemy infiltrators and the rescue of abducted and captured civilians'.[81]

In addition, Grupos Especiais Pára-quedistas (GEPs), were recruited and deployed on a countrywide basis, and were employed by Arriaga as an élite force to spearhead offensives. Both the GEs and GEPs, who underwent training at Dondo barracks outside Beira, were strongly linked with the powerful Beira-based businessman Jorge Jardim. These units were allegedly heavily 'mentalised' – to use the phrase then current – to fight for a Mozambique ruled by Mozambicans, but maintaining links with Portugal.[82] Indeed, Arriaga's friendship with Jardim gave rise to speculation about a settler bid for independence under the stewardship of these two influential figures, and was probably one of the reasons Lisbon looked with suspicion on the process of political indoctrination to which the new black units were subject.[83] At the time when Arriaga and Jardim were establishing the GEs and GEPs, the DGS was establishing a black counter-insurgency force under its separate control.[84] Indeed, this may have represented yet one more manifestation of the friction and sharp rivalry which existed between the army and the DGS.[85] Used previously with some success in Angola, the *flechas* (arrows) comprised commando-trained and helicopter-borne counter-insurgency squads of

[79] Kaúlza de Arriaga, *A Luta em Moçambique 1970/1973*, Braga, 1977, p. 46, and Dr T.H. Cashmore, personal communication.

[80] *Daily Telegraph*, 24 April 1973.

[81] Lourenço Marques radio, 7 April 1973. For the organisation of special units see Abbott and Rodrigues, *Modern African Wars*, p. 34.

[82] Jorge Jardim, *Moçambique: Terra Queimada*, Lisbon, 1976, pp. 142-3.

[83] Henriksen, *Revolution*, pp. 69, 99-100.

[84] Henriksen (p. 111) suggests that Jardim was closely associated with the *flechas*, but in his book Jardim clearly states that his links were with the GEs and GEPs, and also with the élite commando units trained at Montepuez.

[85] Beckett, *Portuguese Army*; Henriksen, *Revolution* pp. 54-55.

about half a dozen men, who were a mixture of local recruits and 'turned' Frelimo guerrillas. Paid bounties for kills, captures and recovery of weapons, and subject to draconian internal discipline, the *flechas* earned an unsavoury reputation for brutality, torture and summary execution.[86] However they only began operations in Manica district at the beginning of 1973 and were never used outside the central provinces of Mozambique.[87]

By the war's end, Portugal had deployed some 65,000-70,000 men in Mozambique. Over half (38,000-43,000) were from the metropole, and the rest recruited locally. More than 90% of the GEs and GEPs were black, as were 70% of the commandos, paratroops and marines, although the proportion in the regular army units was probably nearer 35-40%. The *flechas* were almost all African, apart from the officers.[88] Linked with the establishment of those élite units, Arriaga also claimed a high rate for 'turning' captured guerrillas. Many defections were claimed from Frelimo-controlled areas, including some middle-ranking Frelimo officials as well as peasants complaining of harsh treatment and of being forced to work and grow food for the fighters (in the latter part of 1973 this withdrawal from Frelimo areas was accentuated by a cholera outbreak in Tete and in Beira districts). As in its wars of conquest and of 'pacification' in the late nineteenth and early twentieth centuries, Portugal was beginning to rely on local troops. But this late Africanisation could do nothing to prevent the collapse of military will in Lisbon. After the coup there on 25 April 1974 it did, however, have the effect of leaving a detritus of many thousand black collaborators with military training, some of them associated with atrocities against Frelimo and their supporters. Many fled to Rhodesia, and provided a skilled recruitment pool for later action against Frelimo-ruled Mozambique.

Aldeamentos and liberated zones

The entire social geography of the north was changed by war and

---

[86] Comments by Ron Reid-Daly, former Rhodesian Selous Scouts Commander, reported by Al.J. Venter, 'Why Portugal lost its African Wars' in Venter (ed.), *Challenge: Southern Africa within the African revolutionary context*, 1989, pp. 224-72; see also Henriksen, *Revolution*, p. 155.

[87] Information from J. Borges Coelho.

[88] Henriksen, *Revolution*, pp. 68, 94-5. By the early 1970s Portugal had about 140,000 men under arms in the colonies, of whom just under two-thirds were black. No African appears to have risen above the rank of captain in the armed forces. See Clarence-Smith, *The Third Portuguese Empire*, p. 217.

Portugal's chosen counter-insurgency strategy. Up to 1 million people – perhaps one in eight Mozambicans – were confined to fortified villages, or *aldeamentos*, designed to isolate the guerrillas from their peasant support base. Regroupment first took place in Cabo Delgado where some 250,000 people were moved into 150 villages from a 50-mile strip between the mouths of the Montepuez and Messalo rivers and inland for 100 miles. Arriaga's ambitious scheme was to neutralise infiltration by placing a human 'barrier' along the Rovuma line.[89] Later, the Portuguese regrouped rural Africans either in response to Frelimo infiltration, as in Tete, or in anticipation of it, as in southern Mozambique.[90] The location of these *aldeamentos* was largely dictated by the army's need for free-fire zones and by the proximity of strategic highways, rather than proximity to areas of cultivation; thus production often suffered. In 1973 Arriaga was claiming that the government intended shifting all rural Africans in Mozambique into *aldeamentos* within five to six years: a policy which would in its own way have been as stark an admission of failure as any military defeat.[91]

Especially in the early days, there were ethnic overtones to the *aldeamento* programme. The Portuguese claimed that they were facing risings of tribes who straddled Mozambique's borders – the Makonde in Cabo Delgado, the Nyanja in Niassa – and they played the ethnic card accordingly. The Macua held largely aloof from Frelimo during the liberation war, and the Portuguese attributed this to their historical differences with their Makonde-speaking neighbours to the north, who provided the backbone of Frelimo's fighting force. The large, traditionally more or less politically autonomous Macua village, based on three-generational matrilineages, lent itself to 'fortification' and the formation of self-defence militias.[92] It formed the bulwark of the *aldeamento* programme and was designed to block Frelimo's advance southwards through Cabo Delgado, and indeed was successful in blocking that advance for several years until Frelimo moved westward via Zambia and Malawi into Tete. Similarly, the *aldeamento* programme in Niassa was initially anchored among the Islamised Yao, because Frelimo's early advances in the lake zone between Vila Cabral and the Tanzanian border appeared to reflect the influence of a Protestant-

---

[89] Beckett, 'The Portuguese Army', pp. 156-7.

[90] Henriksen, *Revolution*, pp. 68, 95.

[91] Gallagher, *Portugal*, p. 178.

[92] Edward A. Alpers, 'Ethnicity, Politics and History in Mozambique', *Africa Today*, 21, 4 (fall 1974), pp. 39-52.

educated Nyanja élite, to which the Yao were expected to be impervious.[93]

The Yao were also chosen to populate Arriaga's prestige project at Nangade on the Rovuma river.[94] Nangade *aldeamento* on completion was to be blessed with concrete houses, electricity, medical and educational facilities, a mosque, and closed-circuit television, and was linked to the coast by a tarred road. This proposed model for a chain of similar *aldeamentos* along the northern border with Tanzania, where schools and social services would win the hearts and minds of the locals, formed part of the Portuguese military 'psycho-social action' programme. Materials for Nangade's construction travelled 100 km. along a route strewn with mines and ambushes, to the vivid memory of Portuguese troops who accompanied the convoy.[95] Propaganda requirements for showpiece *aldeamentos* also led to a concentration of resources on model villages elsewhere, such as Chiulugo, near Vila Cabral in Niassa.[96] More typical was the *aldeamento* of Mocimboa do Rovuma in Cabo Delgado. This former administrative headquarters was transformed into a military installation by the addition of an air strip and barracks, with civilian huts in the middle of the complex containing both voluntary residents and unwilling captives. The civilian population lived under suspicion, but served as a recruitment pool for the ranks of the colonial forces.[97] Very large population relocations into *aldeamentos* of this kind were effected in the northern war zones, and extensive areas of countryside were denuded by Portuguese bombing raids, scorched earth tactics and the razing of villages. By early 1974, according to one Portuguese spokesman, 63.3% of the population in Cabo Delgado, 67.7% in Niassa, and 44% in Tete had been relocated in *aldeamentos*.[98]

The situation in Tete was compounded by the ambitious development plan associated with the Cahora Bassa hydro-electric scheme,

---

[93] Brendan F. Jundanian, 'Resettlement Programs: Counterinsurgency in Mozambique', *Comparative Politics*, 6 (1974), pp. 519-40.

[94] C.F. Spence was helicoptered up to see Nangade by the Portuguese authorities on the eve of the 1974 coup, and reports it as populated then by Yao. (We are grateful to Alex Vines for making a copy of Spence's unpublished 'Diary of Events in Mozambique, 25 April 1974-22 March 1976', available to us.)

[95] *Os anos de guerra, 1961-1975. Os Portugueses em Africa. Crónica, ficção e história*, Lisbon, 1988.

[96] Malcolm G. Spavan, 'Rural Resettlement and Socialist Construction: Communal Villages in Mozambique', M.Sc. thesis, May 1981.

[97] *Poder popular e desagregação nas aldeias comunais de Mueda.*

[98] Henriksen, *Revolution*, p. 155.

which became incorporated into the Portuguese strategic defence. Beginning in 1971, some 24,000 people in the area to be flooded by the lake were moved into seven resettlement villages. A key part of the original scheme was to tie peasant agriculture to cash-crop production, largely through research stations run by the Agricultural Research Institute. The aim was to establish state control over all development and, in an area where Frelimo guerrilla actions were becoming increasingly threatening to the Portuguese, to offer good infrastructural facilities to encourage Portuguese settlers to live and work there as a bastion of colonial rule. Three areas of 'rural restructuring' were formed around the key military garrison towns of Estima, Changara and Mutarara. Most of the villages were brought under military administration; even education was taken over by the army as part of the hearts and minds campaign.

Especially in Tete, where a cattle-keeping local population with highly dispersed patterns of settlement took badly to concentration, the Portuguese armed forces, with the current of events running against them, resorted after 1970 to increasingly desperate measures. Following exposure of the notorious massacre at Wiriyamu and nearby hamlets on 15 December 1972, in which several hundred villagers were killed by the 6th Commando Group on orders of the local DGS, other earlier atrocities were publicised by missionaries. Many were linked directly to government efforts in late 1971 and 1972 to force all the population around the town of Tete and even well south of the Zambezi into *aldeamentos*.[99] Two Spanish priests who toured Europe to publicise the massacre at Wiriyamu, Chawola and Juwau told a press conference in London that the road from Beira port to the Cahora Bassa hydro-electric project beyond Tete led past the area and that the armed forces, who had come under attack, were removing the villagers as a deterrent against further guerrilla infiltration. Specifically, the military operations on 15 December were in retaliation for Frelimo attacks on the Beira-Tete road.[100]

The embarrassment in Lisbon was acute. Local enquiries by Jardim, on the instructions of the Governor-General, supported the missionaries' contention that a serious massacre had indeed been perpetrated at Wiriyamu by a Portuguese military unit supported by the DGS.[101] An officer's report later divulged that white and black troops of the 6th Commandos were dispatched by helicop-

[99] See Hastings, *Wiriyamu*, p. 47.

[100] *Daily Telegraph*, 7 August 1973.

[101] Jardim, *Moçambique*, pp. 108-14.

ter to the Wiriyamu vicinity with explicit orders from the Tete military commander to 'mop up the land and kill any living soul, for the area was 100 per cent terrorist'. The Portuguese National Defence Department issued a statement in August 1973 based on its inquiry, which admitted that 'isolated units, contrary to express orders received, had, in at least one case, carried out acts of unjustified violence at another point of the region'.[102] The Governor of Tete District and the Army Commander were among those dismissed.[103] The several official Portuguese reports on the incident have never been made public and remain, more than twenty years after the event, a matter of controversy.[104] For its part Frelimo is alleged to have killed more than eighty chiefs or headmen in Tete district, and a campaign of counter-intimidation is probable, even if numbers have been exaggerated.[105] Although penetration of Tete gave Frelimo access to Manica and Sofala, it also over-extended the group's supply trails. The guerrillas were often compelled to raid the *aldeamentos* for food (although they may also have had support and a clandestine presence in many of them). The cholera outbreak in the latter half of 1973 compounded Frelimo's problems, so that by the time of the coup in Lisbon its position in Tete had suffered some clear reverses.

Over the ten years until April 1974, Frelimo's guerrilla army grew to between 9,000 and 11,000 full-time fighters inside Mozambique, with an equivalent number in training, on stand-by or in the pipeline southwards. More than twice as many youths, old men and women were organised in militias who transported supplies, defended base camps and backed up local raids.[106] The Portuguese estimated in mid-1973 that the numbers of people then living under Frelimo control ran to more than 60,000 in Cabo Delgado, 6,000 in Niassa and 2,000 in Tete.[107] Naturally Frelimo made much larger claims, suggesting there were some

[102] Henriksen, *Revolution*, p. 130.

[103] Interview with Stanley Duncan, British Consul-General and later Chargé d'Affaires, Lourenco Marques 1973, 17 February 1994.

[104] Cf. *Expresso* (Lisbon), 19 December 1992: 'Ex-PIDE acusa Kaulza de mentir sobre Wiriyamu'. An earlier article on Wiriyamu (5 December) drew on interviews with survivors and also participants from 6th Commando and assessed the number killed there and nearby at about 400.

[105] I.M. Kaplan (ed.), *An Area Handbook for Mozambique*, Washington, DC, 1977, p. 199; Beckett states that 55 chiefs were murdered by Frelimo in Tete in 1971.

[106] Henriksen, *Revolution*, p. 41.

[107] René Pélissier, *Le naufrage des caravelles. Études sur le fin de l'Empire portugais (1961-1975)*, Orgeval, 1979.

1.25 million people in its liberated zones, which covered nearly a quarter of the land area of the country.[108] There was, of course, much double-counting, and the liberated zones became such a central plank of Frelimo propaganda that their nature is now clouded in official myth, some of it originating in the bitter internal power struggles within Frelimo over questions of policy and administration which arose in the late 1960s. However, Frelimo's conception of a 'liberated' zone clearly never demanded the elimination of the colonial presence entirely, but encompassed areas where this was confined to military outposts and garrisons; in other words, Frelimo included in its claims of liberated areas those which also contained *aldeamentos*. Thus Samora Machel's clarification of the term:

> 'Liberated zones' does not mean the complete expulsion of the physical presence of the colonialists. There are still Portuguese there but they are isolated in a few small garrisons. The basic question is: who do the people follow? [...] In our zones the work is open. [...] That means freedom from exploitation, from forced labour. That is a liberated zone.'[109]

The liberated zones were also presentationally central to Frelimo's diplomatic offensive, in which the CONCP was a key vehicle. It was effective at the level of the UN General Assembly, where the Afro-Asian states, together with the Communist bloc, could always command a majority. As an umbrella movement for Frelimo in Mozambique, the MPLA in Angola, and the PAIGC in Guinea-Bissau, it had the effect of isolating rival liberation movements, and making them look like splinter groups.[110] The CONCP from its office in Algiers linked the African guerrilla organisations to political currents elsewhere in the Portuguese colonies, and to the underground opposition in Portugal itself. Its alliances with the anti-Salazar Portuguese opposition directly influenced Frelimo's contention that the enemy was to be understood as the Portuguese colonial system but not the Portuguese people, and, as such, could not be defined by race or colour.[111] The Goan intellectual and journalist Aquino de Bragança, once a member of the CONCP Secretariat in Algiers, settled in Mozambique at Samora Machel's invitation after independence, where he filled the role of informal envoy, academic and presidential adviser. Mozambique's own fore-

---

[108] Marcelino dos Santos in *The African Communist*, no. 55, 1973.

[109] *Sunday News* (Tanzania), 2 April 1972.

[110] Newitt, *Portugal in Africa*, pp. 232-3.

[111] See Munslow, *Revolution*, pp. 109, 135.

most Marxist intellectual, Marcelino dos Santos, provided the link
between the Mozambican 'nationalist' movement and the CONCP
of which he was a founder member and then Secretary-General
from its first meeting in April 1961.[112]

Claims to have liberated large numbers of people from effective
colonial control became part of Frelimo's weaponry in its campaign
for international recognition as 'sole legitimate representative' of
the Mozambican people at the OAU, the UN and elsewhere. There
was clearly much exaggeration for propaganda purposes. The emphasis on the liberated zones after Machel's assumption of the
leadership accompanied both the expansion of the war through
Tete in the early 1970s, where the military contest was simply too
fierce for extensive secure areas to develop under Frelimo administration, and the international solidarity campaign which
focused on the Cahora Bassa dam project. In Tete, Frelimo portered
food south for its guerrillas from elsewhere; some was provided
clandestinely by the populations of certain *aldeamentos* and more
was obtained by raids. Agreements were made with local *cantineiros*
and food was quietly given by sympathetic Protestant and Catholic
missions, but the supply was precarious.[113] Nonetheless, some
liberated and semi-liberated zones were carved out, though naturally smaller, less secure and different in character from established
Frelimo areas in the north. In Tete, for example, cassava had to
be introduced as the staple by Frelimo in place of maize, essentially
because as an underground root crop it was less vulnerable to
burning and destruction by napalm.[114] A visitor to Fingwe district
near the Zambia border in August 1971 noted that although the
Portuguese remained in control of Fingwe town and scattered
bases and *aldeamentos*, 7,000 people in the surrounding
countryside came under Frelimo's control.[115]

Foreign visitors were all part of the campaign. They generally
reported that populations living under Frelimo control endured
harsh conditions, but they also noted the presence of an embryonic
political and administrative organisation for the purpose of mobilisation and defence, and some economic activity as well as basic
health and educational services. Frelimo's claim to provide within
the liberated zones services which the Portuguese administration

[112] De Brito, 'Le Frelimo', p. 62.

[113] *Não Vamos Esquecer!*, 2, 4, 1987.

[114] *Ibid.* See also Machel's directives on production at the beginning of the agricultural cycle for 1971-2 in *Mozambique Revolution*, no. 49, October-December 1971,
pp. 20-4.

[115] T. Gifford, 'Struggle in Mozambique' *Third World*, 1, 3, (November 1972).

had so often signally failed to provide were obviously linked to the search for international recognition and support. They entailed some optimistic enhancement, but also represented real aspirations and genuine commitment and effort. Specialised training courses for various officials were introduced in 1971.[116] By 1972 there were reported to be about 190 primary schools operating with 250 teachers and about 20,000 pupils.[117] The conditions were, of course, basic. The focus of teaching materials was on immediately relevant topics, such as the quality of military cadres, arms and enemy attacks, as well as on the policies and programmes of Frelimo. A 'curricular' emphasis on unity and discipline was justified in terms of attempts by the Portuguese to divide and rule, and their corruption of 'traditional' authorities. Health centres were established wherever possible. The first 'provincial hospital' was established in Cabo Delgado in 1968, and by 1972 the number of Frelimo medical and paramedical staff in that province was claimed to have reached some 340. By 1972 Frelimo also claimed that the eastern and western regions of Niassa province each had one regional central hospital, seven district medical posts, nine first aid posts and one quarantine station. In Cabo Delgado, with its much greater population density, there were one provincial central hospital, seventeen district medical posts and sixty first aid posts. However, the progress of the health services was impeded by the shortages of material and qualified staff; besides sending people to study abroad, Frelimo ran its own nursing courses, training an average of two batches of twenty pupils each year, as well as rural medical aids and first-aid assistants.[118] Doubtless this effort reflected the personal interest of Samora Machel, the former hospital nurse, as well as Italian 'solidarity' medical aid.

It was the deteriorating situation in Tete which most disturbed Portugal's regional allies. In 1971 the Rhodesian Central Intelligence Organisation (CIO), South Africa's Bureau of State Security (BOSS) and the DGS formed an intelligence steering committee to exchange information on the situation inside Mozambique.[119] Portuguese concentration on the defence of Cahora Bassa was such that the remainder of the Tete region became a springboard

---

[116] *Tempo*, 248, 6 July 1975.

[117] Anton Johnston, *Study, Produce, and Combat! Education and the Mozambican State 1962-1984*, Studies in Comparative and International Education no. 14, Institute of International Education, University of Stockholm, 1989, p. 78.

[118] *Mozambique Revolution*, no. 51 (April- June 1972), pp. 24-5.

[119] H. Ellert, *The Rhodesian Front War*, pp. 54-5. See also K. Flower, *Serving Secretly*, London, 1987.

from which ZANU guerrillas, with whom Frelimo closely coopera-
ted, could infiltrate into Rhodesia in December 1972. By 1972
Frelimo was beginning to infiltrate, in small groups south and
east from Tete, into the Vila Pery region during 1972, and the
Beira region in 1973, with the Beira railway coming under attack.
After Frelimo crossed the Zambezi and started moving south in
1972, the Rhodesians became more deeply involved in the war
on Portugal's side, while South Africa's direct involvement apparently remained limited to support for the defence of the Cahora
Bassa site by provision of 200-300 paramilitary police on the south
bank of the Zambezi (although it may have allowed Rhodesian
units to recruit from the SADF for combat duty in Mozambique).

The Portuguese counterinsurgency was characterised by containment, stalemate and minimal physical contact, so that western
Tete was written off apart from air strikes. Rhodesian security
forces filled the vacuum. In April 1973 Arriaga disclosed the existence of a 'gentleman's agreement' between Portugal and
Rhodesia enabling their respective troops to cross the common
border in pursuit of Frelimo or ZANLA guerrillas. More and more
of western Tete turned into a Rhodesian battleground with the
involvement of both the Rhodesian SAS and the Rhodesian Light
Infantry (RLI) as well as integration of battle plans between the
Mozambican authorities and the Smith government. The
Rhodesians criticised Portuguese lack of zeal and developed a certain contempt for their reluctance to engage the enemy, and
preference for cooperating with the DGS or the *flechas* rather than
with the army.[120] In the face of a deteriorating situation Rhodesian
forces switched from 'hot pursuit' counter-raids in western Tete
to longer-duration operations into central Mozambique; the incidence of Rhodesian strikes escalated (along with their scale)
from three or four a month in 1971 to at least one a day in early
1974.[121]

The communication routes were now a guerrilla target. As the
Rhodesians were effective in preventing sabotage of the Beira line,
so Frelimo switched its efforts to the Moatize line into Malawi.
The murder of the first white civilian in this area (probably not
the work of Frelimo, which adopted a remarkably restrained policy
that eschewed targetting whites)[122] sparked off riots against the
army in Beira in January 1974. A settler demand for more protection

---

[120] Beckett, 'The Portuguese Army', p. 159.

[121] See Henriksen, *Revolution*, pp. 179-82.

[122] Stanley Duncan interview.

also enabled the DGS to exploit the army's unpopularity in the bitter rivalry which had underlain the entire campaign. SAM missiles made their appearance in the colony in March 1974. Thus, although Frelimo's sphere of operations was, by April 1974, still mainly focussed on the provinces of Cabo Delgado, Niassa and northern Tete, it had managed to establish itself as a presence in the outlying areas of Tete province and, from this base, extend its influence southward towards the central provinces of Manica, Sofala and Zambézia by the end of 1973.[123] However, Frelimo's campaign in Tete was also suffering reverses, and its position there at the end of 1973 was less favourable than at the beginning of the year. Despite war fatigue the Portuguese army, and especially the élite units, could still inflict damage, but 'spread-eagled' across Mozambique, they could not 'prevent infiltration, pacify the countryside or injure fatally the guerrilla infrastructure'.[124] They would not have been able to win. However, few expected the end to come as swiftly as it did, except perhaps for military and intelligence circles in Rhodesia aware of the deteriorating situation in Tete and Frelimo's rapid penetration into Manica and Sofala.[125] But the end, when it came, was a consequence of the collapse of military will in Lisbon and reflected the cumulative effects of thirteen years of wars in Africa and the prospect of eventual defeat in Guinea-Bissau, as well as the deterioration in Mozambique itself.[126]

---

[123] Annette Seegers, 'Revolutionary Armies of Africa: Mozambique and Zimbabwe' in Simon Baynam (ed.), *Military Power: Politics in Black Africa*, London, 1986, pp. 129-63.

[124] Henriksen, *Revolution*, p. 56.

[125] K. Flower, *Serving Secretly*, pp. 300-2; S. Vieira, W.G. Martin, I. Wallerstein (eds), *How Fast the Wind? Southern Africa, 1975-2000*, Trenton, NJ, 1992, p. 18.

[126] See van der Waals, ch. 6, and A.E. Duarte Silva, 'O Vietname português', *Expresso Revista*, 2 October 1993, pp. 44-6.

2

'ANYTHING SEEMED POSSIBLE': THE TRANSITION TO INDEPENDENCE

'To form the true personality of our People, it is necessary to create conditions to unify the habits, customs and traditions and to give them a revolutionary dimension; for this purpose, the Party must create a committee at the national level to gather and analyse all cultural manifestations, such as habits, customs, traditions, plays, dances, songs, tales, poetry, romance, literature, sport etc. – rejecting whatever divides us and gathering together all the common factors of our lives.'[1]

'The outcome was that the white community was engaged in an inner mini-civil war.... Every time a reformed colonialist turned into revolutionary theoretician took to writing an article in the local papers or speaking on local radio stations, a few more hundreds of white settlers would join the queues of airline companies or the cardiologists' consulting rooms. Those skilled people, such as doctors, teachers and technicians, who could more easily find jobs elsewhere, were often the first to leave, thus setting in motion a chain reaction in more ways than one.'[2]

The confused interregnum, April–September 1974

The immediate result of the coup in Lisbon on 25 April 1974 was to put power into the hands of a Junta of National Salvation (JSN) headed by General António de Spínola, whose book *Portugal and the Future* had publicly floated the notion of self-determination for the colonies within a federation dominated by Portugal. However, from the beginning opposing currents within the MFA (Movimento das Forças Armadas) were pushing for a speedy end to the African wars and for complete independence for the colonies with sovereignty ceded to the respective anti-colonial movements.

[1] Resolution of the Mocuba meeting, 16-21 February 1975 in *25 de Setembro: Dia da revolução moçambicana*, p. 132.

[2] António de Figueiredo, *Guardian* supplement on independent Mozambique, 25 June 1975.

Although no differences existed over the need for liberalisation in Portugal itself, there were divergences over the form this should take, so that the main tensions and struggles over policy within the MFA centred on the question of decolonisation. But a convergence of interests on effecting a transfer of power produced a temporary alliance between the colonialist officer corps and its erstwhile opponents, thus introducing an irresistible momentum into the internal politics of Portugal and the timetable of decolonisation in Portuguese Africa.[3]

On 14 July the 'radical' tendency emerged triumphant, with the appointment of a provisional government headed by Colonel Vasco Gonçalves as Prime Minister, and with the adoption of Law no.7/74 which enshrined recognition of the 'right of self-determination, with all its consequences', including independence. However, between the April coup and this decisive shift of policy was an enormously confused period in the African colonies as much as in Portugal, where a variety of political forces struggled for control and authority.[4] The confusion was compounded by competing power structures within Portugal, which made it increasingly difficult to see where real authority lay.[5] Political shifts in Mozambique shadowed the struggles in Lisbon. Colonel David Teixeira Ferreira temporarily replaced Governor-General Pimental dos Santos as the local representative of Portuguese authority; then in mid-May Soares de Melo was named Governor-General and fronted an office headed by elements of the Democratas de Moçambique (of which more below), while the town halls were handed over to administrative commissions, with the (unfulfilled) promise that they would later be replaced by elected bodies. A law of 24 July created military governing juntas in Angola and Mozambique, but one was not appointed in Mozambique because of Frelimo objections.[6] Soares de Melo resigned as Governor-General and powers were transferred to Ferro Ribeiro, who acted as government representative until in September 1974 a Transitional Government was formed to take the country to independence, in accordance with the settlement finally negotiated between Portugal and Frelimo.[7]

---

[3] Kenneth Maxwell, 'Portugal and Africa: the Last Empire' in Prosser Gifford and W.M. Roger Louis (eds), *The Transfer of Power in Africa: Decolonization, 1940-1960*, New Haven, CT, 1982, pp. 337-85.

[4] See *A Descolonização Portuguesa*, Lisbon, 1982, vol. 2, ch. 1.

[5] See Gallagher, *Portugal*, vol. 2, pp. 192ff.

[6] Stanley Duncan interview.

[7] *A Descolonização Portuguesa*, vol. 2, pp. 21-3.

Whatever was decided at higher levels, Portuguese power in the colonies began to disintegrate on the ground immediately after the coup. Morale among regular Portuguese troops crumbled, and a form of unilateral ceasefire affected even élite units such as the commandos, in their case allegedly due to orders from Costa Gomes, Lisbon's Chief of the General Staff, to limit operational activity to defensive action. From the announcement of the opening of a new operational front in Zambézia in July 1974, large-scale desertions from the Portuguese armed forces began to occur. There were reported to be 1,000 desertions in Zambézia itself, while other troops in the province refused to fight; 2,000 men at the Boane barracks near Lourenço Marques refused to be sent to the operational zones. In Nampula, high-ranking officers declared themselves in favour of halting operations against Frelimo.[8] With Spínola's public recognition of the right to independence on 27 July, unofficial ceasefires began breaking out in patchwork fashion all over Mozambique, sometimes directly negotiated between the local army command and Frelimo units.[9] Even without a formal ceasefire agreement, weary and dispirited Portuguese troops were withdrawing to the towns from bases all over northern Mozambique.[10]

The Portuguese community was badly divided in the midst of the uncertainty and physical insecurity and found adaptation to the new conditions of political freedom difficult after years of dictatorship. First and foremost, there was a division between the metropolitan Portuguese working in Mozambique as part of the administration, and white Mozambicans. The former simply wished to return home; the latter, whatever their political stripe, warmly welcomed the prospect of a 'free' Mozambique run by Mozambicans, although their hopes for its political complexion varied widely. Thus a variety of factions emerged among the white population, representing three kinds of responses to the loosening of Lisbon's grip. A significant number of whites, particularly students and professionals, had some sympathy for Frelimo. A second response came from those attempting to bring Frelimo into some kind of 'moderate' government; while further to the right an un-

---

[8] Christie, *Machel of Mozambique*, Harare, 1988, p. 83. *Daily Express* 25 July 1974. The 25 June 1975 edition of *Mozambique Revolution* refers to the struggle in Zambézia in mid-1974 and to the voluntary adherence to Frelimo ranks of 5,000 'patriots', most of them GEs and GEPs. See also José and Vieira in Vieira, Martin and Wallerstein (eds). *How Fast the Wind?*, pp. 22-3.

[9] *Financial Times*, 30 July 1974.

[10] *Sunday Mail*, 28 July 1974.

stable amalgam of white settlers, small businessmen and traders, skilled workers and poor whites, grouped together under the banner of the Frente Independente de Convergência Ocidental (FICO, meaning 'I stay' in Portuguese), encompassed divergent aims ranging from Rhodesian-style unilateral declaration of independence (UDI) to partition under Rhodesian or South African auspices.[11]

'Progressive' whites, especially the Democrats (who had formed the local white liberal opposition to the dictatorship), played an important role in the transition period. They represented and publicised Frelimo positions when the only Frelimo presence in the cities was a clandestine one. Indeed, the Democrats have been accused of seeking to 'capture' strategic posts in the press and radio for this very purpose.[12] Lawyers (and journalists) were prominent in Democrat ranks, and one important initiative they took was the formation of a committee to investigate 'crimes against humanity' which collected 1,000 depositions from ex-prisoners in DGS jails in Mozambique, most if not all of them Frelimo supporters and activists, whose accusations ranged from murder and torture to malnutrition.[13] This evidence was crucial in persuading the Portuguese military authorities to mount 'Operation Zebra' on 8 June 1974, which resulted in the arrest of 600 DGS personnel over the whole country and their detention in Machava prison (though about twenty escaped to Rhodesia and South Africa).[14]

Support for Frelimo also came from white university students in Lourenco Marques who belonged to the Associação Académica de Moçambique (AAM), with its links to clandestine opposition groups in Portugal of leftist persuasion, ranging from pro-Soviet to 'Maoist'. Of course the ranks of apparently 'progressive' whites were swollen by a combination of euphoria, resulting from the events in Portugal itself, and sheer opportunism. An experienced journalist, revisiting Lourenço Marques in August 1974, later commented drily on the sudden emergence of large numbers of white 'revolutionaries':

A larger proportion of the white community than I ever imagined

[11] Middlemass, 'Twentieth Century White Society in Mozambique'.

[12] Rita-Ferreira, *Mocambique post-25 Abril.* The actions of the Democrats are also recorded (sympathetically) by Bernardino G. Oliveira, *Aqui Portugal Moçambique,* 1978.

[13] See *Tortura na Colónia de Moçambique, 1963-1974. Depoimentos de presos políticos,* Porto, 1977.

[14] *Daily Telegraph,* 2 May 1974; Oliveira, p. 167. An estimated 1,000-2,000 Frelimo supporters were freed from jails in Lourenço Marques on 1 May 1974 on the orders of the junta in Lisbon.

had all along it seems been secret followers of Frelimo.[...] Most of them were, of course, unconsciously engaged in a perennial struggle for survival, looking for rewarding positions in which to carry on with a 'civilising mission' in another disguise. And, since Frelimo did not have enough black cadres to go around, many of the white revolutionaries took over control of the media and other key posts, thus exercising an influence out of proportion to their numbers.[15]

Of those who wished to pursue strategies that would incorporate Frelimo in a broader-based government Jorge Jardim was certainly the best publicised, largely through his control of the press in Beira. Even before the April coup he had unsuccessfully pursued a settlement of the war which would have had some regional support. The essentials of his plan included independence for Mozambique within a community of lusophone states which would leave Portugal the leading role; and an elected government of an independent Mozambique with Frelimo participation but without Frelimo hegemony. Jardim succeeded in interesting President Kaunda of Zambia in his ideas, and direct talks took place during July-September 1973 with him or with one of his aides. They resulted in a document known as the 'Lusaka Programme', approved by Kaunda, who tried to persuade Samora Machel to accept it, but it received a cool reception in Lisbon from Caetano.[16]

Although General Spínola held talks with Jardim within two weeks of the coup, Jardim's influence in official Portuguese circles hardly extended beyond the city of Beira. Jardim's own Beira newspaper published proposals at the beginning of May for a referendum on independence within three months; the establishment of political parties, including Frelimo; expansion of the electoral register to include all adults; and finally it was hoped that elections backed by the presence of 70,000 troops would result in a 'moderate' centre party forming the first independent government.[17] These ideas were influential with a section of the white community and with some urban *assimilados* in Beira, the country's commercial centre and second city. Groups and civic associations willing to follow schemes for autonomous government based on Spínola's proposals began forming in May 1974, but it is difficult to discern how far Jardim's influence (and money) may have been behind them, although his personal support seems to have gone to Domin-

---

[15] De Figueredo, *Guardian* supplement.

[16] See D. Martin and P. Johnson, *The Struggle for Zimbabwe*, London, 1981, ch. 8.

[17] *Guardian*, 6 May 1974.

gos Arouca, a black lawyer who had been imprisoned by the Portuguese authorities as a Frelimo supporter.[18] There were, however, important differences of emphasis between Jardim's scheme and Spínola's; and while it seems that Spínola continued to insist on self-rule for Mozambique within an eventual lusophone federation with foreign and defence matters retained by Lisbon, Jardim foresaw a looser arrangement which would give Mozambique more control over its own affairs.[19]

The sudden growth of weakly structured and mainly insignificant black political movements in urban areas – some claiming multiracialism and appealing for white support – appears only to have increased Frelimo's determination to see a clear handover of power to itself (supported in this by a very active campaign by white Frelimo sympathisers against any proposed referendum).[20] The most significant among these parties was the Grupo Unido de Moçambique (GUMO) led by Dr Joana Simeão, a lawyer and a Macua (with, therefore, a potentially large ethnic constituency). It had already published a manifesto demanding economic independence for Mozambique, leading eventually to political freedom, but without necessarily separating the country from Portuguese influence.[21] Dr Simeão came to prominence in the local press before the April 1974 coup, and possibly enjoyed some support from the Portuguese authorities.[22] The size of some GUMO rallies nonetheless suggests that it possessed some political appeal for black city-dwellers.

In May 1974 General Costa Gomes, the most senior member of the junta after Spínola and Chief of the General Staff, made a four-day visit to Mozambique, which was marred by serious racial disturbances in Beira, and a wave of strikes culminating shortly after his departure in a stoppage by more than 1,000 railway workers in Lourenço Marques. He used his visit to appeal to Frelimo for a ceasefire and to enter negotiations to end the war. On two

[18] See T.H. Henriksen, *Mozambique: A History*, London, 1978, pp. 221-4.

[19] *Daily Telegraph*, 6 May 1974. Jardim's fortunes subsequently plummeted. Having taken refuge in the Malawi embassy in Lisbon he fled to Spain in June and died in Gabon in 1982.

[20] De Brito, Le Frelimo, p. 162.

[21] *A Descolonização portuguesa*, Vol. 1, p. 319.

[22] Jardim, *Moçambique*, p. 288. According to Christie, *Machel of Mozambique* (p. 85) a furious Machel, on hearing of the September 1974 revolt – see following page – made accusations to the remaining member of the Portuguese delegation in Lusaka that Costa Gomes had tried to promote an opposition movement to Frelimo under Simeão's leadership.

occasions he stated his belief that the people of the colony would choose something between the 'extremes' of independence and the *status quo* at a planned referendum.[23] But Frelimo saw no need to compromise its demand for full independence under its sole leadership, without any referendum or other popular consultation on the country's future, and refused to concede a ceasefire until its conditions were met. Indeed, increasingly aware of the contradictory currents inside the Portuguese government over decolonisation, Frelimo stepped up the war, calibrating the exercise of military pressure with a negotiating strategy which sought simultaneously to weaken the Spínola faction and to strengthen that line within the MFA (which Frelimo associated with Melo Antunes, a leading Leftist member) favourable to their own position.[24]

In their northern strongholds Frelimo guerrillas had started coming into towns as early as August 1974, before any political settlement had been reached, and openly addressing what were, in all but name, political rallies.[25] Elsewhere, however, the collapse of Portuguese rule had precipitated increasing disorder and violence in rural areas, with looting of rural shops and the destruction, closure or occupation of many rural businesses. At this point many of the *cantineiros* (often of Indian origin) fled to the relative safety of the towns, and the rural commercial networks began to disappear. The transport and communications system had already been severely affected by industrial unrest and by Frelimo attack. Increasingly, specialised and technical staff of the agro-industrial complexes and many private firms transferred *en masse* to those areas of the economy – largely in the urban centres – that were still functioning. White emigration began at the same time.

These were the real pressures that underlay negotiations between Portugal and Frelimo, which finally brought the long-awaited official declaration of a ceasefire by Frelimo on 8 September 1974. Indirect contacts between the two parties took place in May, followed by the first, inconclusive round of peace talks in early June, with the Portuguese side still committed to a referendum and unwilling to concede Frelimo's demands, which comprised recognition of Frelimo as the Mozambican people's legitimate representative; recognition of the Mozambican people's right to complete independence; and the transfer of power to Frelimo. But a secret

---

[23] Martin and Johnson, *The Struggle for Zimbabwe*, p. 117.

[24] See de Bragança, 'Independência sem Descolonização' in *Estudos Africanos* 5/6 (1986), pp. 7-28.

[25] Lourenço Marques radio, 12 August 1974.

meeting in Dar es Salaam beginning on 30 July brought Frelimo
the prize it sought, affirming that the MFA and Frelimo were the
legitimate and authentic representatives of, respectively, the Portuguese and Mozambican peoples. A secret protocol according
Portuguese recognition to Frelimo was then signed. Subsequently,
a larger delegation headed by Antunes, and including Foreign
Minister Mario Soares and Almeida Santos, met Frelimo again in
Dar es Salaam on 14-17 August. It laid the foundations for the
final negotiations in Lusaka on 5-7 September in which Portugal
ceded all Frelimo's demands. The clauses of the agreement, signed
on the 7th, formed the political, military and legal basis for the
transfer of power and contained a ceasefire agreement entering
into force at zero hour on 8 September.

By this means Portugal undertook the progressive transfer of
power to Frelimo until the day of independence, set for 25 June
1975 (the anniversary of Frelimo's foundation). Government and
military structures were to be divided between the Portuguese state
and Frelimo. There were to be a Cabinet dominated by Frelimo
(with two-thirds of the ministers), a high commissioner appointed
by Portugal, and a joint military commission with equal representation from both sides responsible for security and for supervising the ceasefire. Details of the economic and technical aspects
of decolonisation were not announced, although the agreement
declared Frelimo to be responsible for the financial obligations
assumed by the Portuguese state in the name of Mozambique –
provided that these had been assumed in the effective interests
of the territory – and created a Central Bank, so that Mozambique
might have the means to pursue an independent financial policy.
Before the economic and technical negotiations began, the two
sides adopted a timetable whereby all the outstanding points should
be settled by Independence Day. These negotiations took place
in four phases in both Mozambique and Portugal from late January
to June 1975, and included decisions on Cahora Bassa and establishing both the central bank and monetary reserves.[26]

Fighting the internal enemy

Within hours of the finalisation of the Lusaka Agreement the
self-styled 'Dragoons of Death' allied to FICO attempted to wreck
it. Although the events of 7 September were sparked off by an

[26] For an account of the negotiation of the Lusaka Agreement see J. Mittelman,
Underdevelopment and the Transition to Socialism in Mozambique and Tanzania, New
York, 1981.

attack on a lorry in Lourenço Marques flying the Frelimo flag, they had been preceded the previous evening by a demonstration outside newspaper offices controlled by the Democrats. Subsequently the headquarters of the Democratas de Moçambique and the university students' centre came under attack. Calling themselves the Movimento Moçambique Livre, the organisers of the revolt freed former DGS operatives from prison and then occupied the radio station, broadcasting appeals through the night and all the next day for people to resist the handover of power to Frelimo alone, and for those of all races and creeds to join them. Leaders of some small black political parties accepted – foolishly, as it turned out, for their own self-interests. Ex-Frelimo dissidents such as Uria Simango added their presence and voices to the radio appeals. Paulo Gumane even returned from Swaziland to join in the revolt.[27]

There is little evidence of any black Mozambican support for their action – which, after it collapsed, gave Frelimo the excuse and opportunity to move in due course against almost the entire internal African political opposition, grouped since August 1974 under the umbrella National Coalition Party (PCN). Although FICO hoped to recruit Domingos Arouca during the days of the 'coup', he wisely remained aloof from this action and refrained from lending it support in any way. He too, however, later found it necessary to go into exile, in Lisbon.

For the brief period that the revolt lasted, a wave of white enthusiasm in Lourenço Marques was bolstered by a sense of betrayal at the hands of the metropolitan government in Lisbon. The revolt, in its turn, also served to strengthen the Frelimo/MFA alliance. On 8 September, Machel broadcast from Lusaka that, 'in the spirit and letter of the Lusaka Agreement', the FPLM (liberation forces) and the Portuguese armed forces, 'true to their word, will cooperate closely to safeguard public order, defend territorial integrity and guarantee the process of Mozambican independence.[28] The rebellion was in fact peacefully neutralised by the Portuguese military on orders from Lisbon. Late on the 10th, the radio station was surrendered, and those ex-paratroopers holding the airport control tower were instructed to do likewise to avoid bloodshed. For the next two days, however, the African areas of the city were in violent ferment. With news of killings by white mobs in the suburbs, Portuguese troops prevented black crowds

[27] See Clotilde Mesquitéla, *Moçambique 7 de Setembro. Memórias da Revolução*, Lisbon, 1978, p. 97.

[28] BBC Summary of World Broadcasts, 10 September 1974.

from marching on the centre of the city only with intense valleys of rifle fire. Final hospital figures were revised from eighty-two dead and 400-500 wounded, to 115 and almost 600 respectively some two weeks later, but the real number of casualties was certainly higher.[29] The bloody clashes between the 'rebels' and supporters of Frelimo provided the main reason for the agreement to surrender.

What prevented worse casualties was the practical security cooperation on the ground between Frelimo and the Portuguese military. Portuguese reinforcements were brought down from the north, raising the numbers in the capital to 10,000-12,000, and Frelimo units also flew south in Portuguese military transports.[30] More FPLM units were brought in to Beira to patrol the African areas and prevent the spread of violence there.[31] The situation in these southern and central Mozambican cities was in notable contrast to events in the north, where considerable numbers of Portuguese troops and a relatively well-organised Frelimo presence prevented anti-independence demonstrations from erupting into disorder. Although the revolt in Lourenço Marques directly involved about 250 armed militants, it precipitated events which caused some 5,000 whites to flee by rail to neighbouring countries between 11 and 17 September alone; according to official figures the number of refugees over the border later reached 15,000.[32] By early 1975, an estimated 80,000 whites out of the 120,000 enumerated at the 1970 census had left.[33] Of the approximately 100 DGS officials and agents released by FICO from Machava prison during their revolt, only about one-third returned to Portugal. A number made their way to South Africa, where they were they were picked up by BOSS.[34]

Machel himself took no part in the transitional administration and remained in Dar es Salaam, but Alberto Chipande, Frelimo's defence chief and delegate to the mixed defence and security commission established under the Lusaka Agreement entered Lourenço Marques with the Frelimo forces in September. Although, as agreed, two-thirds of ministers were to be Frelimo nominees and one-third Portuguese, two out of the latter three (Alcântara

---

[29] *Guardian*, 23 September 1974.

[30] *Daily Telegraph*, 13 September 1974.

[31] *The Times*, 14 September 1974.

[32] BBC Summary of World Broadcasts, 3 December 1974.

[33] *Financial Times*, 23 May 1975.

[34] João Paulo Guerra, *Os 'flechas' atacam de novo*, Lisbon, 1988, pp. 144-5.

Santos and António Paulino) were also Frelimo sympathisers who went on to occupy high office after independence. This twelve-man Transitional Government was inaugurated on 20 September under the prime ministership of Joaquim Chissano, previously Frelimo's chief of security. He had already been propelled into the public arena by this appeals for calm; his genuine concern at the violence created a universally favourable impression.[35]

Portuguese repatriation of its forces from Mozambique began in October and underlined the continued need for close cooperation with Frelimo to ensure that this proceeded unimpeded by local disorder, while Frelimo's commitment was underscored by its release on 20 September of nearly 200 Portuguese soldiers who were subsequently flown from a camp in southern Tanzania to Nangade. In a speech broadcast on Lourenço Marques radio the following day, Samora Machel expressed due pride that Frelimo's policy of clemency

'...defined by our Central Committee and solemnly reaffirmed at our second congress held in 1968 in the liberated zones of Niassa, laid it down that we were to treat with the utmost respect and humanity all prisoners of war...not a single Portuguese soldier ever suffered any maltreatment at our hands. Not a single Portuguese soldier taken prisoner has died in captivity.'[36]

Further bloody disturbances occurred in the capital on 21 October, following a clash between Frelimo and Portuguese soldiers and subsequent rioting in the black suburbs, resulting in some 50 deaths and 160 injured.[37] The coordinated efforts of Portuguese and Frelimo troops, operating separately to avoid further clashes and in white and black areas of the city respectively, managed to restore relative calm, but further repressive measures were deemed necessary. A combined operation by police and Frelimo on 26-27 October picked up an estimated 1,200 'agitators or lawbreakers'.[38] Subsequently, Decree-Law 11/74 was published, with a view to neutralising 'the action of agitators and subversive elements who seek to oppose by all means, even violent, the process of decolonisation in course'. Mandatory prison sentences were increased by

[35] C.F. Spence's unpublished diary of events in Mozambique, 25 April 1974-22 March 1976.

[36] BBC monitoring report, 24 September 1974. The contrast with the absence of Frelimo prisoners-of-war in Portuguese hands has often been remarked on, but Frelimo prisoners were, of course, 'dealt with' by the DGS.

[37] *Daily Telegraph*, 23 October 1974.

[38] *Times*, 28 October 1974.

50%, and sentences for more serious offences fixed at between two and eight years, detainees remaining in the custody of the military authorities until brought to justice. Provision for habeas corpus, only recently introduced by the post-revolution Portuguese authorities, was eliminated in Mozambique.[39]

This was the context in which 're-education camps' were established. Initially at least, they appear to have been an emergency measure to feed, house and process large numbers of detainees (although political re-education of prisoners began in Frelimo's liberated zones in 1966, where 'turning' enemy agents in this way was seen as an alternative to execution and part of the newly-adopted policy of clemency towards members of the Portuguese colonial forces).[40] The first camps were established at the end of 1974 on abandoned *colonatos* outside the capital. One such, created in December 1974 at Inhassume (Inhambane province), housed 160 '*marginais*' from Lourenço Marques and existed alongside several agricultural cooperatives; its inmates were described by the press as engaged in agricultural cultivation and benefiting from political education and literacy classes.[41] There is little doubt that conditions in many others were considerably worse.[42] In October 1975 the newly-created National Security Service (SNASP) was empowered to consign people to the re-education camps without trial, its powers being made retroactive to September 1974. In the early days large numbers were so consigned, including prostitutes, drug addicts and 'deviants' of various kinds, as well as Jehovah's Witnesses. The anti-Frelimo dissidents implicated in the radio station revolt also found their way there after independence, having been snatched by Frelimo from their countries of refuge during the period of the Transitional Government and held temporarily at Nachingwea (these included Uria Simango, Mateus Gwengere and Lazaro Nkavandame).[43] In March 1975 Machel personally paraded 240 Mozambican collaborators before the press at Nachingwea including Nkavandame, Simango, Gwengere, Gumane and many other well-known names; a similar parade the following month

---

[39] Rita-Ferreira, 'Moçambique pos-25 de Abril'.

[40] *Justiça Popular*, no. 8/9 (Jan/June 1984), p. 13.

[41] *Tempo* 239, 27 April 1975, pp. 47-53.

[42] *Guardian* 25 February 1975.

[43] Jorge Jardim charges in *Moçambique* that Paulo José Gumane (whom Banda had never liked) was arrested in Malawi and handed over to the Portuguese authorities at Milange, he and his companions being taken, handcuffed, to Frelimo and immediately transferred to Dar es Salaam.

included Joana Simeão, who had arrived there only three days previously.[44]

Re-education camps were also used to remove dissidents within Frelimo. Its soldiers expected to enjoy something of the fruits of victory; and although many former guerrillas were drafted into government or to fill posts in the administration, and others were sent out into the countryside in an organising capacity, there were grievances in the towns and especially in Lourenço Marques about lack of pay and the absence of ranks and promotion. Meanwhile the privileges of those members who had been given government posts were all too apparent. Lack of leave, particularly for the Makondes, led to indiscipline and finally, after Machel's disciplinary counter-measures (beginning in July/August), to the open mutiny of 400 soldiers at Machava barracks.[45] Over the next six months, the army was purged of dissidents and converted into a conventional defence force allied to, but separate from, Frelimo. Its numbers were kept up by recruitment; the chief threat to national security was seen as a Rhodesian invasion.[46]

In the rather chaotic circumstances of the transition Frelimo increasingly understood its difficulties as the machinations of an 'internal enemy' which worked through rumour, conspiracy and economic sabotage to undermine its policies and defeat the revolution. The identity of this internal enemy was shifting and ill defined, and was characterised rather by decadent and corrupt attitudes than by class position. The important 8th Session of the Frelimo Central Committee (enlarged to include members of the Frelimo Executive Committee and the FPLM) defined the 'permanent enemy' of the Mozambican people as 'imperialism' and the world capitalist system. It explained that 'agents of imperialist reaction' were recruited from the colonial bourgeoisie and from the small and medium national bourgeoisie. But almost everyone was suspect, including the peasantry outside the liberated zones. Even the working class was described as vulnerable to the manouevres of the enemy because of its poorly developed class consciousness. The

---

[44] *Daily News* (Tanzania), 18 March 1975; *Guardian*, 23 April 1975. An Africa Watch report *Conspicuous Destruction* (July 1992), suggests that a number of these detainees, including Nkavandame, Simeão and Simango, were executed in 1983 when the government feared they would be freed by South African agents and recruited to Renamo.

[45] See 'Vencer a batalha de classe' (Report of the 4th National Conference of the Frelimo Defence Department, 25 July-2 August 1975), which lists a number of FPLM cadres dismissed for corruption and indiscipline.

[46] Middlemass, 'Mozambique: Two years of independence'; see also de Brito, 'Le Frelimo', pp. 200-4.

'internal enemy' comprised all the various hostile or obstructive forces by which Frelimo felt itself beleaguered. This would play an increasingly important part in the party perception of the political difficulties it faced.

'Dynamising' Mozambique

While Chissano and his team worked in Lourenço Marques to build the foundations for independence – this involved dealing with the departing Portuguese over complex technical issues such as debt, the future of Cahora Bassa, development aid, relations between the Mozambican airline and the Portuguese TAP, white civil service pay and pensions – Machel remained based in Tanzania, along with other Frelimo leaders responsible for the party, the army and the mass movement.[47] He travelled in December 1974 to East Germany, Bulgaria and Romania, and in March 1975 to China and North Korea, to make agreements on future economic cooperation. In May he toured Tanzania and Zambia to express appreciation for their support during the independence struggle. Finally, on 24 May he began a month-long tour of Mozambique from the Rovuma river in the north to the Maputo river in the south, addressing mass rallies along the way to explain Frelimo's policies. In his broadcast to the Mozambican people on the eve of the transitional government, he outlined its intentions in uncompromising terms:

> 'To decolonise the state means essentially to dismantle the political, administrative, cultural, financial, economic, educational, legal and other systems which, as an integral part of the colonial state, were destined exclusively to impose foreign domination and the will of the exploiters on the masses.'[48]

On 25 June 1975 Frelimo nationalised land and, a month later, the social sectors of law, medicine, education and funeral services. The size of the adverse Portuguese reaction and the devastating economic implications of the exodus which followed were probably entirely unforeseen by Frelimo. The nationalisation of rented property (on 3 February 1976, the same day that Lourenço Marques was renamed Maputo) accelerated the flight. These measures dispossessed not only the administrative and rentier classes, as Frelimo

[47] Middlemass, 'Mozambique: Two Years of Independence'.

[48] *Notícias*, 24 September 1974, quoted in Rita-Ferreira, 'Moçambique pos-25 de Abril', p. 135.

intended, but also skilled white artisans in the ports and railways whose savings had traditionally been invested in property. By the end of 1976, some 90% of whites had left, a few to be accepted in South Africa, roughly 25,000 in Rhodesia, and the rest as penniless refugees in Portugal or Brazil. The majority of those who had taken Mozambique citizenship after independence reverted during 1976 to Portuguese status, and many whites who had genuinely sought to live under the new conditions were forced out – contrary to Frelimo intentions; following the enactment of a law enforcing the choice between Mozambique citizenship or expulsion, the majority of these fled in chaotic conditions.[49]

The flight created dramatic economic problems. Businesses were abandoned, tens of thousands of domestic servants lost their employment, and the rapid collapse of the building boom and the tourist industry threw many thousands more out of work. As the settler exodus gained momentum, the pool of skilled and semi-skilled workers shrank, losing not only white Portuguese but also literate black Mozambicans or *mestiços* who had formed a significant proportion (up to 30%) of the skilled working class. In particular many *assimilados* had, as investors, been adversely affected by the nationalisation of rented property, and joined the exodus to Portugal.[50] The commercial network throughout the countryside, much of it dependent on Portuguese or Indian traders, continued to unravel, industries collapsed, and farms were left without managers and technicians. Social services disintegrated and the whole administrative network lost the bulk of its qualified staff. Frelimo's immediate response was to assume control over as much as possible of what the settlers left, in order to maintain production and keep the economy operating. State control through a so-called 'intervention' process was thus assumed not so much as part of a premeditated strategy, 'but rather as a defensive measure to stave off a greater evil – the total collapse of economic activity'.[51] The intervention law (Decree-Law 16/75 of 13 February 1975) allowed the state to take over the running of an abandoned or sabotaged business, permitting the former owner to reclaim it later under certain circumstances. By the end of 1976 more than 300 businesses had been subjected to this process.

Portuguese administrators also disappeared, leaving a vacuum

[49] Middlemass, 'Mozambique: Two years of independence'.

[50] Landeg White, personal communication.

[51] Grete Brochmann and Arve Ofstad, *Mozambique: Norwegian Assistance in a Context of Crisis*, Fantoft, 1990, p. 13.

which, given the dearth of skills, could not be easily filled: at independence there were, for example, only about forty Mozambican university graduates in the whole country. With no relevant organisational experience, and cadres forged in armed struggle who had exercised some degree of control in only four provinces, the movement suddenly found itself forced to disperse over the entire national territory and to grapple with an economic and administrative apparatus constructed to serve the colonial regime. About 5,000 members of the FPLM were placed in government posts and provincial administrations, and during 1975 many of the remaining troops were sent out to the countryside, to mobilise the people, and to try to deal with such major problems as the future of abandoned estates, colonatos and the *aldeamentos*. FPLM officers were also frequently assigned to fill such roles as that of district administrator. In its first session, the Council of Ministers decided on the abolition of the *regedorias*, thereby stripping the *régulos* of their role and powers.[52] In practical terms, the only unit which initially remained operational below the district was that of the village, or in larger towns the ward (*bairro*). Thus entire layers of local administration disappeared, and the structure at the local level was further confused by a division of the country into liberated and other areas. In the liberated areas the local party unit was the *círculo* (circle or cell), to which all Frelimo's local wartime supporters belonged, but there was little organised Frelimo presence on the ground outside these areas.

Beyond this deployment of available cadres the hope seemed to be that 'popular solutions' would somehow resolve the intractable and anti-democratic nature of the state apparatus, and suggest how it might be transformed. Thus Frelimo's main answer to its lack of effective presence over large areas of the country was to tap the great popular upsurge of energy and enthusiasm released by the end of the war through the dynamising groups – *Grupos Dinamizadores* or GDs – whose establishment was announced by Machel in September 1974. Their appointed task was to apply the directives of Frelimo and of the Transitional Government and to exercise vigilance against sabotage by 'agents of colonial reaction'.[53] They were essentially *ad hoc* groups of eight to ten people set up in urban areas, villages and workplaces. Their members were sometimes militants known to Frelimo from underground activities, but more often they were simply local volunteers (though Frelimo

[52] De Brito, 'Le Frelimo', p. 181.

[53] Rita-Ferreira, 'Moçambique'.

members were expected to provide leadership) who were then confirmed in their posts at public meetings. Their role was at first largely defensive: preventing anti-white violence in the black suburbs, as during the incidents in September and October, and economic sabotage by the remaining settlers. In Frelimo's official account the GDs were:

> ....our basic weapon in the struggle against all forms of economic sabotage, and against all attempts to confuse, divide, corrupt and subvert the workers. In the transition period, the activity of the GDs restrained the escalation of capitalist manoeuvres and put the reactionaries on the defensive. They kept hundreds of abandoned farms working. They organised the workers to be vigilant, and deepened their awareness of the nature of the enemy, his objectives and methods. [...] The reactionary provocation in the capital in December 1975...collapsed completely thanks to the firm and prompt action of the FPLM, supported by the people organised in the framework of the Dynamising Groups.[54]

But it also fell to the GDs to hold regular community and workplace meetings to explain Frelimo policies and to 'dynamise' people by stimulating them to take initiatives themselves. They took over more and more official functions from the steadily collapsing colonial apparatus.[55]

Yet despite their enthusiasm, even the more uncritical could not fail to note shortcomings. 'Like the committees in the liberated areas before them, they were somewhat unstructured and variable in form, and of course their success record also varied.'[56] Some GDs clearly wrought havoc with enthusiastic abandon, creating more problems than they solved. There were frequent purges, and those expelled were usually denounced by Frelimo as opportunists who sought to use membership of the GDs for personal advancement, although 'infiltration' by former DGS agents and others was also alleged. However, diagnosis of the difficulties was no straightforward matter. Frelimo's first national Plenary Meeting inside Mozambique at Mocuba (Zambézia province) in February 1975, with 372 delegates from Frelimo's district committees in

---

[54] Third Congress Central Committee Report.

[55] See J. Hanlon, *Mozambique: the Revolution under Fire,* London, 1984, pp. 49-50.

[56] John Saul, 'The Content: A Transition to Socialism?' in John Saul (ed.), *A Difficult Road: The Transition to Socialism in Mozambique,* New York, 1985, pp. 75-151, p. 71 See also the assessment of GDs in A. Isaacman, *A Luta Continua: Creating a New Society in Mozambique,* Southern Africa Pamphlets no. 1, 1978; and Munslow, *Revolution,* p. 153.

attendance, concluded on the matter of their failings and appropriate disciplinary action:

> One must distinguish between ideas or erroneous tendencies – such as, for example, superstition, witchcraft and polygamy – from the deviation of policy or reactionary manoeuvre, such as those who support the reconciling of opposing ideologies. In many cases, the distinction is not an easy one because no clear line exists between deviation and error. [...] Revolutionary discipline is the sentinel of the political line of Frelimo. All forms of undisciplined behaviour, such as so-called 'leftism', liberalism, lack of respect for hierarchy, spreading rumours, intrigue are ideological deviations.[57]

A national conference on ways to improve the GDs was held in May 1975, but the same problems still preoccupied the government eighteen months later, as party leaders continued to call for the purging of reactionary elements and former opponents of Frelimo who were seeking to gather strength for renewed opposition from inside the party.

Just as serious was the confusion of responsibilities at local level, particularly the conflict between the administrative cadre (some the remnants of colonial personnel) and the GDs. In Marromeu (Zambézia province) power was shared between a small army detachment, the administration, the political commissar and the GD. It was impossible to find out who had final responsibility, and there were occasions when the Governor of Beira had to intervene personally to prevent bloodshed.[58] Initially lacking any form of model or central direction, it seems that the GDs did offer a useful forum for Frelimo's exhortations and political education, but they not only failed to galvanise production, but by their interventions hampered work patterns and such management as still remained. It has been suggested that the GDs interfered increasingly and damagingly in the management of businesses and services, their denunciations leading to many workers being jailed. A whole series of Frelimo directives aimed at moderating and disciplining their behaviour had little discernible effect. Finally Machel was compelled to intervene, and in a key speech on 13 October 1976 which cited the severe economic problems the country was facing he announced the launching of the 'Generalised Political

---

[57] The final conclusions of the meeting were published in the collection *25 de Setembro. Dia da revolução moçambicana*, pp. 103-63.

[58] Leroy Vail and Landeg White, *Capitalism and Colonialism in Mozambique: A Study of Quelimane District*, London, 1980, p. 393.

and Organisational Offensive on the Production Front'. Part of this offensive was the creation of Production Councils, which in practice relegated the GDs to second place. 'But during the two years of their almost uncontrolled activity they managed to drive many owners, managers, and technical cadres in private firms to despair – and the decision to abandon everything.'[59]

In these circumstances Frelimo's instincts precluded any fundamental restructuring of the state apparatus. The continuity was very much a case of a swamped Frelimo administration afraid of the consequences of dismantling any part of the state apparatus. Some suggestions for fundamental alterations were made in the early days, but were not then judged feasible: the Cabo Delgado delegation, for example, came to the Mocuba conference of February 1975 armed with concrete proposals for greater financial and administrative autonomy at provincial level, an improvement in communications, simplification of bureaucracy, and a remodelling of the existing structures and administrative divisions, but Armando Gurbuza, Frelimo National Commissar and Minister for Internal Administration in the Transitional Government, urged caution, condemning 'the implicit demagogy in the precipitate attempt by the Provisional Government to substitute for the present administrative structure an unrepresentative system of municipal administration, while ignoring the problems existing outside the urban centres'.[60]

Creating the new society

Yet despite 'the *confusão*', the new government remained optimistic. 'In 1976 Frelimo and Mozambique were carried forward on a wave of enthusiasm. They had beaten the Portuguese and they had kept the country going, despite the exodus and sabotage. Anything seemed possible.'[61] Thus as they struggled to consolidate their hold on the country the Frelimo élite also sought to fashion their vision of the new society to be created. For this they drew on the image of the liberated zones which shaped what might be described as a 'strategic politico-moral map' of the country. As Machel had explained in 1971:

---

[59] Rita-Ferreira, 'Moçambique pos-25 de Abril', pp. 150-2.

[60] *Tempo*, no. 231, 2 March 1975.

[61] Hanlon, *Mozambique: The Revolution under Fire*, p. 51.

Everything has a content determined by the zone in which it is, by the kind of power that prevails in that zone. In the capitalist and colonialist zone, schools, fields, roads, courts, shops, technology, laws and education – everything serves to oppress and exploit us.

In our zone, because we have power, because it is the peasants, the workers, the working masses who plan and lead, everything is directed towards liberating man, serving the people. This is what happens with the hospitals, the health services.[...]

Whereas the capitalist hospitals have links with the exploiters, the settlers, because that is whom they serve, our hospitals have links with the people, because they are there to serve them. [...]

In a Frelimo hospital there are no tribes, no regions, no races, no religious beliefs – there is nothing to divide us.[62]

This characterisation was inspired by an appropriately military imagery deriving from the defence of territory, on the one hand, and liberation of ground from the enemy, on the other. With the collapse of the Portuguese, Frelimo found itself having to fan out into, try to administer, and eventually win over, whole areas of the country hitherto regarded as enemy terrain, with a social and economic organisation at the service of colonial exploiters. But 'liberation' was a notion further loaded with social and spiritual values and associations, and Frelimo's 'liberated zones' had become invested with layers of meaning: so too were enemy-occupied zones, but with converse negative values, in direct opposition.

Gradually, Frelimo was defining its policies through a series of conferences and meetings. Those meetings which began to provide policy guidelines included the first national agricultural conference at Beira in September 1975, a first education seminar (January 1975), a national seminar on technical education (December 1975), a conference on the state apparatus and the public service (October 1976), a seminar on cooperatives (also October 1976), the 2nd conference of the Organização das Mulheres Moçambicanas (November) and the 8th session of the Central Committee in February 1976.

Not surprisingly the main effort was focused on the field of social services, where colonial discrimination had been most apparent. In the educational field all colonial curricula were discarded, political education was introduced to the schools, and the syllabuses for history, geography and cultural activity were

---

[62] Samora Machel, *Mozambique: Sowing the Seeds of Revolution* (Harare, 1981), p. 43.

'nationalised'. In broad outline, new programmes for general education from pre-primary to pre-university level were hastily drafted to come into effect during 1975, based in part on the material used by Frelimo during the armed struggle. In July 1975, education was nationalised, separating church from state, formally removing religion from the curriculum and ending mission control of schools. The official stance involved a rejection of any indigenous forms of educational practice.

> ....during the period of colonisation, there were two kinds of education, reflecting the existing forms of social organisation: traditional education and colonial education.
>
> The first, which corresponds to traditional society, was characterised by superstition, by the oral transmission of tradition elevated into dogma, by the fight against the appearance of new ideas. This resulted from a superficial knowledge of nature, and from the mode of production of traditional society, based on subsistence agriculture.
>
> The second was aimed at perpetuating the domination of the colonial bourgeoisie through the inculcation of foreign cultural values.[63]

Significantly, education was the number-one budgetary priority during the period of transitional government. Much enthusiasm and popular involvement were chanelled into it, and adult literacy was perhaps the one sphere where the GDs made a positive impact. It was already an area of considerable Frelimo effort: by the time of the Lusaka Agreement in September 1974, it was claimed that more than 30,000 Mozambicans had already received primary-level or literacy training inside liberated Mozambique.[64] Shortly before the Lisbon coup of 25 April 1974, a Frelimo seminar with participation from all the liberated zones had reportedly already decided on launching a 'national literacy campaign' which emphasised the training of monitors and their progressive use as literacy teachers, but implementation was naturally interrupted by events.[65] However, the Mocuba meeting of February 1975 put it back on the agenda. Noting that Mozambique was nearly 90 per cent illiterate, and that illiteracy 'made it difficult to spread to the people

---

[63] Literacy and Adult Education in the People's Republic of Mozambique', anonymous paper delivered at a conference on Adult Education and Development, Dar es Salaam, 21-26 June 1976.

[64] J. Marshall, 'Making Education Revolutionary' in Saul (ed.), A Difficult Road, pp. 156-210.

[65] From 'Literacy and Education'.

Mozambican culture, Frelimo's political line, science, and the direct knowledge of the experiences of other peoples', the meeting charged the GDs with responsibility 'at the level of the circle, work establishments, districts and provinces' to organise militants to teach adult education classes, while political party members were to mobilise all schoolteachers in the circles and localities to participate during their spare time in the literacy campaign.[66] (The language of instruction and study was to be Portuguese, the necessary language of national unity.) During 1974/5 Frelimo's Department of Education and Culture moved itself and the pupils studying in Tanzania into Mozambique, and many in the higher levels entered enthusiastically into the task of literacy teaching.[67] Thus the collapse of Portuguese education combined with a mass demand for education, the experience of the liberated zones and Frelimo mobilisation to produce an outburst of energy in which hundreds of *ad hoc* literacy classes were organised in factories, residential areas, hospitals and commercial establishments.[68]

Second only to education as a field of government activity was health, with the accent on 'primary health care', which once again sought to build on the experience of the liberated zones where nurses and health workers, some trained in Tanzania and in other countries abroad, taught basic skills in first aid and simple preventive measures to guerrillas and peasants.[69] Outside the liberated zones, there were in all only about 600 doctors in Mozambique in mid-1974, 350 of them in the capital, about fifty in Beira and another twenty in the north, either treating soldiers or in psycho-social programmes. The rural population was virtually without modern health care. The Transitional Government restructured the health services and legislated to prevent government-employed health workers engaging in private medical practice.[70] As a result trained health workers of all kinds were soon leaving for Portugal. At independence, Mozambique was left with only thirty trained doctors for the entire population of 12 million. As a further consequence of the nationalisation of health services in July 1975, rural mission

[66] Final conclusions of Frelimo's plenary meeting at Mocuba.

[67] See Anton Johnston, 'Study, Produce and Combat!'

[68] Isaacman, 'A Luta Continua', pp. 72-3.

[69] G. Walt and A. Melamed (eds), *Mozambique: Towards a People's Health Service*, London, 1983, p. 6.

[70] Portaria 15/74 of 7 November 1974 created a commission to make recommendations for such a restructuring; a despatch setting out the competences of the central organs of the Ministry of Health and Social Affairs was published in a supplement to the *Boletim Official*, 1st series, 144, of 12 December 1974.

hospitals or health posts were abandoned. A few were kept going by untrained *serventes* – health orderlies – who administered what aid they could from experience. In the liberated zones of the northern provinces *socorristas* continued to provide simple care, although many were sent on retraining or refresher courses and provided the basis for future village health workers.[71] By 1976, however, the government had recruited almost 500 medical workers from more than twenty different countries and had inaugurated a national health programme, allocating the health services between 13 and 15% of the national budget.[72] A vaccination campaign in 1976-8 reached 95% of the population and provided an accurate forecast for the 1980 census.[73]

The private traditional health sector existed on sufferance until the time when scientific medicine became easily accessible and available throughout the country.[74] As in education, the official attitude towards anything 'traditional' was hostile. Traditional healers were prohibited from charging fees, although it is unlikely that this was capable of effective enforcement. But in reality it was the entire magico-religious world view that provided an explanatory context and symbolic vocabulary for their healing activities which Frelimo wished to displace with its modernising and 'scientific' ideology. Frelimo recommended a survey of spirit mediums and traditional healers in each province, with a view to ascertaining which ones had some useful empirical knowledge of medicines which, if disentangled from superstition, might be useful.[75]

The overwhelming problem facing the new government, however, was how to stem the economic collapse and especially the collapse of agricultural production. The abandonment of settler farms and the virtual disappearance of the distribution network threatened both the urban food supply and cash-crop production for export. Between 1974 and 1976, marketed output of export crops fell by more than 40% and there were considerable declines in production of maize and cassava.[76] In response to these problems,

---

[71] C. Barker, 'Bringing health care to the People' in Saul (ed.), *A Difficult Road*, pp. 317-46.

[72] Isaacman, 'A Luta Continua', p. 74.

[73] Hanlon, *Mozambique: Who Calls the Shots?*, 1991, p. 9.

[74] Walt & Melamed, *Mozambique: Towards a People's Health Service*, pp. 10-11.

[75] 'Documentos. II Conferência Nacional do Trabalho Ideológico', Beira, 5-10 June 1978.

[76] See *African Development* November 1976, and M. Wuyts, 'Money, Planning and Rural Transformation in Mozambique', *Journal of Development Studies*, 22 (1985), pp. 180-207.

policies exhibited both compromises with established realities and certain immediate contingencies, as well as the beginnings of a strategic vision. Samora Machel spoke during his 'Rovuma to Maputo' march of the need to create throughout the country 'communal societies' of at least 500 families, which would be the base unit in the struggle against underdevelopment. He expressed optimism that 'no problem' existed in installing such communities in the liberated zones, even though the population in some areas was still dispersed because of Portuguese bombing.[77] It was announced that the organisation of communal villages, state farms, collective farms and production and sales cooperatives would be the first major objective. In addition the *aldeamentos* were to be retained and expanded to serve as one major base for collectivisation of the rural economy and society. Guidelines for the construction and development of communal villages were ratified at the 8th session of Frelimo's Central Committee in February 1976.[78]

The situation was of course considerably messier than the policy documents implied. More than 1 million people, mainly in the north of the country, were already living grouped in *aldeamentos*. Communal villages were also established for all sorts of other reasons: the need to house the Mozambican war refugees from Tanzania, Malawi and Zambia who numbered some 110,000; strategic and defence purposes in border zones and areas of political insecurity; spontaneous action in some villages, by peasants responding to Frelimo exhortations; the need to rehouse populations made homeless by natural disasters (accounting for at least fifty communal villages in Gaza, where the February 1977 Limpopo floods led to the construction of communal villages on higher ground with the aid of $4 million from the World Food Programme); and, finally, for settlements established around centres of wage employment, to create a settled labour force (for example, around state farms in the Limpopo – although the initial stimulus came more from floods creating the need for resettlement).[79] In some places, abandoned settler farms were turned over in part to state farms and in part to co-operatives.[80] In others, peasants from *aldeamentos* moved on to better colonato land nearby, farming communal villages.[81]

---

[77] *Tempo*, 245, 8 June 1975.

[78] For text of the resolution see *Notícias numero especial*, 25 June 1976.

[79] Spavan, 'Rural Resettlement and Socialist Construction' pp. 60-4.

[80] See Helen Dolny, 'The Challenge of Agriculture' in Saul (ed.), *A Difficult Road*, pp. 211-52.

[81] *Financial Times*, 23 May 1975.

In the struggle over the fertile lands of the Limpopo *colonato* the black *colonos*, the middle-ranking peasants of the region, took advantage of the GDs and increased the pressure on the Portuguese by threats and intimidation, forcing their exodus.[82]

But in the economic as in other spheres the various measures taken after 1975 were not simply reactions to events, or 'pragmatism'; rather they drew on an (increasingly idealised) account of the liberated zones as nurseries for national unity, where people from different areas and cultures were engaged side by side in the common struggle for liberation and economic production and where they had practised 'people's power' through the creation of a pyramidal structure, the different levels of which (circle, locality, district, province) were directed by their respective committees and secretariats, chosen by the people under the direction of FPLM political commissars. As Frelimo had put it in 1970:

> ....the most important victory we are winning cannot be measured in figures – how many soldiers we have killed, how many square kilometers we control; it is valued in the new system of life led by people. Exploitation does not exist in the liberated zones; the cause of the vices which characterise colonial society – theft, drunkenness, prostitution (in sum, corruption), crimes, are being gradually removed. A new, pure and healthy society is being born in Mozambique. The people want this society and are building it.[83]

As Frelimo continued on the path of the construction of the new society, it was perhaps inevitable that it would turn to the political language that appeared most closely to articulate its own political experiences and its vision of a pure and healthy society.

---

[82] See K. Hermele, *Land Struggles and Social Differentiation in Southern Mozambique,* Uppsala, 1988.

[83] Published in the collection *O Processo Revolucionário da Guerra Popular de Libertação. Artigos coligidos do orgão de informação da Frelimo 'A Voz da Revolução' desde 1963 até 1974,* Colecção textos e documentos da Frelimo, Maputo (undated), p. 131.

3

THE TURN TO MARXISM

'It was impossible to build a People's Democracy with the Front.'[1]

'The Soviet representative presented President Machel with a large red flag bearing a picture of Lenin. Not to be outdone, the East German representative then handed over a bust of Karl Marx.'[2]

In February 1977 Frelimo held its 3rd Congress and declared itself to be a Marxist-Leninist party (announcing that it would retain the same name, but now calling itself Partido Frelimo). This was not a sudden or surprising development. From the early 1970s onwards Frelimo had increasingly talked about itself in Marxist terminology. The history of the organisation was described as a struggle between two lines, one representing the reactionary interests of the exploiters and the other the revolutionary interests of 'the people'. The fight against Portuguese colonialism was portrayed, in its later stages at least, as a struggle for the 'correct line' and as much part of a revolutionary process as one of national liberation. The practices of the anti-colonial struggle were not simply effective methods for fighting the Portuguese but were themselves part of a revolutionary transformation – the beginning of the creation of the 'New Man'. Finally, as part of this process the leadership of Frelimo, cleansed of reactionaries and exploiters, came increasingly to have the quality of a vanguard leadership – a leadership for whom the defeat of Portuguese colonialism was merely the first part of a much larger process of transformation that would culminate in socialism.

---

[1] Samora Machel's closing speech to the 3rd Congress, SWB ME 5435/BI-4, 10 February 1977.

[2] *The Times*, 5 February 1977.

Frelimo's Marxism

If politics is in part theatre, then the least that can be said is that Frelimo did not fluff its lines. The sheer volume of Frelimo's documentation attests to a serious effort to present its history and the struggle against Portuguese colonialism as a revolution. From 1977 onwards Frelimo's Marxist discourse became, as it were, official. The party began to profess an 'orthodox' Marxism-Leninism, although this was clearly marked by a concern to establish the equality of legitimacy of revolutionary endeavours, a point invariably made at set-piece gatherings of the Communist bloc countries and parties.[3] Frelimo's leaders stressed both the universality of scientific socialism on the one hand and the specific features of national revolutionary experience on the other. These two strands, the universality of socialism (and thus the denial of any special kind of 'African socialism') and the assertion of the uniqueness of the Mozambican revolution, could be brought together with the notion of Marxism as a 'science of the people', for sciences were 'intrinsically collective...the result of the effort, the sweat and the reflections of our contemporaries and ancestors'.[4]

What was the nature and significance of this transformation from a broad front to a party with a very specific ideology? There can be little doubt that the regional and international circumstances of Mozambique's transition to independence played a considerable part. Only the Soviet bloc countries (and China) had been prepared to supply arms to anti-colonial movements, and after independence was secured they appeared to offer some protection against pressures from both the West and the potential local enemies, Rhodesia and South Africa, as well as advice and assistance in the pursuit of development. In addition, the suddenness of Frelimo's victory as well as the mass exodus of Portuguese settlers meant that the party faced independence desperately lacking cadres with 'modern' skills. This relative vaccum was bound to attract those latter-day carpetbaggers of revolution, the 'red feet' *cooperantes* who, having found other forms of African socialism a grievous disappointment, came in search of new terrains of revolutionary endeavour.[5] The

---

[3] See Machel's speech to the East Berlin Conference on Marxism, 'Cada revolução é uma contribução para o Marxismo'. The point was emphasised even more strongly in an interview on East German television, *Notícias*, 14 March 1983.

[4] Machel speech, 1 May 1976, at Eduardo Mondlane University; SWB 5199/B 2-3, 4 May 1976.

[5] For Africanist 'red feet' see P. Chabal, 'People's War, State Formation and Revolution in Africa: A comparative analysis of Mozambique, Guinea-Bissau and Angola', *Journal of Commonwealth and Comparative Politics*, 21 (1983), pp. 103-25. For the

two groups of 'red experts', Soviet and Western, by no means saw eye to eye, but both brought with them analytical stances, assumptions and prejudices of a recognisably Marxist provenance.

But it would be far-fetched to imagine that all Frelimo's ideological effort was no more than an elaborate ruse (to secure Soviet bloc aid and obscure élite tensions), or that the Frelimo leadership was over-awed by foreign advisers (which is not to deny that such factors have not been part of Mozambican political life). Yet efforts to go beyond these explanations have been limited either to those that offer little more than a simple-minded repetition of Frelimo's discourse coupled with assertions that it *really is* Marxist or, in a mirror image, those that measure that discourse against some template and pronounce it *not really* Marxist at all.[6] In fact the significance of Frelimo's Marxism is not to be sought in the appropriation of an intellectual and political tradition or the utilisation of a method of socio-political analysis. There is little evidence that Frelimo's leadership committed itself to a serious appropriation of that tradition. While the specificity of the liberated zones was stressed, and this provided an additional advantage in enabling Frelimo to distance itself from the Sino-Soviet conflict, little attempt was made to suggest that they constituted any special Mozambican contribution to Marxism. Except perhaps for a brief period in 1979, when the Machel personality cult appeared to extend to theory, no Frelimo leader was ever presented as an important theorist.[7] There seems to be no evidence of factions within Frelimo identifying themselves in any kind of Marxist terms, or much evidence of Frelimo using Marxism as a means of analysis.

Of course Frelimo itself made much of its Marxism 'coming from experience', in this as in much else faithfully echoed by its academic admirers who often suggested that 'the Marxist tradition in Mozambique is not an academic tradition, but one which comes

---

general phenomenon see P. Hollander, *Political Pilgrims*, New York, 1981. It is only fair to say that many *cooperantes* were motivated by a more personal and less obtrusive idealism – but arguably they had little political effect.

[6] See for example S. Kruks, 'From Nationalism to Marxism: The Ideological History of Frelimo 1962-77' in I.L. Markowitz (ed.), *Studies in Power and Class in Africa*, Oxford, 1987. For the other view see M. Cahen, *La révolution implosée*, Paris, 1987. *Pace* Cahen, this problem is not resolved in his 'Check on Socialism in Mozambique', *Review of African Political Economy*, no. 57, 1993, pp. 46-59, although it is full of other insights.

[7] Cf. Marcelino dos Santos in his speech decorating Machel as *Heroi da Republica*: 'Sob a tua direcção esclarecida e o teu pensamento de grande teorico comunista....' (*Notícias* 26 June 1982). For the full text see *Tempo*, 612, 4 July 1982.

straight from the experience of armed struggle.'[8] Yet this apparent
disdain for 'Marxism-as-books' was based on ignorance, not experience. Indeed far from Frelimo's Marxism 'coming from
experience' the truth was almost the exact opposite – again, like
much else, Frelimo's Marxism was imported from outside. A Faculty
of Marxism-Leninism at Eduardo Mondlane University taught a
rather indigestible dialectical and historical materialism. Almost
all the teachers were from the Soviet bloc, and one of the few
who were not, the Canadian socialist John Saul, suggested that
by 1983(!) 'it was apparent to party structures that they [the stu-
dents] had been given little in the way of *analytical tools* with which
they could grapple with concrete realities in the field.'[9] The
response to this belated discovery was to close down both the
Faculty and the party school.

An explanation of Frelimo's Marxism must therefore lie elsewhere. Its appeal lay in providing a language to account for the
past, a vision of the future and an understanding of the struggle
to attain that future, in terms which had the greatest affinity with
Frelimo's own political-military experience. Frelimo's political experience and thinking were formed and shaped by a Portuguese
colonialist and assimilationist ideology whose theory and practice
were desperately humiliating for those Mozambicans who aspired
to education and 'modernity'. As Machel put it, 'the colonial bourgeoisie...wanted to mould society to such an extent that it reached
the point of forcing a Mozambican to deny his personality, to
transform himself into a little black Portuguese.'[10] Even the apparent openness to those who 'assimilated' (and this appears to
have included Machel himself) was greatly undermined in reality
by Portuguese racism which only rubbed salt in the wound. Those
Africans who did assimilate were not treated as equals and risked
racial insult.[11] The psychological strain induced by Portuguese
colonialism in African aspirants to modernity was then peculiarly
intense. The colonial power was modern and 'progressive' but it
also imposed overt humiliation and exclusion on its subjects. The
centres of 'civilisation' and therefore of exclusion from 'civilisation'
were of course urban. The special nature of Portuguese urbanism
in Africa helped shape these feelings:

[8] J. Depelchin, 'African Anthropology and History in the light of the History of
Frelimo', *Contemporary Marxism*, no. 7 (1983), pp. 69-88, 85.

[9] John Saul, 'The Content: A Transition to Socialism?' in J. Saul, *A Difficult Road*,
p. 143.

[10] Machel's speech to first People's Assembly *Notícias*, 1 September 1977.

[11] See the discussion in G.J. Bender, *Angola under the Portuguese*, London, 1978.

In perhaps no other region of Africa has the presence of a colonial power been so clearly impressed as on the cities and towns of Portuguese Africa. In a sense they are Portugal. In the most ancient coastal cities or in the newest towns of the interior, the architecture, the streets, the city squares, the gardens and the parks, the color, the spirit, the whole way of life is fundamentally Portuguese.[12]

The leaders of Frelimo were aspirants to modernity who found that they themselves were excluded from it or at least that their progress within it was blocked on racial grounds.[13] This induced a simultaneous veneration and hatred for 'civilisation' as represented by Portuguese colonialism. The latter was not just a matter of political control and economic exploitation: it was also a 'real act of rape' – but at the same time the rapist was the bringer of progress, even if in a distorted way.[14]

Yet the obvious alternative to colonial civilisation – African tradition in its various forms – was not an acceptable one for two reasons. First, there was the familiar dilemma of accounting for the colonial conquest and subjection, an accounting which had both to explain that conquest and to preserve the dignity and equality of the conquered. This conquest had been made possible by the manipulation of the divisions within African societies, but the leaders of resistance to the colonialists could be seen (as elsewhere) as proto-nationalists. Secondly, the Frelimo élite and the social strata to which it appealed were profoundly convinced of the superiority of modern civilisation and the need to 'catch up' with it. The only way to resolve these dilemmas was to see 'the people' as empty, but possessing the potential to develop. It is not what 'the people' are but what they can be that is important. The old world is backward and unscientific, the colonial world is corrupt and oppressive. Further, there is a sinister link between the two because the corrupt colonial world took and indeed reinforced the worst traditions of the old ways and lost the best.[15] 'Feudalism' and 'capitalism' neatly encapsulated the twin enemies.

[12] James Duffy, *Portuguese Africa*, Cambridge, MA, 1959, p. 2.

[13] This very much reflects Machel's own personal life. See his remarks in the special issue of *Tempo*, 677, 2 October 1983.

[14] S. Machel, 'Knowledge and Science should be for the Total Liberation of Man', speech made at Ahmadu Bello University, 10 December 1977, *Race and Class*, 19, 4 (1978), pp. 399-404.

[15] S. Machel, 'Fazer da Escola ume Base para o Povo tomar o Poder', Maputo, July 1974.

Thus in Frelimo's usage a *marxisant* terminology was reshaped
to articulate national and racial concerns. Concepts of class were
not used in any sense of economic agents generated by a mode
of production, nor were they deployed in any kind of 'class analysis'
in the conventional sense. Rather, they designated a whole series
of colonial experiences, including status hierarchies and notions
of racial inferiority and division. Ideas of exploitation referred
not to economic relationships but rather to experiences of racial
humiliation and unfair and discriminatory treatment. Machel's
repeated and passionate references to 'exploitation' concerned
unfair trading practices of the kind perpetrated on African peasants
by traders; they were always about unfair exchange. This explains
in part why Frelimo's first and most enthusiastic nationalisations
were not of the means of production but of such things as funeral
parlours.[16] Indeed, the formal condemnations of colonialism as
a system of production were almost completely overshadowed by
the emotional intensity of the charge of moral degradation levelled
against colonial society: '*A unica cultura portuguesa que eu conheco
sao os bailes, que sao feitos de noite nos bares.*... They said this culture
was civilising. This culture was never condemned as immoral in
Mozambique. It was a culture which began at nine o'clock at night
and finished at four in the morning.'[17] Machel repeatedly turned
to the issues of alcoholism, drug addiction and sexual corruption.[18]
The instruments of 'neo-colonialism' were said to include decadent
fashions in dress, cabarets and undermining Frelimo cadres
by introducing them to drugs.[19] As Henriksen put it, 'Frelimo
castigates capitalism more as a wicked instinct than as a mode of
production.'[20]

First and foremost, then, Marxism enabled Frelimo's élite to
convey the essence of the colonial experience. In its most general
aspects there is perhaps nothing especially Mozambican about this.
It has been said of the Arab world that 'Marxism furnished an
ideology capable of denying tradition without seeming to surrender
to Europe; it allowed one to evade a particular form of European

---

[16] For bitter and typical remarks by Machel on this issue see 'A nossa luta é uma
revolução', 24 July 1975.

[17] Quoted in Rita-Ferreira, p. 144.

[18] For an astonishing harangue on prostitution see his speech at a public rally in
Gaza, *Tempo*, 600 (11 April 1982). Machel's obsession with these matters deserves
more serious analysis than we have been able to give it here.

[19] Samora Machel, Frelimo Anniversary Address, 25 September 1975, SWB ME/5018
B3-5.

[20] T. Henriksen, 'Marxism and Mozambique', *African Affairs*, 77 (1978), p. 460.

society but did not compel one to return to tradition.'[21] It offered an historical labelling that restored both the dignity and the historicity of African peoples – their capacity to participate in progress. Beyond the moral decay of colonial society was a vision of progress and enlightenment to be attained by discipline and relentless struggle, and here also Marxism in a general sense had much to offer. There is a long Marxist/Leninist tradition of military analogy and rhetoric, of metaphors of struggle that are both transformative and liberating. Frelimo's Marxism shared that characteristic fully – it was a language of unending combat, enemies, offensives, victories, iron discipline and constant 'mobilisation'. In so far as Frelimo's leaders (along with other Southern African anti-colonial movements) were interested in or attracted to 'Maoism' it was as the science of mobilisation of peasants. This quasi-military understanding of discipline clearly reflected a certain political practice and style developed during the anti-colonial war, and continued to resonate with Frelimo's self-understanding and public presentation. This also shaped its use of 'Marxist' categories. Thus 'liberalism' and 'petty-bourgeoisie', for example, functioned not as forms of analysis but as indications of failure of personal will.[22]

But there was a concern also with discipline in a more general sense that linked it with order and planning. As Machel put it, 'Everything must be organised, everything must be planned, everything must be programmed.'[23] Marxism in all its variants provides a powerful secular vision of transcendence and renewal in which divisions have disappeared and new institutions have emerged to ensure progress, purity and harmony. The appeal of this to the leaders of a society notable for its divisions is hardly surprising. The political experience of the Frelimo leaders, as well as their historical image of colonialism, included a painful recognition of the damaging effects of disunity. As a young man Marcelino dos Santos wrote home: 'We must instruct, cultivate and educate ourselves to improve our culture and raise our standard of living – parochial issues must be subordinated to general concerns and personal and group interests must be subordinated to collective

---

[21] A. Laroui, *The Crisis of the Arab Intellectual*, Berkeley, 1976, p. 121. It has been argued that this dilemma characterised Lenin's own position. See A.J. Polan, *Lenin and the End of Politics*, London, 1984, ch. 4.

[22] See *Notícias*, 11 August 1977, where 'liberalism' is defined as not reporting your colleagues to the authorities if they are late or drunk. More generally see commentary on 'how the enemy behaves', SWB ME/5578/B1/2 August 1977. English text in *People's Power*, no. 9, July-September 1977.

[23] *Notícias*, 18 November 1976 speech to the OMM conference.

interests.'[24] The speeches of Frelimo's leaders are full of such assertions. Both 'development' and 'nation-building' were seen as matters of discipline and mobilisation. The 'New Man' was born in the liberated zones characterised by the collective values of liberation and creative initiative. But this 'New Man' was of course born in combat.[25]

In important ways Marxism provided support for entirely familiar nationalist aspirations, as de Brito has emphasised : 'The formation of the nation, the creation of national unity, antitribalism formed the dominant themes in Samora Machel's interventions.[...] "Marxist-Leninist" discourse served without doubt as an ideological support for this national project.'[26] But it also provided, or at least brought with it, intellectual content for those nationalist aspirations. In this context it was precisely because of its lack of Marxism that the Frelimo leadership was ill-equipped to assess outside sources of advice critically, whether from Soviets or *cooperantes*. As Luis Cabaco put it (in the context of development), 'The abstract nature of Mozambique's brand of Marxism complemented all too neatly the empty formalism which had infected the planning process itself.'[27] Frelimo's protean ignorance of the great books (dismissed by Frelimo's leaders as irrelevant academic affectation) extended to the actual economic and political experiences of the Marxist states (however defined).[28] For example, there was almost no familiarity with the history and mechanics of Soviet-style planning or with the debates about one-man management or the history of collectivised agriculture and the use of class analysis in the creation of that agriculture.[29] But many of these ideas and practices were adopted as matters of faith without much thought as to whether they were appropriate for Mozambican realities. Frelimo's leaders were not, of course, the first political activists who, proclaiming from the housetops their reliance on 'experience', proved to be the prisoners of the most implacable abstractions.

---

[24] Quoted in Penvenne, 'A Luta Continua', p. 125.

[25] See the interview with Machel, *Le Monde*, 27 April 1976.

[26] De Brito, 'Une relecture necessaire', pp. 15-27.

[27] Quoted in John Saul, 'The Content: A Transition to Socialism?' in Saul (ed.), *A Difficult Road*, p. 145.

[28] See Machel interview in *Africa*, August 1979.

[29] Comparison with the Soviet experience remains interesting. See, for example, M. Lewin, *Russian Peasants and Soviet Power*, London, 1968.

Constructing the party-state

Thus Marxism had profound effects on Frelimo's politics, along with other influences which are not always easy to disentangle. Perhaps the most important of these was the conception of the instrument of the process of social change. The Leninist tradition, at least as understood by Frelimo, provides a clear language of state construction, offering solutions to the problems of the structure and operation of a modernising state and the relations between that state, the party and the people. The attraction here is the vanguardism and revolution understood as discipline. Frelimo sought to become a vanguard party whose internal practices would be regulated by democratic centralism (understood in the 'classical' Leninist fashion) and which would direct the state and indeed the wider society in the construction of the new order.

Frelimo formalised its own structure at the Third Party Congress (though much of the preparatory work had already been done), endowing itself with a Central Committee and an Executive Committee, the latter constituted by the key leaders of the party. As a vanguard party it aimed to draw in the most ideologically advanced members of the oppressed classes and to regulate their lives to a considerable degree. New rules for membership of the party required not only the usual characteristics of energy, zeal and so on but also a rejection of the old society and the adoption of the tenets of 'scientific socialism'.[30] 'Each militant must also engage himself in an equally important internal fight against the vices and effects of the old society.'[31] There was a continual emphasis placed on the necessity for party cells to be active in all the most important spheres of social life. In the party restructuring campaign which followed the congress (from 3 February to 25 September 1978) recruitment was focussed very much on factories, communal villages and the armed forces.[32] According to a Central Committee announcement, only those 'living exclusively by their labour' were to be recruited.[33] Potential aspirants were subject to a process of proposal and then vetting by their workmates, and final decisions on admission to party membership were made by provincial

[30] Building the Party in Mozambique, p. 51. See interview with Machel in *Tempo*, 431, 7 January 1979.

[31] 8th session of the Central Committee.

[32] For a sympathetic account of recruitment in one factory see P. Sketchley, 'Problems of the Transformation of Social Relations of Production in Post-Independence Mozambique', *People's Power*, winter 1979.

[33] SWB ME/5700/B/6, 30 February 1977.

brigades. Although *Grupos Dinamizadores* continued to exist at the neighbourhood level they were eventually, in theory at least, to be constituted into party branches.

The wider society was conceived of as, on the one hand, a progressive alliance of class forces consisting of the peasantry and the working class, and on the other (and somewhat vaguely) various reactionary elements. The connecting link between the vanguard party and the 'popular masses' comprised the democratic mass organisations. In 1977 Frelimo clearly envisaged the eventual creation of a number of such bodies, but formally at least the most important were the Organização das Mulheres Moçambicanas (for women), the Organiazação da Juventude Moçambicana (for young people) and the embryonic forms of trade unions, the classic mass organisations of the Communist world. Communal villages were supposed to play a similar role in the rural areas. In various other ways the party sought to ensure its guiding role in society. The press and all other media were effectively (if not formally) under party control, and all key appointments (e.g. Rector of the University and senior judicial officials) were party decisions.[34] The principles of 'democratic centralism' were inscribed by law into the structures of non-party organisations.

The party's central position in the new political order had already been established by the Independence Constitution of 25 June 1975 which was 'proclaimed by acclamation' by the Central Committee of Frelimo. The 'fundamental aims' of the state were identical to those of Frelimo and included the elimination of the structures of colonial and traditional oppression and exploitation and the mentality underlying them; the extension and strengthening of democratic people's power; the building of an independent economy and the promotion of cultural and social progress; the defence and consolidation of independence and national unity; the building of people's democracy and the construction of the material and ideological bases of socialist society; the establishment and development of relations of friendship and cooperation with other peoples and states; and the prosecution of the struggle against colonialism and imperialism. This Constitution further laid down in its general principles that power belonged to the workers and peasants united and led by Frelimo, and exercised through the organs of people's power (Article 2), and that the Republic itself was guided by the political line defined by Frelimo, the leading force of state and society (Article 3). Transitional provisions vested

---

[34] For the judiciary see A. Gundersen, 'Popular Justice in Mozambique: Between State Law and Folk Law', *Social and Legal Studies*, 1, 2 (1992), pp. 257-82.

competence to amend the Constitution in the Frelimo Central Committee 'until the coming into being of an Assembly vested with constituent authority' (Article 70), while Article 72 determined that legislative authority should rest with the Council of Ministers until the People's Assembly was created. The party's vanguard character in relation to both state and society was further buttressed in constitutional provisions implemented after 1977. The constitutional design effectively prescribed that all paths to power converged on Frelimo and specifically its leader. The latter was automatically head of state, head of the government and commander-in-chief of the armed forces.

As soon as the immediate difficulties of the transition to independence had passed, attempts were made to construct new state structures. The People's Assembly, formed in 1977, was at the apex of a pyramid of indirectly elected assemblies. Direct popular voting took place only at the lowest (locality and city) level. District and provincial assemblies were in turn indirectly elected from below. Provincial assemblies then elected the National Assembly. The assemblies were to operate according to the prescriptions of democratic centralism; that is, they functioned as a channel for central directives downwards. The legislation laid down that the deputies 'do not serve or represent the particular interests of any village, locality, district, province, region, race, tribe or religion'; rather they were mandated to serve the interests of workers and peasants as a whole in the materialisation of Frelimo orientations. Deputies could be dismissed if they 'lost the confidence of the masses'.[35]

Finally there was the structure of the state itself, the instrument guided by Frelimo in the implementation of its line. Here again the party's documentation articulated conventional Marxist-Leninist aspirations: 'The old state is to be destroyed and replaced by a new one.'[36] A major conference took place on the state apparatus in October 1976, chaired by Oscar Monteiro and given extensive press coverage.[37] Familiar Marxist-Leninist themes were applied to the Mozambican state. The old state was a class state to be supplanted by a state of the people, itself based on the embryonic state in the liberated zones.[38] Despite this emphasis, not much

[35] Electoral Law, articles 9 and 10.

[36] Samora Machel speech to the 8th session of the Central Committee, *Notícias*, 1976 special issue.

[37] See *Notícias* 15, 18, 20 and 22 October 1976. Its Proceedings were published as *Vamos Construir um Estado do Povo ao Serviço do Povo*.

[38] For this emphasis see interview with Machel, *Notícias*, 18 December 1976.

on the liberated zones is to be found in Frelimo's state discourse. Rather this relied on a trinity of principles generally labelled the unity of power, democratic centralism and the principle of double subordination – which, despite the distinction made between them, overlapped somewhat.[39] The first reflected a familiar Marxist view that political power is always the power of a class and that the supposed 'separation of powers' in the Western constitutional tradition is no more than a sham. The class power of the bourgeoisie was to be replaced by the class power of the proletariat. Organs of the state were a part of and subordinate to the People's Assemblies at the appropriate level. Democratic centralism was construed by Frelimo to mean both the subordination of lower to higher state bodies (as well as a rather vague concern with discipline more generally), while the principle of double subordination entailed that any state body was subordinate both to a higher state body and to the Assembly at its level.

Following the guidelines of an Assembly resolution on the basis of a people's democratic state, 1978 saw a flood of legislation dealing with the Council of Ministers, provincial and local government and the judicial system.[40] Within this context the regime's concern with discipline (as so often linked with science and planning) surfaced in new regulations for the public service as well as attacks on 'liberalism'.[41] For the purposes of sub-national government the country was separated into provinces (10), districts (128) and localities largely along territorial lines inherited from the colonial period. The provincial government comprised the Governor, the provincial council and the provincial directors of state agencies. With the abolition of the colonial *Cameras Municipais*, a number of cities were allowed municipal executive councils comprising a president (selected by the national President) and a number of other senior state and party representatives in the area. While the territorial shape of the new state did not greatly depart from the colonial legacy, its range of responsibilities was of course enormously extended. Municipal structures were largely modelled on national and provincial ones and therefore comprised (at least in principle) departments dealing with finance, housing, services,

---

[39] See Machel's speech to the 1st session of People's Assembly, *Notícias*, 1 September 1977. Virtually identical formulations were provided in a Frelimo text, *Noções sobre o Estado*, Maputo, 1980.

[40] For the formal structures see D. Martins da Silva, 'Como se organiza o Estado Moçambicano', *Justiça Popular* 10 (June 1985), pp. 21-5.

[41] See *Normas de Trabalho e Disciplina no Aparelho de Estado* (Documento Informativo serie A 1979-1-02).

agriculture, education and culture, health, public order, transportation, planning, construction and commerce. Financial resources were largely provided from the centre, almost entirely through the provincial administrations.[42]

Politics and the state after the 3rd Congress

At the very least, then, there was in Mozambique for some years after 1977 a considerable attempt to deploy a Marxist discourse and to set up the formal structures of a Marxist-Leninist party and state as they have generally been understood.[43] But having sought to account for the place of Marxism in Frelimo's political development in a way which neither dismisses it as rhetoric nor takes its own theses as literally true, we must place this Marxist option in the wider context of the development of Mozambican politics after independence. Marxism did speak to real elements in the Frelimo élite's political experience, but any account of the effects of its adoption must be careful neither to attribute every aspect of the regime to it nor to dismiss it as irrelevant.

The Frelimo regime was completely dominated by the leadership group (essentially the party politburo and some of Machel's close associates), among whom there was a remarkable capacity for consensus and who, over a long period, rotated all the key offices of party and state between themselves. The longevity of the core Frelimo leadership (hardly changed until the late 1980s) is notable by any standards.[44] Within the leadership group Machel was the central figure and the voice of the regime.[45] His prestige with the army and the central positions held by Chipande and Mabote secured the loyalty of the armed forces. His ability to communicate with the mass population is well attested and, even if it is exaggerated, he far outstripped in appeal any other figure in the senior leadership. Machel's personal commitment to non-racialism secured

---

[42] For sub-national government, see World Bank, *Mozambique Public Expenditure Review*, vol. 2, and J. Sidaway, 'Contested Terrain: Transformation and Continuity of the Territorial Organisation in post-Independence Mozambique', *Tijdschrift voor economische en sociale geografie*, 82, 1991, pp. 367-76.

[43] For discussion of this issue see S. White, 'What is a communist system?', *Studies in Comparative Communism*, XVI, 4, 1983, pp. 247-63.

[44] Between the 3rd Congress in 1977 and the 5th in 1989 and excepting the death of Machel and the inclusion of Monteiro in 1983 the composition of the Politburo did not change at all.

[45] *Rand Daily Mail*, 15 March 1976; *The Times*, 17 November 1976; *Guardian*, 4 August 1976.

the support both of the coterie of *marxisant* intellectuals, often of Indian origin (Rebelo, Vieira, de Bragança), who provided much of Frelimo's political language, and the radical wing of the rump of the Portuguese community who identified with Frelimo's aspirations and were disproportionately visible at the senior levels of both party and government because of the desperate shortage of skilled people. Some members of the élite group were real outsiders (notable Veloso) but their personal connections with Machel and intimate knowledge of Frelimo's affairs made them indispensable.[46] Finally there were those in the leadership group who could be described as technocrats in that they possessed essential administrative skills and experience, had often been professionally successful before the end of Portuguese colonialism and had maintained (or claimed to have maintained) clandestine relations with Frelimo during that period.

At the heart of Frelimo's leadership style lay an apparent ambiguity between, on the one hand, a commitment to *poder popular*, mass participation and popular needs and, on the other, a puritanical and top-down vision of social progress and the hierarchical and centralised means to attain it. Frelimo's thinking and propaganda did indeed make much of the need for popular solutions, listening to the masses, unleashing their creative energies and so on. The Frelimo revolution was about freedom in the obvious anti-colonial sense but (like all revolutions) also made claims to provide 'emancipation' in a broader human sense. Yet this process of transformation (like all revolutions?) was to be guided by an élite of revolutionaries with very clear ideas about the content and direction of this emancipation – ideas that were not to be subject to popular veto, questioning or indeed debate. But precisely because modern revolutions are about 'emancipation', the masses must be mobilised around and in support of their 'universal' truths – mere compliance is not enough. Frelimo certainly belonged to this tradition, its nationalist-Marxist ideology shaping the leadership's image of itself as an embattled vanguard of 'fighters against darkness and superstition' surrounded by legions of enemies, shepherding the masses towards progress and enlightenment.[47]

The awareness of bearing a lofty vision as well as being embattled on all sides made for strong tendencies towards demonisation of 'the enemy' and the attribution of all failures to malevolence and

[46] For an interesting if jaundiced comment on white élite Mozambicans see *Africa Confidential*, May 1986.

[47] 'Colher no 25 de Setembro força renovada para o combate'. For Machel as the quintessential 'new man' see *Tempo* 667, 24 July 1983.

lack of will. Failures could only be understood as a matter of poor implementation, and failures of implementation could only be dealt with in the short-term by 'trouble-shooting' by members of the leadership; also by ever more insistent calls for renewed effort and mobilisation and denunciations of 'the enemy'. 'The enemy' was identified according to a taxonomy of moral failings – laziness, corruption and self-indulgence. The important speech in which presidential '*ofensivas*' were launched, glossed as a 'sharpening of the class struggle', consisted of denunciations of alcoholism, unpunctuality, indiscipline generally and lack of hygiene – Machel's pet subject.[48] A radio broadcast in April 1983 justifying new security laws suggested that there were

> ....active within our society unarmed bandits, black marketeers, speculators, hoarders, saboteurs, armed robbers, kidnappers, evildoers, rapists who attack minors, enticers, people who use minors in committing crimes, foreign currency and narcotics traffickers, smugglers, rumourmongers, intriguers, slanderers, pamphleteers, thieves, and those who foment negligence, disruption and [in?]discipline. These bandits operate to bring about famine, shortages, lower production, the flight of currency, corruption, economic chaos, social disorder, instability, and poor living standards, particularly those of the urban centres.[49]

The cartoon figure Xiconhoca, widely used in propaganda, represented just such a composite enemy.[50]

It was within this discursive space that much of Frelimo's practice towards 'the masses' was inscribed. Despite the considerable efforts devoted to mass organisations within both the state structures (assemblies) and the party, it is clear that these bodies had at most ratificatory functions. The central value commitments of the regime were beyond question or debate. This applied not merely to the charter statements but to general political practice. The prerogatives of leadership were an important part of the Felimo style which replicated itself down the line of command. Crises and difficulties were usually met with the despatch of a senior figure to resolve the issue. The model for this was the '*ofensivas*' begun by Machel in 1979, which involved unannounced visits to a variety of organisations at which all kinds of corruption and incompetence

---

[48] 'Transformer O Aparelho de estado no Instrumento da Vitoria', 7 February 1980.

[49] SWB ME/7298/B3-5, 5 April 1983.

[50] See *Guardian*, 9 November 1976, and *The Times*, 17 November 1976. See also *People's Power*, no. 9.

would be uncovered and sundry miscreants who were deemed responsible dismissed or worse.[51] These efforts formed part of a quasi-populist strategy to effect an alliance with the 'people' over the heads of the bureaucrats. The people would maintain a vigilance over the state, 'with the task of participating in the cleaning-up', as Machel put it.[52] But the state remained the privileged apparatus in the implementation of Frelimo's directives.

The counterpoint to *poder popular* was a strong stress on the rights of leadership (and its associated privileges, including material ones) and command, along with vigorous denunciations of 'liberalism'. This concern with hierarchy also expressed itself in an elaborate and highly developed sense of protocol within the leadership group (though this was also very much a matter of Machel's personal style). There was a veritable obsession with status. There were to be first-class restaurants in Maputo into which ordinary workers would not be allowed; women must not breastfeed their children in public; people must not sit on the grass in public parks. The President took time in public speeches to describe what kind of hedge-cutters were to be used in parks.[53] In Beira, 'whenever a motorised high-level delegation was passing, all traffic on the streets was halted and pedestrians were made to stand to attention.'[54] With the passing of time these tendencies became stronger within the Frelimo leadership so that, 'increasingly hierarchical and bureaucratic and marked by the military organisation of the guerrilla period, the new party consolidated a more and more decorated leadership whose heroic nostalgia continued to separate them from the concerns of the population.'[55]

This leadership style did much to shape the form that Mozambican politics took after 1977. The core group, while it retained great internal stability and coherence, remained extremely small and enormously stretched. The regime was so centralised and top-

[51] For the style of the offensives see *Guardian*, 30 January 1980 and 15 February 1980; *Le Monde*, 22 March 1980; SWB ME/6349/B/8, 19 February 1980.

[52] Speech, 'Desalojemos o Inimigo Interno do Nosso Aparelho de Estado', 18 March 1980.

[53] An exhaustive list of such references would fill many pages. For a sample see Machel's speech of 21 May 1983 denouncing at great length spitting, sleeping in parks, jeans and other examples of moral degradation, *Tempo* 659, 29 May 1983. For the grass-cutters see translation in B. Munslow (ed.), *Samora Machel: An African Revolutionary*, p. 103.

[54] B. Egero, *Mozambique: A Dream Undone: The Political Economy of Democracy, 1975-1984*, Uppsala, 1987, pp. 190-1.

[55] C. Meillassoux and C. Verschuur, 'Les paysans ignorés de Mozambique', *Le Monde Diplomatique*, October 1985.

heavy that Frelimo itself recognised the problem and even before Machel's death the post of Prime Minister had been created to relieve the burden on the President, though in fact it appears to have made little difference. The classic communist separation of party from state, with the former guiding and monitoring the latter, remained almost fictional as at all the strategic levels the same people occupied both party and state roles. Within Frelimo a tradition of revolutionary puritanism and periodic but rather mild purges of middle-level cadres enabled the leadership to maintain a loyal and generally competent corps of second-level leaders and to control the armed forces. Periodic 'mobilisation', always of course directed from on high, ensured intermittent party activity. But with the larger task of creating a continually active nationwide Marxist party there is little evidence that Frelimo had much success. Even within the state apparatus itself party cells were more or less moribund.[56]

Thus much of the institutional fabric created by Frelimo remained highly formal. This was most clearly the case with the assemblies, supposedly exempt from the 'electoral farces of the bourgeoisie'.[57] Notionally the instruments of *poder popular*, these bodies had no autonomy of any kind. Indeed, none published any record of its proceedings. All the legislative work of the National Assembly was done by its Permanent Commission, which comprised the senior Frelimo leadership. Not surprisingly, 'deputies of the Popular Assembly do little work in this capacity between sessions of the Assembly.'[58] This situation was of course replicated lower down the hierarchy, where there was even less clarity about the formal responsibilities of such institutions. Thus in Nandimba (Cabo Delgado province) 'the Assembly had never, since it was formed and up to the end to 1983, had a meeting on its own, separate from party cell or other meetings of "responsables" in the village.'[59] In any case, at the lower levels the assemblies had no legislative or fiscal powers, their function being simply to retail legislation at the provincial or district level. In the words of one provincial assembly chairman his assembly's function was to advise on the 'lines of application of central laws'.[60] Even this modest task was to be carried out in

---

[56] See for example report on the Ministry of Internal Commerce, *Tempo*, 637, 26 December 1982.

[57] Machel's phrase, *Notícias*, 1 September 1977, faithfully reproduced in *New African*, December 1977, and *People's Power*, 11 (1978).

[58] Egero, *Mozambique*, p. 129.

[59] *Ibid.*, p. 159.

[60] J. Sidaway, 'Contested Terrain', p. 374.

two meetings a year lasting only a few days. The evidence points to the conclusion that the assemblies failed to function – indeed it is rather difficult to see what they were supposed to do at all.

Despite these features there is no doubt that the values of the leadership group rapidly communicated themselves down the chain of command, at least rhetorically. Mozambican politics became suffused with technicist state-led assumptions about modernity, though here also there was doubtless a colonial legacy as well. In many spheres of policy, distinctions between 'the technical' and 'the political' appeared, the former invariably identified with modernity, science and 'progress'. In the economic field, 'state farms were to be defined first and foremost as an 'investment question'. In contrast, the peasant-based cooperatives were defined as primarily an 'organisational question, a matter of "mobilisation", a front to be left in effect to party workers and not economic planners'.[61] In general the modern was the new and the technical. It was by no means in the field of education alone that 'traditional technology was considered to be of little value; the "big", the "mechanised" was automatically seen as the path to the future.'[62] There were of course few rewards in being out of line. It was not merely in the field of journalism that the regime 'rewarded mediocrity and punished those who raised awkward questions'.[63]

Much of this, however, appears to have remained largely rhetorical, with lower-level subordinates in both party and state having only the haziest idea of key concepts in the regime's discourse or indeed actually having read party and state documents.[64] Party policy was of course implemented – often with almost comic results. In rural areas it was reported:

> The villagers have loyally carried out the party's directives to set up branches of the OJM and the OMM but there seems to be little comprehension of the distinction between these mass organisations and the party itself. The result is the anomalous situation

[61] John Saul, 'The Content: A Transition to Socialism?' in Saul (ed.), *A Difficult Road*, pp. 116-17.

[62] J. Marshall, 'Making Education Revolutionary' in Saul (ed.), *A Difficult Road*, p. 180.

[63] Jose Cabaco, *Mozambiquefile*, August 1991.

[64] A research team from the Centro de Estudos Africanos reported that local state functionaries did not know the cooperative law. *A Situacao nas Antigas Zonas Libertadas*, 1983, p. 44.

whereby the vanguard party actually has more members than the mass organisations.[65]

In the wake of Machel's 1979 May Day speech (which denounced *inter alia* tight trousers and long hair) a representative of SNASP, chairing a meeting of the People's Vigilance Groups, informed them that 'people who go around the streets badly dressed are imperialist agents, for imperialism, as usual, attacks everything that we have built for the welfare of our people.'[66] Party meetings were stilted and formal, all higher party bodies made decisions 'unanimously', and the 'mass organisations' faithfully parroted the party-line – all in the name of democracy. Here, as elsewhere, 'democratic centralism' reaped its terrible harvest.

Finally and inevitably, Frelimo's leadership style entailed a clear priority for the state as the agent of modernisation. From the beginning Frelimo produced the right Marxist phrases about 'smashing the old state' and replacing it with a new type of state, but while a great deal of formal structural change was made in the state departments and other state agencies, these were in-cremental changes in the old state machine. Indeed it was perhaps an effect of Frelimo's Marxism that what was wrong with the old state was invariably seen in terms of functions (the activity of the state) or social interests (the class basis of the state) rather than internal structures or mode of operation. There seems to have been no detailed analysis of structural issues, and it remained unclear what exactly the problems of the old state were.[67] Thus much continuity remained, including the very territorial shape of the state itself. The colonial provincial boundaries, with minor modifications, were preserved.[68] Local government officials were simply Maputo appointees, effectively responsible to the provincial governor.[69] The provincial structures of power shadowed those of the centre – indeed provincial governors fashioned much of their political style on that of the president. Machel was not exaggerating or criticising when he suggested (in Nampula) that 'everything

---

[65] *Sunday Mail*, 27 September 1981.

[66] SWB ME/6115/B3, 14 May 1979.

[67] This is not to suggest there were not specific complaints. See for example remarks about 'departmentalism' in Council of Ministers communique, SWB ME/5544/B2-7.

[68] Arguably some really radical thinking about such matters, especially the position of the capital city, might have been helpful here.

[69] Interview with the deputy governor of Nampula province, May 1990.

here depends exclusively on the Governor'.[70]

Certainly there were concerns about the degree of political reliability of the incumbent cadres (though the solution to this was seen largely as a matter of changing wills), but the evidence for a 'state bourgeoisie', obstructing Frelimo policies, seems rather thin. The leadership was able to establish control of the state in the formal sense, and the evidence generally points to a situation in which Frelimo party documents and the President's remarks were taken as the main guidelines of policy. What was critical here was rather the virtual paralysis of the state machine below the senior leadership without instruction from that leadership. Even then, as a senior Frelimo figure put it, 'we are reaching a point that the president says something, the Minister says something, and nobody moves.'[71] Had Frelimo feared a state bourgeoisie, it might well have set up different kinds of structures at provincial and local levels – but it did not.

Frelimo never engaged in constructing a 'new type of state' precisely because the state under its control was to be the main vehicle of social change. As Cabaco rightly suggests, 'within Frelimo the culprit was less technocratic bias than the surfacing, in the first flush of victory over the Portuguese, of an overweening self-confidence.'[72] And indeed the capacity of this state should not be underestimated. Frelimo's early prestige and popularity, combined with the existing state's capacities, enabled the regime to implement a population census, a currency reform and a fairly extensive vaccination programme. But these were all standardised tasks imposed from the centre which involved little more than carrying out clear and elementary instructions. The Frelimo state was of course required to do far more. It grew enormously in size, controlling most of the economy and also the whole of the health and education sectors. The Frelimo leadership laid down extremely ambitious programmes of transformation for society as a whole and within each sector of policy, which it was simply beyond the ability of the Mozambican state to implement, either materially or culturally. As a result, there was a constant short-circuiting of the implementation of policy guidelines. This was caused, first, by a failure to establish appropriate bureaucratic mechanisms and, secondly, by arbitrary interventions of the leadership,

---

[70] *Tempo*, 713, 10 June 1984.

[71] Cabaço quoted in J. Nunes, 'Peasants and Survival: The Social Consequences of Displacement Mocuba Zambezia' (unpublished paper), p. 27.

[72] Quoted in John Saul, 'The Content: A Transition to Socialism?' in Saul (ed.), *A Difficult Road*, p. 125.

especially Machel's own tendency suddenly to announce policy imperatives in public speeches or to implement decisions by presidential decree.[73] These two features were often linked. Operation Production began as a Machel initiative in Nampula province, but as it began to be implemented 'local authorities went into action before either a proper plan had been worked out or any instrument created for the identification of people without work or resident [*sic*] rights in Maputo city.'[74]

Even where they were not so intimately connected, virtually all fields of policy were crippled by these structural difficulties, a result both of material and personnel shortages as well as the almost complete absence of the kind of organisational cultures that Frelimo's vision required. In the field of education 'the effective and immediate control of the education process necessitated enormous efforts for which we had insufficient resources, either human or material.'[75] Most areas of policy were desperately short of trained people. It was not only that the state had taken on too much – it was simply incapable of operating the structures required. 'In fact new programs and structures were created in abundance, and directives on all manner of activities bombarded provincial and district education offices on a regular basis. These offices, however, lacked the capacity to implement them.'[76] In the field of planning, 'policy was usually made in Maputo and transmitted to the provinces without taking into account local conditions.'[77]

Frelimo and Mozambican society

The effectiveness of states, considered as their capacity to determine policies, extract resources and deploy and control agents, cannot

[73] The closure of the Law Faculty at the University in 1983 was suddenly ordered by Machel.

[74] Egero, *Mozambique*, p. 189. For more on Operation Production, see ch. 4.

[75] Graça Machel (Minister of Education) quoted in J. Marshall, 'Making Education Revolutionary' in Saul (ed.), *A Difficult Road*, p. 167.

[76] J. Marshall, 'Making Education Revolutionary' in Saul (ed.), *A Difficult Road*, pp. 174-5.

[77] J. Sidaway, 'Urban and regional planning in post-independence Mozambique', *International Journal of Urban and Regional Research*, 17 (1993), pp. 241-59, esp. 248. For documentation in other areas of policy see for housing P. Jenkins, 'Mozambique' in K. Mathey (ed.), *Housing Policies in the Socialist Third World*, London, 1990, and Verschuur, pp. 140-1. For the inadequacies of the Land Law see Egero, *Mozambique*, pp. 161 and 167. For the failure to sort out migrant labour see W. James, *Our Precious Metal: African Labour in South Africa's Gold Industry, 1970-1990*, London, 1992.

of course be understood in isolation from the wider society of which they are part. Such capabilities rest, in part at least, on their degree of 'fit' with that society. For example, it is clear that Frelimo took a risk in adopting a variety of political and economic strategies which required large quantities of skilled manpower from a society which could not (rapidly) provide them. Even if (as was the case) manpower shortages were to be supplemented from elsewhere, such transfers create their own difficulties in that such manpower is not familiar with the local terrain. As a senior official in the Ministry of Education put it, 'the very weaknesses that make us need your assistance in the first place mean that we won't be able to use either the people or the materials and equipment you send us to maximum effectiveness.'[78] Conversely, various limitations on state capabilities can be compensated for by high degrees of legitimation. At the time of independence and indeed for some time afterwards Frelimo did indeed enjoy considerable legitimacy, drawing credit from a mass population for the ousting of an un-popular colonial regime and support for a broad programme that was generally perceived to portend great improvements in people's material lives. Rural people expected the gradual improvement in their lot that had begun to occur towards the end of the colonial regime to continue.[79] But there is no reason to suppose that there was mass support for a programme for revolutionary transformation in anything other than a narrowly anticolonial sense.[80] It is a Western conceit (fully shared by Frelimo) that people who want medicine or literacy or wells necessarily also want to adopt 'modern' (Western) modes of conduct or beliefs.

But as Frelimo's political language and policy-making began to be more coherent after 1977, so its societal project began to deviate sharply from any kind of political consensus which had given it strength as an anti-colonial movement. The effectiveness of the state relied increasingly on a top-down coercion which placed a high premium on the state's capacity to reach out and mould society, while the legitimacy of the state, having eroded other bases, came to rest precariously on its ability to provide material improvement in people's lives. As became apparent, the Frelimo state was both over-extended and underdeveloped, and the dual

---

[78] Quoted by J. Marshall, 'Making Education Revolutionary' in Saul (ed.), *A Difficult Road*, p. 176.

[79] See J. Nunes, 'Peasants'.

[80] For some early and sensibly sceptical remarks on this see P. Chabal, 'People's War'.

crisis of both effectivity and legitimacy eventually brought it shuddering to a halt.

The erosion of legitimacy in post-independence Mozambique took various forms, partly overlapping yet also retaining distinct characteristics. Several clusters of features of the society created difficulties for Frelimo. One concerned the racial and regional origins of the party's own leadership, in large part a legacy of the anti-colonial struggle. The leadership group, consisting not only of the politburo but also including close Machel favourites such as Bragança and Vieira, were mostly southern Mozambicans, *mestiços* and white intellectuals. This was indeed a major part of the regime's self-presentation as having moved beyond racism, tribalism and regionalism. A frequent feature of Machel's public rallies was to present different members of the élite group to the audience, stressing their Mozambicanness irrespective of skin colour.[81] Such a degree of racial mixing at the senior levels has been unusual in post-colonial African regimes (except the lusophone ones), and was connected in part at least with Frelimo's rather Jacobin notions of nation-building.

Because of this stance, however admirable in the abstract, it was impossible to confront questions of ethnic, racial and regional origin – they were simply taboo subjects. But it is clear that the make-up of the regime, as well as some of its practices, remained a source of difficulties.[82] It was widely felt in the northern provinces, not without foundation, that both party and state were biased towards the south. Recruitment to the country's only university was also heavily skewed towards students from the southern provinces.[83] There was considerable resentment in the provinces at the priority given to Maputo, and the central region and in particular Beira remained resentful of the terrible damage done to them by the conflict with Rhodesia.[84] There were persistent grumbles about the absence of whites in the armed forces which occasionally surfaced publicly (as in the letter of the *antigos combatentes*).[85] In a later political climate when opinion was more freely expressed, the furious debates about the nationality law in 1990 showed the

[81] See the account of such meetings in the *Guardian*, 13 July 1983.

[82] Most African regimes have resolutely denied the pertinence of 'tribal' or ethnic affiliations while engaging in complex ethnic balancing acts. There was probably a certain amount of this in Mozambique (it may explain why Chipande kept his post as Minister of Defence) but much less so than elsewhere.

[83] Figures in de Brito, 'Le Frelimo', pp. 227-8.

[84] For Beira see Finnegan, *A Complicated War*.

[85] For the letter see *Politique Africaine*, 29 (March 1988), pp. 115-30.

depth of feeling about such issues. Yet these kinds of ethno-regional and racial sentiments, virtually universal in Africa if not the world, remained literally invisible to the regime.

A second major feature of Mozambican society that confronted Frelimo with major problems of legitimation was the rural-urban divide. The considerable tensions on these matters within Frelimo have already been noted. Its thinking and sentiments undoubtedly included an element of anti-urbanism, seeing cities as dens of iniquity and colonial corruption. On his triumphal return journey to Maputo in 1975 Samora Machel noted in Quelimane:

> 'So, we entered the transitional phase, of occupying the cities, towns and barracks left by the enemy: a difficult task since we had to cross the line of demarcation between our zone and the zone of the enemy. We came to the cities where vice, moral and material corruption and all the vestiges of colonialism are strongly implanted.'[86]

But this anti-urbanism coexisted with a deep contempt, verging on hatred, for rural 'backwardness' (including 'obscurantism') and 'hut habits'. There was a strong sense in which for the Frelimo leadership 'the secret is in the school...the secret is the book'. Without such secrets it was impossible to plant crops or even to wash oneself.[87]

What seems to have been critical in determining which of these elements predominated was a shift from a Marxism of peasant insurrection to one of development and nation-building. Although its roots lay in rural insurgency, for many in Frelimo the knowledge it had acquired to fight a successful anti-colonial struggle no longer seemed pertinent to the new tasks. Its vision of rural transformation certainly became entirely urban: 'The communal village transposes the town to the countryside and its conception follows a model in which the individual only exists by and in the state.'[88] Whether this concerned economic or political institutions the rural world was essentially empty, waiting for the new vision to be implanted on it. This kind of understanding has been aptly termed by Geffray the ideology of the 'blank page' – conceiving Mozambique 'as if the rural population had been a vast collection of individuals – men, women, the old and children – outside history and social

---

[86] Quoted in Rita-Ferreira p. 142.

[87] For 'hut habits' see footnote 71. For 'the book' see speech at a public rally in Inhambane province in February 1982, *Tempo*, 599 (4 April 1982).

[88] De Brito, 'Le Frelimo', p. 250.

relations as if, fallen from the sky, they had been waiting for Frelimo to organise them as they had never been historically organised before'.[89] These deep-seated attitudes helped shape the failure of villagisation as both an economic and a political project. The imposition of communal villages took little account of either the economic or cultural practices of rural people. They were simply sunk in '*torpeur millenaire*'.[90] Peasant cultivators were to be brought to 'higher' relations of production by state farms that would diffuse science ('the book') among them. Little account was taken of the intensely varied rural terrain including pre-existing patterns of land tenure and lineage. 'Frelimo's new legal code on the use of land gave certain rights on the basis of the fact of occupation, but no recognition of the basis of such rights or occupation in customary land tenure.'[91] In fact, the earlier proposals for the design of communal villages, while apparently drawing on the 'experience and creative imagination' of the members, were so meticulous as to leave nothing to the imagination at all.[92]

Such assaults generated both resistance and evasion, though usually the latter and that of a rather sullen and passive kind. Nunes' generalisation that 'most peasants in Namanjavira tried to avoid major confrontations with local institutions and often showed an apparently subservient attitude' could probably be extended to the whole of Mozambique.[93] This did not of course exclude more creative strategies which utilised the official language of the regime as a way of subverting its effects. In Mueda peasants abandoned the official communal villages to set up their own 'communal' villages, in reality 'autonomous villages established in the forest by peasants who had abandoned the centre village of Ngapa, but used the designation cooperatives in an effort to legitimise their undertaking in the eyes of the authorities'.[94]

Finally, there were the divisions within Mozambican society that may be characterised, however inadequately, as 'traditional' and 'modern'. Whatever qualifications need to be made to these terms, it is beyond dispute that there was a sharp divide between Frelimo's

---

[89] C. Geffray, 'Fragments d'un discours du pouvoir (1975-1985). Du bon usage d'une méconnaissance scientifique', *Politique Africaine*, 29 (1988), p. 78.

[90] A senior Mozambican official cited in de Brito, 'Le Frelimo', p. 247.

[91] J. Sidaway, 'Urbanity, Image and the State in post-colonial Mozambique' (unpublished paper), p. 18.

[92] See documents discussed in de Brito, 'Le Frelimo', pp. 250-3.

[93] Nunes, 'Peasants', p. 27.

[94] L. Rudebeck, 'Conditions of People's Development in Postcolonial Africa', p. 44.

vision of modernity and a number of widespread indigenous or indigenised practices and beliefs which, while not necessarily a coherent and certainly not a timeless whole, did inform the lives and behaviour of many Mozambicans – especially, though by no means only, in the rural areas. At its most ambitious this vision involved a wholesale assault on many such practices and beliefs and, even though such assaults tended to be intermittent and locally variable, Frelimo's modernising ideology and its tendencies to demonisation provided considerable obstacles to any kind of nuanced understanding of 'traditional' Mozambique. Thus all chiefs were the handmaidens of colonialism, 'feudal' and backward; all traditional beliefs were '*obscurantismo*'; all traditional practices were 'oppression'. In sum, all values and habits that did not square with modern (Western) notions of progress and propriety were illegitimate.

While Frelimo particularly singled out the Catholic Church for its association with the colonial regime, both religious belief and religious institutions were to be attacked and vilified and deprived of any social role, although they were formally permitted by the state. 'Although protected in the constitution religious practice was mocked and derided when it was not simply a reason for preventing entry to the party.'[95] Until about 1982 the regime was characterised by a diffuse hostility to organised religion generally, although practice on the ground was uneven and seems to have been dependent on the inclinations of local officials. Certainly there was a considerable degree of harassment, including 'petty vindictive actions by local officials, ranging from football matches in front of churches during the Sunday morning service to throwing pigs into mosques'.[96] Virtually all religious communities lost property during the nationalisations, and this property often contained schools or facilities for religious observance. Religious associations were forbidden, and attempts were made to prevent religious activities anywhere but in churches.[97] The Muslim community was also subject to some harassment, again locally variable.[98] It was

[95] C. Verschuur *et al.*, *Mozambique. Dix ans de solitude*, Paris, 1986, p. 163.

[96] J. Hanlon in the *Guardian*, 14 January 1983. See also interview with D. Manuel Vieira Pinto, Bishop of Nampula, in *Expresso*, 11 August 1984.

[97] The story of religion in post-independence Mozambique remains obscure. For official hostility to the Catholic church see *Notícias* 20 May 1979 and 23 May 1979. See also 'Inside Mozambique' (*The Tablet*, 1 July 1978), *Le Monde*, 8 June 1979, and *Zambia Daily Mail*, 23 May 1979.

[98] See its response to the state at the December 1982 meeting Supplement to AIM *Information Bulletin*, 78.

forbidden to build churches of any kind in communal villages (into which the state proposed to shift most of the rural population), and in some areas at least the holding of services was prevented.[99]

The special hostility to the Catholic Church derived in part from its associations with the colonial authorities and Salazarist Portugal generally. Frelimo's criticisms of these associations were well founded, despite courageous opposition to the Portuguese role by individuals within the church.[100] But Frelimo's post-independence hostility was driven also by intense suspicion of Catholic 'internationalism', itself a threat to national strategies in the regulation of ecclesiastical institutions and especially to the principles of the secular state, which Frelimo's ideologues articulated in a Marxist idiom (although they are a common legacy of the Enlightenment). It was this position that enabled the Catholic Church to call for talks with the regime's enemies and to demand the restoration of its property. Both these demands touched very sore points with the regime. Consequently the attack on the Catholic Church was at times ferocious and came from the highest level, with Machel himself denouncing 'imperialism's agents in cassocks' in a May Day speech in 1979, itself the culmination of weeks of hostile press and radio propaganda against the church.[101] This hostility continued into the 1980s, and was only moderated as the damage caused by destabilisation and Renamo made almost any allies acceptable. The organised churches were at least a force to be reckoned with. Less organised 'traditional' practices were to be given short shrift. According to Frelimo's Department of Ideological Work, 'animism' was to be 'extinguished' largely by education and the development of productive forces. Generally, obscurantism was to be 'dispersed' by science.[102] As a recent Mozambican commentator has put it, 'the new developments attempted the brutal elimination of most of the pre-existing values.[...] The introduction of new values did not take account of the existing cultural context, and in the end represented great violence towards the population.'[103]

---

[99] O. Roesch, 'Rural Mozambique since the Frelimo Party Fourth Congress: The Situation in the Baixo Limpopo', *Review of African Political Economy*, 41 (1988), 73-91, esp. p. 85.

[100] See his fairly measured speech at the meeting with religious leaders Supplement to AIM *Information Bulletin*, 78.

[101] 'Fazer viver a linha do Partido em cada trabalhador', May 1979. See report in *Africa*, 95 (July 1979).

[102] Departamento do Trabalho Ideologico, documents of 2nd Conference in Beira, 5-10 June 1978.

[103] Helder Muteia in *Notícias*, 28 May 1993.

The institutions of legitimation created by Frelimo were fatally disabling in the face of these characteristics of Mozambican society. The party itself excluded all those not committed to its notion of modernity – in a one-party state that is effectively to accuse the bulk of the population of potential treachery.[104] The district and provincial assemblies and the mass organisations, subject to the rigours of democratic centralism, simply could not articulate these issues as problems, except of course as problems to be removed. Frelimo deliberately excluded non-party intermediary bodies (the churches, 'traditional' structures) from any area of policy-making, and it rapidly became disillusioned with the results of its own populist tendencies and increasingly preferred centralised solutions. Yet this centralised power, while able to impose many arbitrary decisions on society, was often bureaucratically ineffective and certainly insufficiently coercive to impose the transformations the Frelimo leadership dreamed of. Had the regime been able to achieve the steady improvement in the material well-being of the population while slowly consolidating its grip on society, and had it been left free from meddling and interference from outside, things might well have been different. But the fundamental contours of its politics coloured its choice of economic strategies, and while these might not have been as ruinous, as it has subsequently become fashionable to suggest, in combination with the regional and international factors they proved too much. It is thus to economic strategy and international relations that we must now turn.

---

[104] For the exclusion of polygamists from public office see Egero, *Mozambique*, p. 157.

4

THE PATH TO DEVELOPMENT

'The victory of socialism is a victory of science, it is prepared and organised scientifically. The plan is the instrument of scientific organisation of this victory.'[1]

'A curious sight greets the visitor to a showpiece state farm which the government has established 60 miles west of the capital.[...] Some 50 new bright red British tractors are lined up outside the farm office, their wheelless chassis propped on blocks and slowly rusting in the humid air of the coastal plain.[...] Few of these vehicles have broken down for mechanical reasons but because in normal day-to-day use their tyres have been punctured and since farm labourers [do not] have the means or the knowledge to repair inner tubes.[...] In the case of the state farm tractor tyre punctures are repaired by cannibalising whole wheels from previously immobilised vehicles, a practice which naturally diminishes the number of road-worthy tractors very quickly.'[2]

An essential underpinning of the new political order was a new kind of economy. While the immediate post-war period was dominated by improvisation and *ad hoc* measures, this was not simply a matter of drift or reacting to events. Frelimo's economic thinking, while vague in detail, had already taken a definite shape. Even before independence, and particularly after the defeat of the Nkavandame faction, the condemnation of the 'exploitation of man by man' had become a regular part of the movement's propaganda.[3] And just as the liberated zones of the guerrilla war had foreshadowed new forms of political organisation, so also the embryonic forms of socialist practice, including collective produc-

---

[1] Samora Machel quoted in *Voz da Revolução*, 73 (June 1981), p. 32.

[2] James MacManus in the *Guardian*, 19 May 1979.

[3] *Mozambique Revolution*, 52, p. 2. See Marcelino dos Santos, 'The revolutionary perspective in Mozambique', *World Marxist Review*, 11 (1968), pp. 43-5, and interviews with dos Santos in *African Communist*, 55 (1973), pp. 23-53, and *Sechaba*, 4 (1970), pp. 15-18, 22-7; the comments of Samora Machel quoted in P. Spacek, 'Nation building in Mozambique', *Sechaba*, 4 (1970), pp. 12-15.

tion, heralded the ending of exploitation and would form the building blocks of the new society.[4] The formula that agriculture formed the base and industry the dynamic factor in economic development had also been widely promoted and indeed written into the first post-independence constitution (Article 6). Thus, even before the official turn to Marxism, Frelimo had a rudimentary analysis of the colonial economy, a view as to what would replace it and some idea of the mechanisms, both economic and political, required to implement such a vision.

Development: discourse and strategy

But the relative generality of Frelimo's economic thinking and the *ad hoc* nature of its practices in the immediate post-independence period had to give way to something more formal and structured. This was elaborated in a series of key documents from the Economic and Social Directives of the 3rd Party Congress to the 1980/1 Plan (the PPI or Plano Prospectivo Indicativo). As in other policy areas, Samora Machel's speeches were a major part of the policy process and often led to important shifts in emphasis. These core documents consistently argued that the particular form of Portuguese colonialism had produced a distorted colonial structure in which the economy was heavily dependent on supplying labour services and transport facilities for the stronger economies of the region, notably Rhodesia and South Africa. These features, combined with the unique characteristics of Portuguese racialism and the need to provide employment for Portuguese immigrants, had created an economy which even by colonial standards was peculiarly backward and devastating in its effects on the African population – who, as a result, were largely excluded from the modern sector in both consumption and the acquisition of skills of all kinds.

The economic dimension of Frelimo's thinking about independence followed logically from this analysis and consistently stressed three points. The first was that independence would make possible the construction of a national economy, which would, at least in time, remove the colonial distortions. Secondly, independence would make possible the satisfaction of the people's 'basic needs' in the sense of material consumption and social services. And thirdly, the economy would be transformed in a modern but socialist direction; this transformation would be state-led and planning would

<hr>

[4] See Machel's speech at the party school, *Tempo*, 319 (14 November 1976).

play the key role. Frelimo's programme spoke of the necessity for 'the state-owned sector of production [to] become dominant and determinant, so that the establishment of state-owned firms is a priority objective'.[5] It stressed the centrality of planning, asserting that 'the building of socialism demands that the economy be centrally planned and directed by the state'.[6]

These general positions on the overall strategy of development clearly had major implications for sectoral strategies which required further elaboration. These sectoral strategies, it should be understood, were not exclusively economic. They were intended to have the double objective of immediate increases in production and the transformation of social and economic structures; with the latter would come political and ideological transformations as well. Inevitably considerable attention was devoted to the rural sector. Traditional peasant cultivation was seen as backward and indeed as an obstacle to modern agriculture and expansion of agricultural output. To overcome this backwardness a two-track strategy was to be pursued, involving both the creation of large state-owned farms and the villagisation and collectivisation of peasant farmers as part of a general policy 'to introduce the new socialist production relations into the countryside'. The state farms were seen not only as rational and highly productive, but as having dynamic effects on the surrounding desert of agricultural backwardness.[7] As a long-term aim, they would become 'dominant and determinant'.[8]

The process of villagisation was presented not only as an essential precondition of agricultural modernisation but also as the solution to the problems of the effective delivery of social services to a highly dispersed population. Organised thus, the agricultural sector would be able to play its 'basic' role of feeding the population, supplying the raw material needs of industry, and helping through exports to finance the imported goods essential for further economic transformations. In relation to industry, stress was laid on its essential contribution to genuine economic development; in the short term to attain previous levels of production, particularly in those industries supplying the basic needs of the population, and in the longer term towards the development of heavy industry and the harmonious development of all sectors. As with agriculture, there was an emphasis on the formation of cadres and a workforce

---

[5] Frelimo 3rd Congress Central Committee Report (MAGIC 1978), p. 44.

[6] Central Committee Report, p. 43.

[7] Ibid., p. 46.

[8] Economic and Social Directives in *Tempo*, 333 (20 February 1977), p. 40.

both in the sense of technical competence and as a class-conscious proletariat supporting the state and its political leadership.[9]

Thus Frelimo's economic thinking and practice, while from the beginning buffeted by problems and difficulties, retained a consistent shape that formed part of its vision of social transformation and dovetailed with the chosen instrument of that transformation, the modernising state. Yet, as has already been suggested, the Marxist categories adopted, while they undoubtedly had effects, were not fundamentally a means of analysis. Marxism's intellectual coherence and the success of the Soviet model in effecting rapid industrialisation of agrarian societies almost certainly ensured that they played a pre-eminent role in providing the discursive means to articulate a vision of economic development. But this vision, and indeed the intellectual and political traditions on which it drew, shared certain elements with other forms of thought and practice. This was not 'contradiction' (though it doubtless caused considerable confusion), but simply a reflection of the fact that in the context of 'undeveloped' societies many of the requirements of socialist planning are not greatly different from those of capitalist production. They involve a capacity to mobilise resources and agencies as well as an extensive capacity for monitoring and surveillance, which in turn implies requirements of literacy and various organisational capabilities – in a word, 'modern' organisational behaviour. Thus Frelimo's Marxism attracted to itself elements of other visions of modernisation including those of Portuguese colonial practice (which certainly involved forms of economic planning) and the (then) routine assumptions of Western aid agencies and donors.[10] This rather inchoate mix prevailed particularly among lower and middle-level state functionaries whose Marxist political culture was rudimentary if not negligible.

A number of clear elements were nevertheless discernible in this mix. Material improvements and 'catching up' with 'progress' were almost inseparable. So while it was in a sense true that 'victory over underdevelopment was defined largely in material terms', paradoxically this cannot be understood in a narrowly material sense that takes no account of the effects of a whole psychology of exclusion from modernity.[11] Sympathetic economists who (doubt-

[9] Economic and Social Directives, p. 43.

[10] See M.L. Bowen, '"Let's Build Agricultural Producer Cooperatives": Socialist Agricultural Development Strategy in Mozambique, 1975-1983', unpubl. Ph.D. thesis, University of Toronto, 1986, pp. 124-5.

[11] J.E. Torp, *Mozambique: Politics, Economics and Society*, London, 1990, p. 32. There are interesting parallels with Soviet assumptions: see M. Ottaway, 'Soviet Marxism

less rightly) suggested that, for example, the government might have concentrated on the production of staples for the African population rather missed the point of what 'progress' meant to Frelimo, and that it was driven by powerful feelings of humiliation and exclusion.[12] Once asked why Mozambique could not feed itself, Samora Machel angrily replied:

> 'It is the fault of Europe and the United States. You are the ones who are ultimately responsible for hunger because you were the colonialists, the ones who sowed illiteracy and ignorance among our people. As a result, we now have no technology, engineers, agronomists, veterinarians and doctors. We have no scientific knowledge. This is all because of colonialism.'[13]

In this perspective development was not about modest and gradual improvements in material well-being but about 'becoming modern'.[14]

Such an intensely-felt vision of social progress also made the separation of 'the economic' from 'the political' virtually impossible. 'Catching up' could not possibly wait for long-term historical processes but could only be carried out by the state, which would concentrate resources in the strategic sectors as well as creating the New Man. As Marcelino dos Santos enthused on a visit to the country's largest state farm, 'Here, besides rice, Man is being produced. There has been a growth of Man here. This is already a victory. Mozambican man has grown in Chokwe.'[15] The role of popular needs has also to be seen in this context. These were to be mobilised for developmental purposes (indeed Frelimo made much of 'relying on our own efforts'), but within a framework of élite guidance based on unquestioned (and unquestionable) assumptions about progress. For Frelimo state-led planning was about both production and social discipline; about the destruction of the 'class enemy' and the creation of the class basis of the Frelimo state. The general thrust of such thinking almost inevitably produced strong tendencies to see all economic problems as matters of will and command in a context of sacrifice and moral worth.

---

and African Socialism', *Journal of Modern African Studies*, 16, 3 (1978), pp. 477-85.

[12] P. Raikes, 'Food Policy and Production in Mozambique since Independence' (paper presented at SOAS, July 1983). For the difficulties produced by decisions to produce European crops see O. Roesch, 'Rural Mozambique', pp. 76-7.

[13] Samora Machel, Maputo radio, 16 November 1983, SWB, 29 November 1983.

[14] For a direct statement see interview with Machel, *Africa*, 107 (July 1980).

[15] *Tempo*, 568 (30 August 1981), p. 6.

The attractions of a rhetoric of struggle proved strong: 'We should be aware that PPI is a people's victory of great significance whose fulfillment requires great and profound sacrifices. There is no victory without sacrifices. The success of a battle is the result of great sacrifices.'[16]

Building the socialist economy

The thinking and policy commitments of the regime were quite clear. To what extent did they inform policy and practice, and with what results? To a considerable extent Frelimo's stated policies were implemented even if the circumstances were not those of 'classic' socialist transitions. Even before the 3rd Congress Frelimo had been careful to ensure that abandoned land was not seized by the peasants – the rural GDs were mobilised to prevent this.[17] 'Frelimo's policy was to "advance and transform"; abandoned land would not be distributed to individuals but would be gathered into state farms and cooperatives.'[18] Private ownership of land was abolished in the first post-independence constitution, and land nationalisation gave the government the authority to convert abandoned agricultural land to state farms or cooperatives. There was a further wave of nationalisations in December 1977/January 1978 in which the oil refinery, the Moatize coal mining company and the Cahora Bassa dam were taken over.[19] Simultaneously there was a nationalisation and restructuring of the banking sector which left a Central Bank and a People's Development Bank, while one private sector bank (Standard Totta) was allowed to function. There was a third round of nationalisations in late 1978/9 which brought into the state sector the Companhia Moçambicana de Navegação, the main (Portuguese-owned) cement company CIMPOR, the Industria Mocambicana de Aco and the country's main glass manufacturer. By the early 1980s the nationalised sector consisted of enterprises in which there had been 'intervention', plus some others

---

[16] Machel, AIM supplement, October 1981, pp. 6-7. See also Machel, 20 May 1981, SWB ME/6370/B2-3.

[17] See *AIM Bulletin*, 64, (October 1981), and reports of an interview with Agriculture Minister Joaquim de Carvalho in U. Semin-Panzer, 'Transformation der Landwirtschaft und Überwindung von Underentwicklung in Moçambique', *Afrika-Spectrum*, 13, (1977) p. 301.

[18] Helen Dolny, 'The Challenge of Agriculture' in Saul (ed.), *A Difficult Road*, p. 224.

[19] See *AIM Bulletin*, 18.

such as the banks and the oil refinery which had been deliberate nationalisations.

During 1980 a certain amount of state property, largely in the retail sector, was denationalised.[20] But the retreat from the retail sector was based on the feeling of the senior leadership that the real economic dynamic lay in other sectors. As Machel explained, 'Marxism-Leninism does not concern itself with garages, it does not concern itself with selling eggs in the market.[...] Marxism-Leninism concerns itself with major economic development projects.'[21] Denationalisation of certain assets was not so much a retreat as a focusing of energies on what Frelimo had always regarded as the central core of economic policy – a planned and predominant state sector. Overall state control of the economy was enhanced. In large-scale trade and production the state sector became dominant, as party policy had required. By 1981 it accounted for 65% of total industrial output, 85% of transport and communications activity, 90% of construction and 40% of commerce, although these official figures probably exaggerated the size of the state sector.[22] The area covered by state farms rose to 100,000 hectares by 1978 and 140,000 by 1982. The significance of this state sector was not simply its formal extent, but that it attracted the lion's share of available investment funds and that the largest sector of the Mozambican economy was subjected to certain kinds of planning practices.

Just as there can be no doubt that the Frelimo regime sought to control largely the economy, there can be no doubt that it also sought to plan it. The major strategic characteristics of the planning system were the subordination of the economic ministries to the CNP (National Planning Commission) with state enterprises subordinate to their respective ministries, and the main means of planning was the state budget which centralised all financial resources and provided for their allocation in accordance with the central plans.[23] The National Planning Commission was designed to concentrate the expertise and statistical information that would be necessary for a national planning exercise. Most of the East German

[20] For details see the *Guardian*, 20 March 1980 and 11 November 1980; *Financial Times*, 3 April 1980.

[21] News conference, 22 March 1980, SWB ME/6379/B 6-8.

[22] M. Mackintosh and M. Wuyts, 'Accumulation, Social Services and Socialist Transition in the Third World: Reflections on Decentralised Planning based on the Mozambican Experience', *Journal of Development Studies*, 24, 4 (1988), pp. 136-79, esp. p. 141.

[23] CNP set up by Presidential Decree 33/78, 18 May 1978.

and Soviet advisers were concentrated there. Sectoral plans for the economy were the responsibility of different ministries under the guidance of the Commission.[24] Planning units had already been established in ministries in June 1975.[25] In agriculture the ministry created a Directorate for the Organisation of Collective Production. This was divided into two branches that dealt with state farms and cooperatives respectively, with the first of these receiving the great majority of the available technical manpower.[26]

In August 1979 the Council of Ministers resolved to elaborate a National Plan for 1980-90 to which Machel periodically alluded in speeches, although the actual formal announcement to the People's Assembly was not made until towards the end of 1981.[27] Machel presented the plan as 'the highest stage of implementation of the Third Congress directives.'[28] The plan, which was kept secret then and has never been formally published since, built on three major goals of structural transformation: socialisation of the countryside (designated as the principal task), industrialisation of the country and formation of the workforce. Described as the application of Marxism in a creative way to the 'concrete conditions of our development', the plan had among its targets the construction of communal villages for 5 million people by 1990, as well as laying the foundations of heavy industry.[29] As part of these processes of transformation GNP would rise 17% per annum and agricultural production would increase fivefold.[30]

The implementation of this plan involved the further development of new instruments of planning and control, as well as extending the powers of those already in existence. A National Commission for Salaries and Prices was created in 1979 to replace DINECA (which had itself replaced the old colonial price-setting structures). This was followed in 1981 by the setting up of Agricom to run agricultural marketing, and the state began to set producer

---

[24] *25 de Septembro*, 88 (1978), p. 32.

[25] See F. Cardoso, 'Some experiences in economic development particularly in industry after the fall of colonialism in Mozambique', *Wissenschaftliche Beiträge*, supplementary issue (1977), pp. 111-18. For a slightly different account see J.E. Torp, *Industrial Planning and Development in Mozambique* (Uppsala: Scandinavian Institute for African Studies, research report 50, 1979).

[26] Dolny, pp. 225-6.

[27] See for example the speech of 20 December 1979, SWB ME/6305/B/1.

[28] *Tempo* 575 (18 October 1981), p. 21.

[29] *Tempo* 574 (11 October 1981), p. 8.

[30] Hanlon, *Mozambique: The revolution under fire*, p. 84.

and consumer prices for such goods.[31] The state budget became the principal instrument of financial planning. New taxes, an income tax and a turnover tax were introduced and the banking system was reorganised. The commitment to planning was reinforced by making annual plans legally binding on enterprises. The development of enterprise structures and management largely paralleled the setting up of macro-economic planning structures. In the period during and immediately after independence the government had relied on the GDs to keep the economy at a minimal level of functioning. Confiscated enterprises or state enterprises were run by government-appointed administrative commissions supervised by a control office in the Ministry of Industry and Commerce.[32] This rather chaotic arrangement was gradually changed following a speech by Machel in October 1976 in which he insisted on the necessity for a separation of administrative and political functions within the enterprise.[33] The former was clarified by a law promulgated in April 1977 on state enterprises, which laid down that management would be carried out by a directorate appointed by the appropriate Ministry.[34] This structure was further modified by a new law on state enterprises in 1981, which shifted towards one-man management, giving each state enterprise a general director with full decision-making powers.[35] This law complemented the extended planning system, in that state enterprises were subordinated to targets laid down in the National Plan, fulfilment of which was a legal obligation, and their surpluses were to be returned to the state budget. The 'political' side of enterprises was formalised on an experimental basis in Maputo in late 1976, and then throughout the country during 1977, by the introduction of Production Councils as the major instrument which would allow workers to combat indiscipline and raise production and productivity, as well as helping to shape a proletarian class-consciousness.[36] The Production Councils were split into five departments covering economic matters, social issues,

---

[31] V. Tickner, 'Structural Adjustment and Agricultural pricing in Mozambique', *Review of African Political Economy*, 53 (1992), pp. 25- 42.

[32] Cardoso, 'Some experiences', p. 114.

[33] S. Machel, 'Produzir é um Acto de Militancia' in B. Munslow (ed.), *Samora Machel.*

[34] See *Tempo*, 345 (15 May 1977).

[35] See *AIM Bulletin*, 14 (October 1984), and *Tempo*, 574 (11 October 1981).

[36] For a triumphalist account see 'Workers' Control in Mozambique' in *People's Power*, no. 10. See also *Commissão de Implementação Sobre Restruturação dos Sectores e Estruturas*, p. 64.

hygiene and safety, training and cultural matters, but all of these were to be answerable to a Control and Discipline Committee. From the beginning these councils were seen as prototype trade unions.[37]

The politics of economic transformation, 1977-1982

Such were the fundamental assumptions and their institutional embodiments that governed Frelimo's management of economic policy – tactical adjustments and 'pragmatism' notwithstanding. They had powerful effects, of which the most important was the persistent identification of economic modernisation with the centralised planning of an increasingly large and eventually dominant state sector. Non-state sectors were viewed as islands of backwardness, or at best temporary necessities, but in either case as sectors which were eventually to be absorbed into 'higher' relations of production. These beliefs and their accompanying practices had the effect of constantly biasing resources towards the state sector and obstructing attempts to assess the rationality and utility of this bias. They clearly shaped the state's interventions in the ownership and control of material resources. While it is indisputable that many 'interventions' took place in a situation of severe economic collapse rather than as premeditated nationalisation of the 'commanding heights' of the economy, it cannot of course be inferred from this that there was not a strategy of increasing state control or that Frelimo policy was simply carried along by the need to 'keep the economy going'.

There is always more than one way to keep an economy going, and repeated protestations by the regime that everybody had a place in the new Mozambique were no substitute for a strategic alliance with existing producers and traders which could have been the basis for a different kind of economic strategy, and have included the Portuguese settler population.[38] In fact the government and Party remained hostile to domestic private enterprise well into the 1980s for perfectly good political and ideological reasons – the reality was that while 'publicly Frelimo has always said that there is a place in Mozambique for private business, [it] gave it no encouragement or support in the early years of independence'.[39]

[37] *Notícias*, 26 August 1982. See *Tempo*, 682 (6 November 1983), also M. Cahen, 'Etat et pouvoir populaire dans le Mozambique indépendant', *Politique Africaine*, 19 (1985), pp. 36-60.

[38] K. Hermele, *Country Report: Mozambique 1988*, SIDA Planning Secretariat, p. 6.

[39] Hanlon, *Mozambique: the revolution under fire*, p. 195.

Throughout the earlier years official Frelimo statements frequently denounced the petit bourgeoisie and the bourgeoisie as classes and consigned them to the 'dustbin of history'.[40] The official self-presentation of the Mozambican state was equally explicit:

> The aim of Frelimo is the destruction of the capitalist system and the construction of a society free from the exploitation of man by man. The historic mission of the Frelimo party is to direct, organise, orient and educate the masses for the construction of socialism.[41]

Or, as the weekly magazine *Tempo* put it more succinctly, 'There can be no good Mozambican capitalists'.[42]

The commitments to state-led growth and political control helped shape both investment decisions and the form of operation of economic planning. Investment increased sharply after 1977, though actual investment was always less than planned because of the limited absorptive capacity of the economy and the shortage of funds. In the period 1978-82 some 31% of this investment went into agriculture, as well as a considerable proportion of investment classified statistically under construction (see Table 4.1). These resources went overwhelmingly to the state sector. 'Of agricultural investment in 1977-83, 90% went to the state sector, two percent to cooperatives, and virtually none to the small-scale "family" farming.'[43] A large part of this investment went to the mechanisation of state farms. The showcase for this kind of strategy, the Lower Limpopo Complex (CAIL), a major project that was to integrate farming, animal breeding, processing and warehousing, was alone responsible for some 50% of investment in the agricultural sector during 1977.[44] In the longer term it was intended to expand CAIL by 1990 to employ some 350,000 people.[45]

[40] Marcelino dos Santos in *Notícias*, 30 August 1977.

[41] Information on Mozambique Doc. Info. no. 1 CEDIMO Serie E 1979.1.11.

[42] Quoted in K. Middlemass, 'Independent Mozambique and its Regional Policy', p. 222.

[43] Wuyts and Mackintosh, 'Accumulation', p. 145.

[44] K. Hermele, *Contemporary Land Struggles on the Limpopo: A Case Study of Chokwe, Mozambique, 1950-85*, Uppsala, 1986, p. 86.

[45] See B. Munslow, 'State Intervention in Agriculture: the Mozambican experience', *Journal of Modern African Studies*, 22 (1984), pp. 220-1. For CAIL see also *Tempo* 570 (13 September 1981).

Table 4.1. SECTORAL ALLOCATION OF INVESTMENT[46]
(*million meticais*)

Sector	1978/9	1980	1981	1982
Agriculture	1,095	2,271	4,181	4,826
Industry and energy	561	1,227	3,349	3,493
Transport and Communication	177	155	345	468
Construction	5,457	3,346	3,270	2,424

Nor was the bias limited to material resources alone, but virtually all available human resources were directed towards the state sector, as Machel had demanded in a speech in July 1979.[47] It is clear that this bias was not simply reducible to questions of resources but reflected definite choices:

> Even in areas where little investment was required there was no progress in the development of the cooperative movement. [...] Little was done to encourage animal traction, to organise bank credit for cooperatives and to adjust price structures to give special benefit to cooperatives. In addition there was no attempt to organise consumer cooperatives in the rural areas so that members of agricultural producer cooperatives would be guaranteed access to the distribution of scarce goods.[48]

It has already been suggested that the Mozambican state was over-extended and underdeveloped. The over-extension of the Frelimo state was indeed most vividly exhibited in the economic sphere and made almost intractable by the forms of planning adopted. The planning structures do not appear to have been set up with any detailed knowledge of or background in the history of socialist planning, although their major features, at least as formally established, clearly drew on that tradition. Whatever the case, many of the preconditions of modern planning were simply lacking in Mozambique, except among a small proportion of the élite. It cannot be said that the political leadership was unaware of these facts (though possibly it did not understand all their ramifications), and in part awareness of them explains that leadership's constant concern with social discipline of all kinds. As Samora Machel pointed

---

[46] Commissão Nacional do Plano, *Informação Estatistica, 1975-1984.* The World Bank Public Expenditure Review uses essentially the same figures but provides some useful contextualisation.

[47] '*Organizemos os nossos Recursos para resolver os problemas do Povo.*'

[48] Bowen, p. 130 (emphasis added).

out, the People's Assembly was full of people who could not read the Constitution.[49]

So the imposition of such forms of planning by an élite that had little awareness of the tradition of economic planning (and certainly did not encourage public debate about it) on a society almost completely unfamiliar with such an organisational culture could not but induce massive, and massively dysfunctional, rigidities in the management both of the national economy and of individual enterprises. Across a range of policy areas and instruments such rigidities and lack of organisational capacity caused immense difficulties. At the national level there was a failure to think through the relations between the state sector and the rest of the economy. Whatever decisions were made by the political structures, the administrative weight and discretion of the Planning Commission were considerable; and as there was always a shortfall of funds in relation to projects, its rationing powers were extensive and were almost always exercised to the advantage of the state sector.[50] Planning itself was highly inflexible, with targets being set according to assumed norms which had no basis in existing capacities. In agriculture, 'since the targets are intended to reflect national priorities, they do not take account of such niceties as crop-rotation, economic viability, or even whether the pattern of products chosen is feasible in terms of labour requirements.'[51]

These difficulties were replicated at the sub-national level. The form of planning adopted for the state farms was a highly centralised one, with plans formulated in hectare targets which production units would aim at satisfying with virtually no consideration of cost. Planned prices were rarely adjusted to changed conditions; there was no effective coordination of state purchasing by different state institutions, and 'Mozambique did not have the high level of administrative capacity required for an effective and flexible operation of the system, and when frequent and rapid price changes became necessary they were not undertaken.'[52] Large numbers of important economic enterprises proved incapable of carrying

[49] S. Machel, 'A luta contra o subdesenvolvimento é uma batalha cultural', 3 July 1978.

[50] See M. Wuyts, 'Money, Planning and Rural Transformation in Mozambique', *Journal of Development Studies*, 22 (1985), pp. 180-207, esp. 195.

[51] Raikes, 'Food Policy and Production', p. 8.

[52] F. Tarp, 'Prices in Mozambican Agriculture', *Journal of International Development*, 2, 2 (1990), pp. 172-208, p. 191.

out fundamental management tasks. The state oil company Petromoc produced no financial accounts for seven years.[53]

Finally, economic growth was seen essentially and simply as the sacrifice of current consumption.[54] The other side of this coin was that all economic difficulties and even criticism of the approaches pursued were externalised, either as a legacy of the past or as the work of malevolent forces, internal or external, or as a result of poor implementation. Whichever rationalisation was favoured, the essential commitment to socialist policies, however it might have been understood, remained beyond question and discussion, at least in the public arena. The available options were heroic sacrifice or moral degeneration. This set of assumptions inevitably induced commandist, punitive and even arbitrary modes of economic management, so that failures were to be remedied by more 'mobilisation' and campaigns of moral exhortation, by endless restructuring of state bodies, or by the replacement of personnel. The *ofensiva* style was carried over into economic policy and management both by Machel himself and by the provincial governors following his lead.

These tendencies were most evident in the area of villagisation. For Frelimo socialist agriculture was a mechanism for achieving essential political and ideological objectives in the control of the countryside as well as something that embodied the supposed virtues of scientific agriculture. Peasants were to lose much of the best land to collective farms but also to be 'encouraged' into communal villages. The aim of communal villages was 'to change all aspects of rural life – not simply to make production more efficient'.[55] In principle such communal villages were supposed to practise collective forms of production, though this only rarely occurred. That Frelimo was more concerned about communal villages as a way of concentrating rural populations than collective production reflected a real worry about the possibility of peasants being out of state control. As Machel put it, 'The communal villages are a political instrument because they unite and organise us and thus enable us to exercise power. We must realise that if we are dispersed and disorganised we will not be able to exercise that power.'[56] This apprehension about dispersed peasants was linked

[53] UNDP/World Bank, *Mozambique: Issues and Options in the Energy Sector*, p. 52.

[54] *Notícias*, 5 February 1982, and *Tempo*, 591 (7 February 1982).

[55] First national Agricultural Conference in Beira quoted in Spavan, 'Rural Resettlement', p. 44.

[56] Machel in *Notícias* 26, October 1982.

to a fear, in the words of Marcelino des Santos, that 'economic growth without socialisation would lead to class differentiation in the countryside' and by implication that such differentiation would generate political opposition.[57] Thus long before security considerations became a factor, the CAIL project had involved the forcible removal of people from their land.[58] As peasants displayed less and less enthusiasm for communalisation, forced villagisation increased so that 'peasants frequently talk of houses being burned and people moved at gunpoint'. The commandism of the top leadership replicated itself down the chain of authority. In Manica province the Governor set a goal of total villagisation by the end of 1982 (rather than the end of the 1980s projected in the official plan), but his 'crash programme had neither the political nor the technical cadres to carry it out'.[59] The same style governed the day-to-day management of labour in both the state and the cooperative sectors of agriculture. Generally 'state farm workers were told forcibly to 'carry out the plan'.[60] Observers of rural conditions noted that, 'one finds cases in which...a farm or block manager plants (say) maize, several months after the last date on which a reasonable harvest could be expected, because the seeds arrives late and because the "plan must be fulfilled".'[61] Among cooperatives it was often the case that 'the plan is calculated by the Ministry of Agriculture without the cooperativists' participation and is usually completely unrealistic.'[62]

Nor were attitudes to urban labour much less authoritarian. Despite the ritual obeisance to *poder popular* and the notion that this power rested on a worker-peasant alliance, there was considerable suspicion of urban workers in Frelimo circles. In one of his more important speeches to workers, Samora Machel virtually accused them of helping the Portuguese war effort in exchange for higher wages.[63] The various reforms introduced in the manage-

[57] *AIM Bulletin*, 64 (1981) p. 2. It was a view echoed by Soviet bloc advisers e.g. Nicolae Grib, *Notícias*, 27 September 1985.

[58] K. Hermele, *Contemporary Land Struggles*, p. 87.

[59] Hanlon, *Mozambique*, p. 219. For tacit admission of brutal action against the peasantry, see Machel's 'Address to the People's Assembly', in *SWB* ME.8138/B 1, 13 December 1985.

[60] Bowen, 'Let's Build Agricultural Producer Cooperatives', p. 140.

[61] Raikes, 'Food Policy and Production', p. 9.

[62] Wardman, 'The Cooperative Movement in Chokwe, Mozambique', *Journal of Southern African Studies*, 11, 2 (1985), p. 302.

[63] See S. Machel, 'Produzir è um acto de militancia'. See also H. Schröer, 'Der Kampf an der Produktionsfront. Die materiellen, sozialen und politischen Bedin-

ment of economic enterprises, despite their democratic and participative labels, were in fact entirely authoritarian. The endless meetings were purely formal or ritual occasions in which little or no attempt was made to learn from the workers' experience and hardly any information was given to them on the success or otherwise of their activities. Although planning documents laid down an important role for workers, this did not occur and workers were simply informed of their production targets:

> The workers' production councils were at times asked to check on the information provided and report directly to central levels, but there is no evidence that they managed to fulfill this task and significantly alter the situation.[64]

The workers did not see the various structures in the enterprise as representing their interests, but simply as part of the authorities who must be obeyed. Members of enterprise-based GDs uniformly reported their role as being one of 'mobilisation' and the meting out of punishment for indiscipline'.[65] Because economic difficulties were invariably seen as moral or character failings, there was frequent recourse to criminal penalties. Thus in 1982 it was made a criminal offence to submit faulty production data to the planning authorities, which had the effect that many firms preferred not to submit data at all.[66]

Those not engaged in productive labour could hardly expect to be treated any better by state functionaries, spurred on as they were by constant leadership denunciations of the idle, unproductive and morally vicious. On many occasions the authorities resorted to virtual forced labour. In the biggest exercise of this kind, labelled Operation Production, numerous 'marginal' people were rounded up by the security forces and transported to the countryside, supposedly to engage in productive labour. Indeed Armando Guenbuza, the director of the operation, suggested somewhat optimistically that its fundamental objective was the elimination of underdevelopment.[67] In fact many of the people moved had no rural experience, and in any case conditions in the areas they

---

gungen der Industrialisierung Mozambiks' in F.J. Couto *et al., Eigenständige Entwicklung in Mosambik*, Frankfurt, 1982, p. 55.

[64] Egero, Mozambique: *A Dream Undone*, p. 100.

[65] H. Schröer, *Frelimo und Industrierarbeiter in postkolonialen Konflikten*, Saarbrücken, 1983.

[66] Egero, *Mozambique: A Dream Undone*, pp. 99-100.

[67] *Notícias*, 10 April 1984.

were sent to were not conducive to agricultural labour.[68] It was reported that 'many people were taken from their homes in Maputo at night, and arrived in Niassa with only the clothes they were wearing.'[69] Operation Production took place in a general atmosphere of repression, including the empowering of military tribunals to deal with cases of 'economic sabotage', which was made punishable by flogging or death.[70]

The Mozambican economy, 1977-1982

Economic institutions, discourse and practices always function in a wider national and international context of other agencies and contingent events, the operation and occurrence of which require all sorts of tactical adjustments and responses. In this Mozambique was obviously no exception, but it remains extraordinarily difficult to disentangle – put at its simplest – the internal and external determinants of its economic trajectory. To place the emphasis on the internal factors, especially the policies pursued by Frelimo, by no means requires acceptance of current liberal dogmas about 'free' markets or the 'impossibility' of socialism. What is clear, however, as has been stressed and as in a sense Frelimo was aware, is that many of the processes involved in both capitalist and socialist forms of economic 'modernisation' are similar, and they require social and cultural changes that go far beyond narrowly 'economic' ones. In this context Frelimo's strategy was an extraordinarily ambitious one, aiming at both rapid growth and the structural transformation of the economy in a socialist direction, when many of the preconditions for such a transformation appeared to be lacking.

To say the least, the external and contingent circumstances were not propitious. The country laboured under immense difficulties, some (though not all) of which were outside its control and would have seriously constrained any strategy. While cycles of adverse weather conditions were not of course unknown, their exact occurrence could not be predicted, even if 'to a certain extent the impact of these national disasters could have been reduced had the agricultural sector not been in such a depressed

---

[68] See Meiallasoux and Verschuur, 'Les paysans ignorés de Mozambique', *Le Monde Diplomatique*, October 1985, and *Africa Confidencial* (Lisbon), no. 1.

[69] J. Hanlon in the *Guardian*, 17 April 1984.

[70] See Amnesty International, *The Use of Flogging in the People's Republic of Mozambique*, February 1984, and *The Use of the Death Penalty in the People's Republic of Mozambique*, July 1983.

state and had the distribution and marketing of locally grown produce been better organised'.[71] The Limpopo and Incomati rivers flooded in early 1977 (the worst floods in living memory), making some 400,000 people homeless and causing some $34 million worth of damage. The Zambezi flooded in early 1978, resulting in some $60 million worth of damage of damage and affecting some of Mozambique's most fertile zones.[72] Serious water shortages in some parts of the country (especially Inhambane) turned into full-scale drought in 1980, leading the government to make an urgent appeal for international food aid.[73] By the end of 1980 the drought was seriously affecting about 1.5 million people in six of the country's ten provinces.[74] Mozambique also incurred costs involved in assisting displaced populations. The conflict with Rhodesia had severe economic consequences. Closing the border in March 1976 caused the country considerable losses from transit traffic and tourism as well as those from the closure to (Mozambican) migrant labour. This was in addition to the considerable damage to infrastructure carried out by the Rhodesians in cross-border operations. Sanctions induced damage was estimated at £250 million and direct damage at some £21 million.[75] Finally, Mozambique was hit hard by international economic trends in the late 1970s and early 1980s, resulting in a deterioration in its terms of trade, and it was hard hit by the oil price rises.

By 1980 the economic situation was grim though not yet disastrous. While the economy seemed to have 'bottomed out', pre-independence levels of production, with one or two exceptions, had not been attained (see Table 4.2). The brief upturn reflected in Table 4.2 in the figures for 1980 and 1981 (and emphasised by many commentators whose primary concern was to discredit South Africa) was conjunctural, not tendential, and was basically made possible by a combination of good weather conditions after several years of bad ones, the end of the Rhodesian war, and an increase in imports due to the availability of new credit lines, especially from OECD countries such as France and Italy.[76] Two

---

[71] British Overseas Trade Board Tropical Africa Advisory Group Trade Mission to Mozambique, 15-29 October 1980, p. 6.

[72] Economic Report 1984, p. 34.

[73] *Guardian*, 29 July 1980 and 30 August 1980.

[74] *Le Monde*, 10 November 1980.

[75] *Guardian*, 27 December 1979, and *Rhodesia Herald*, 28 December 1979. Machel speech to 5th Session of People's Assembly, SWB ME/6305/B/1-5, 28 December 1979.

[76] Hermele, 'Mozambique', p. 10. Trade with the latter two countries virtually

developments were threatening even that modest recovery. First, imports were growing at a rate unsustained by foreign exchange (see Table 4.3). Agricultural exports in particular remained sluggish

Table 4.2. GLOBAL SOCIAL PRODUCT AT CONSTANT 1980 PRICES[77]
(× 1 *million meticais*)

Sector	1975	1977	1980	1981	1982
Agriculture	26.1	30.6	33.4	33.3	32.5
Industry	26.4	27.8	30.7	31.6	27.2
Transport	9.1	7.8	8.1	9.0	8.4
Other	9.5	8.8	10.0	9.8	9.8
Total GSP	71.1	75.0	82.2	83.7	77.9

Table 4.3. BALANCE OF PAYMENTS CURRENT ACCOUNT [78]
(× 1 *million meticais*)

Trade	1976	1977	1978	1979	1980	1981
Imports	13,068	16,335	16,000	18,500	23,200	25,783
Exports	4,851	4,950	5,340	8,300	11,817	13,115
Invisibles						
Payments	3,168	2,970	2,500	2,370	3,060	3,132
Receipts	8,019	6,600	6,540	6,600	7,830	8,210

or were actually declining (see Table 4.4). The government had to introduce strict import controls in 1979. Secondly, state companies were already making losses. As a result, the state budget was building up huge deficits, or rather subsidies 'were growing rapidly off budget in the form of bank credit covering losses'.[79]

---

quadrupled between 1979 and 1981. See CNP, *Informação Estatística 1975-1984*, Table 13.3.

[77] Commissão Nacional do Plano (CNP), *Informação Estatística, 1975-1984*.

[78] Figures derived from Bowen, 'Let's build agricultural producer cooperatives', p. 83, in turn derived from UN information. For rather different figures see CNP, *Informação Estatística, 1975-1984*, and M. Mackintosh and M. Wuyts, 'Accumulation', p. 143. All show the same general trend, which is the point being emphasised here.

[79] World Bank, *Public Expenditure Report*, p. 97. Despite optimistic accounts, this was pointed out at the time. Cf. B. Caplan, 'Mozambique beckons the West', *The Banker*, 130, 658 (December 1980), pp. 33-9, and J. Fitzpatrick, 'The Economy of Mozambique: Problems and Prospects', *Third World Quarterly*, vol. 31, January 1981, pp. 77-87, esp. 82.

Table 4.4. AGRICULTURAL EXPORTS[80]
(× *1,000 tons*)

	1973	1975	1976	1977	1978	1979	1980	1981	1982
Cotton	51.0	17.8	16.3	6.3	12.8	16.1	5.7	1.5	13.7
Cashew	29.0	21.2	21.1	17.0	18.4	17.1	15.6	12.2	16.7
Tea	17.5	11.0	12.7	12.3	13.5	23.3	30.0	16.0	25.1
Sugar	178.9	50.7	71.9	37.4	24.6	118.7	63.8	63.1	28.5
Copra	48.2	30.5	41.1	36.5	34.4	29.1	19.4	12.2	12.2
Sisal	19.8	11.7	10.1	13.9	11.3	14.0	7.0	5.8	5.7

Even allowing for unfavourable domestic and international circumstances, things were going wrong. While much of the detail remains obscure, the broad outlines of what happened seem clear. In narrowly economic terms Frelimo's development strategy was a conventional one, based partly on squeezing an investment surplus out of agriculture by means both of the output of state farms and of 'unfair' terms of trade with the peasants, and partly on attracting foreign investment and aid flows to create rapidly a modern industrial and agricultural sector. None of the components of this strategy proceeded according to plan, and their respective failures were interlinked. The state sector manifestly failed to attain its targets. Its mode of operation and its failures both excluded and antagonised the peasantry, whose response was an increasingly sullen refusal to cooperate. Given the centrality of peasant production, attempts to bypass it by means of rapid investment financed by foreign grants and loans were unrealistic. Neither the West nor the East ever showed any inclination to meet the full costs of Frelimo's socialist vision.

The state farms failed despite the huge resources put into them (it is estimated that some 80% were imported). As the area they cultivated expanded, their productivity per hectare consistently declined.[81] A large proportion of this investment was in the form of mechanisation. Mecanagro (the state enterprise formed in 1978 to handle agricultural machinery) controlled some 5,200 tractors

---

[80] The 1973 figure derived from CNP, *Informação Estatistica. Alguns Indicadores Economicos e Sociais*, May 1980. Other years from CNP, *Informação Estatistica, 1975-1984*, May 1985.

[81] Adolfo Yanez Casal, 'A Crise da Produção Familiar e as Aldeias Comunais em Moçambique', *Revista Internacional de Estudos Africanos* 8/9 (1988), pp. 157-91, esp. 162.

and 120 combine harvesters, and the state sector absorbed about 75% of its activity.[82] But the real problem was tractors in the hands of a state which was incapable of using them. The level of mechanical knowledge appears to have been extremely limited – 'most of CAIL's [the Lower Limpopo Complex] tractor drivers know nothing about how to care for their machines beyond lubricating them.'[83] The problems of managing large-scale enterprises with few experienced personnel and inappropriate and ill-understood forms of planning ensured that returns on this investment were low, if not negative. One observer noted a case where 'costs of production, excluding amortisation, seemed to amount to some 3-4 times the value of output.'[84] In 1981 the Ministry of Agriculture admitted that not one state farm was profitable. In the same year type race yields at CAIL, despite immense effort, were the lowest since the state farm had begun.[85] The state farms constituted in fact a source of 'disaccumulation'.[86]

Nor were these failings compensated for by dynamism in the peasant sector or by successes in cooperativisation. Cooperatives suffered from many of the problems of state farms. It was imagined that they would develop spontaneously via 'mobilisation' and that they would bring about immediate increases in output. Neither of these assumptions proved to be reliable.[87] The modern sector certainly failed to dynamise the 'backward' sector. Worse, it actually soured relations between the state and the peasantry:

> The failure to meet their own targets meant that state farms gave little help to cooperatives, and the attempts at extensive growth of surface area cultivated alienated the neighbouring peasantry, many of whom also formed part of the work force of the state farms themselves, where poor working conditions and disregard of their views further alienated them.[88]

[82] R. Tibana, 'The Politics of Mozambique's Famine', paper presented at Political Studies Association annual conference, Plymouth Polytechnic, April 1988, p. 17.

[83] Paul Fauvet in *Zambia Daily Mail*, 7 July 1982.

[84] Raikes, 'Food Policy and Production', p. 7.

[85] Bowen 'Let's Build Agricultural Producer Cooperatives', p. 123.

[86] De Brito, 'Le Frelimo', p. 275.

[87] M. Bowen, 'Beyond reform: Adjustment and Political Power in Contemporary Mozambique', *Journal of Modern African Studies*, 30, 2 (1992), pp. 255-79.

[88] G. Littlejohn, 'Central Planning and Market Relations in Socialist Societies', *Journal of Development Studies*, 24, 4 (1988), pp. 75-101, esp. 90.

There were indeed several element to this alienation. Many peasants anticipated that after independence land would be made available to them. Instead much of it was seized for collective farms and then not utilised. In some areas this resentment even took the form of robbing the state farms and sabotaging their harvests.[89] Secondly, the state farms provided little assistance to peasant farmers. Thirdly, the state planning authorities never really got to grips with the problems of the labour effects of different agricultural cycles, a problem that was in part a legacy of colonial practices with regard to agricultural labour. State farms were unable to coerce labour, and the wages they paid at seasonal peaks did not provide sufficient income over the year as a whole. In addition, such wages increasingly lost value as there were so few goods to buy. In such circumstances the family farm remained the bedrock of security.

> Chronic shortages of foodstuffs and consumer goods in the local economy obliged all state farm workers to continue relying on their individual family plots for their food needs, thereby engendering serious problems of labour instability, and labour allocation conflicts between the state farm and the peasant family sectors.[90]

In their general relations with the state beyond the state farms, the peasants' response was determined by the poor prices they were offered as well as by the growing shortages of both consumer goods and implements for agricultural production. While the evidence on price effects is still unclear, the internal terms of trade seem to have discouraged the production of most crops by peasants.[91] A major effect of the massive commitments to the state sector was to reduce drastically the resources available for the peasant sector, both investment goods and goods for exchange. The state sector of industry failed especially in the production of goods necessary for the improvement of agricultural productivity. Domestic production of hoes declined during the period 1975-9.[92] On the basis of the Ministry of Agriculture's own calculations,

---

[89] Casal, 'A Crise', pp. 180-1.

[90] Roesch, 'Rural Mozambique', p. 76.

[91] See discussion in Gregor H. Binkert, *Agricultural Production and Economic Incentives: Food Policy in Mozambique* (Harvard Institute for International Development discussion paper no. 154). For a different view see Tarp, 'Prices'.

[92] Tibana, 'The Politics of Mozambique's Famine', p. 18.

there had developed by 1980 a shortage of 2,677,000 hoes and 542,000 cutlasses.[93]

The situation with consumer goods was no better. 'Each person in Mocuba district will be able to buy less than one- twentieth of the sugar and soap guaranteed to each Maputo resident. There have been no bicycle tires or parts in the district for three years.'[94] Nationally, Wuyts suggests a decline of 8% in consumer goods available in 1981.[95] This had its own effects on the peasants' production. Study of Nampula by a team from the Centro de Estudos Africanos concluded:

> The problem of delivering/supplying basic consumer goods, which in the final analysis represents production problems of the industrial sector, is more important than the prices *per se*. There is a serious lack of basic consumer goods – sugar, salt, petrol, cooking oil, hoes, hatchets, and particularly textiles at reasonable prices. These shortages were attacked by the peasants and merchants whom we contacted.[96]

In these circumstances the peasant sector not surprisingly became increasingly unwilling to exchange with the state. This in turn ensured a slow growth or stagnation in exports, which exacerbated almost all other economic difficulties. The state sought to resolve this problem by selling consumer goods via Agricom only in return for crop sales, but even this strategy of consumer goods for crops was undermined by other parts of the public sector itself. Not only state farms but construction companies and even the army bought peasant produce at non-official prices. It meant also that peasants resorted to parallel markets, which continually undermined the value of the currency.

Frelimo's high-risk strategies might have been more plausible, and effective, if other sources of investment funds had been available on the scale required. Frelimo's 'pragmatism' had always inclined it to welcome in principle aid and investment from Western countries.[97] Indeed the PPI was definitely linked to appeals for foreign investment in export industries. Far from being a pragmatic retreat (it did not, for example, offer a formal investment code), these steps were a measure of Frelimo's political confidence that

---

[93] Casal, 'A Crise', pp. 165-6.

[94] *Guardian*, 20 August 1982.

[95] Wuyts, 'Money', p. 191.

[96] CEA 1981 study of Nampula quoted in Binkert, *Agricultural Production*, p. 53.

[97] See *Marchés Tropicaux*, 216, September 1980, pp. 2341-3.

with the regime politically self-disciplined and the economy state-controlled, foreign participation would not put at risk the fundamental goals of the regime. But it had also been a consistent part of Frelimo strategy to strengthen Mozambique's relations with the CMEA (Council for Mutual Economic Assistance) countries. This led to a concerted effort to redirect trade towards the Soviet bloc, and Mozambique seriously pursued an application for membership of the CMEA, which appears to have been supported at least by East Germany and Bulgaria (the Soviet bloc countries with which Mozambique had the closest relationships).[98] It had concluded barter agreements with some CMEA countries and had made some effort to reorient its trade with the bloc. The high-powered delegation led by Machel to Moscow in 1980 at the height of Mozambican support for Soviet positions on world affairs was clearly concerned with economic matters, as it included the Planning and Agriculture Minister (Machungo), the Governor of the Central Bank (Viera) and the Industry Minister (Branco).[99] These general agreements presaged a growing number of cooperative ventures between Soviet and Mozambican organisations, including those concerning the news agencies (AIM and TASS), oil and gas prospecting, water projects, the supply of a floating dock and assistance with fishing projects, as well as mutual high-level visits. In mid-July 1981 it was reported that Mozambique was joining the CMEA but dos Santos, returning from a CMEA meeting in Sofia, clarified the position by stating that Mozambique was 'moving down the road to membership' of the organisation and that the CMEA needed to develop new arrangements for the socialist developing countries.[100] In fact the CMEA economies were all facing considerable difficulties in the late 1970s and early 1980s which were a function of their own economic structures, and Mozambique's application was refused. The exact circumstances still remain obscure.[101]

---

[98] East Germany seems to have been Mozambique's strongest supporter. Its ambassador suggested in October 1983 that his country would support Mozambican membership of the CMEA. See *Notícias* 6 October 1983.

[99] *Guardian*, 18 November 1980.

[100] *Guardian*, 14 July 1981; *Africa Economic Digest*, 17 July 1982. The expression of this latter point was by no means new. Cf. S. Vieira: 'We would not like to be a model of "poor socialism". This is a particularly sensitive question in Africa.' *World Marxist Review*, March 1979, p. 60.

[101] For the general background see C. Lawson, 'Socialist Relations with the Third World: a case study of the New International Economic Order', *Economics of Planning*, 16, 3 (1980), pp. 148-60.

Finally, there is the vexed question of South African 'destabilisation' in terms of both its economic effects and its intentions. Mozambique had traditionally been an area of recruitment of South African mine labour, and the arrangements were covered by various kinds of conventions. While Frelimo was hostile to migrant labour in principle, it accepted in the short term that this could not immediately be brought to an end. Until the early 1980s, however, neither the South African state nor the mining companies had a political interest in reducing the supply of Mozambican labour. The problems of the late 1970s, and in particular the precipitous collapse during 1976, resulted from a combination of Frelimo's inability effectively to introduce new passport procedures and changes in attitudes towards labour supply among the mining houses.[102] There was a sharp drop in the number of such labourers employed from Mozambique – from 113,000 in 1975 to 32,000 in 1976 – but the very high 1975 figure is partly explained by Malawi's temporary withdrawal from the scheme: in 1974, for example, only 86,000 Mozambicans went to work in South Africa's mines. In 1976 Mozambique closed seventeen of the twenty-one WENELA (Witwatersrand Native Labour Association) recruiting centres. It also declared old passports invalid and was slow to produce the replacements, 'but by the time the new immigration procedures at last became properly operational, the Chamber [of Mines] had in fact altered its labour policies.'[103] Higher mine wages in South Africa were generating more domestic labour and the mining houses decided to diversify their foreign sources of labour supply. Recruiting of labour in Malawi, the other traditional area outside South Africa, was also restricted but no-one suggested this was a 'sanction' against that country or an attempt to destabilise it.

In relations between South Africa and Portuguese Mozambique, gold and trade had, historically been linked by an agreement of 1928, by the terms of which the mines deferred part of Mozambican miners' wages in gold valued at the official price. With the introduction in 1969 of a two-tier pricing system, the difference between the official price and a free-market price produced a large surplus.[104]

---

[102] This was occasionally observed at the time (e.g. *Daily Telegraph*, 14 June 1976; *Rand Daily Mail*, 11 March 1977) and repeatedly pointed out by South African mining house spokesmen. It is confirmed by research reported in J. Crush *et al.*, *South Africa's Labor Empire*, Boulder, CO, 1991 p. 110, and W. James, *Our Precious Metal*, p. 35.

[103] James, *Our Precious Metal*, p. 31.

[104] Cahen suggests Frelimo pursued secret negotiations to continue this agreement (*Révolution Implosée*, pp. 109-10) but cities only confidential sources. His account

In 1977 the International Monetary Fund (IMF) changed the rules, abolishing two-tier pricing, and not surprisingly the South Africans announced that they would no longer pay the premium. Mozambique's own Director of Planning, J.M Brum, was quoted as saying that 'the South African policy change was not unexpected'.[105] The gold payment arrangements came to an end in April 1978 when the Republic revalued its gold at the free-market price.[106]

Finally, in the area of transit trade the figures show that there was no sharp fall until after the collapse of the Rhodesian regime.[107] The initial declines were due to losses in efficiency leading exporters to use other ports in spite of a 'concerted effort by South African Railways to persuade exporters to keep using the route'.[108] There was no concerted effort to reduce traffic through Maputo after independence; indeed quite the reverse, as the intensity of South African government pressure to continue the use of Maputo brought protests from South African business circles.[109] This commitment included agreement between South African and Mozambican railways to develop cooperation.[110] Maputo, Matola and Nacala registered slight increases in their traffic in 1979.[111]

The fact of the matter was that while Mozambique began its independent life facing all sorts of hazards, before 1980 the overt hostility of the South African state was not one of them. Indeed, as Samora Machel himself put it, 'South Africa needs us as much as we need it. I do not spend sleepless nights over our relationships with South Africa.'[112] Tragically for him and his country, it was political not economic forces which would produce many sleepless nights over that very question.

does seem plausible.

[105] *Rhodesia Herald*, 5 June 1978.

[106] *Financial Times*, 11 March 1978.

[107] National Planning Commission Economic Report 1984, p. 30. See also Cahen, *Révolution Implosée*, p. 110.

[108] *Financial Times*, 31 May 1977.

[109] *Ibid.*, 30 January 1978.

[110] *Ibid.*, 28 February 1979; *Le Monde*, 28 February 1979.

[111] *Financial Times*, 17 December 1980; Economic Report 1984, p. 30.

[112] Samora Machel quoted in *Rand Daily Mail*, 11 March 1977.

5

THE REVOLUTION FALTERS

'Machel appeared to be unworried about the MNR in those days. He seemed to think it would disappear along with its creator, the Rhodesian regime.'[1]

'It would be naive to expect the country [South Africa] to renounce the destabilisation option for at least as long as black states remain committed to destabilise it.'[2]

The most pressing external problem Frelimo faced on assuming power was Rhodesia, though its close relationship with ZANU began with cooperation in Tete from 1971 onwards. As a result of that experience, the Frelimo leadership gradually became convinced that ZANU was the most serious of the movements fighting for Zimbabwean independence and increasingly channelled its aid in that direction.[3] Mozambique's independence opened up a huge new border area to operations by ZANLA guerrillas, much of this area being mountainous and ideal for guerrilla infiltration. The thrust of Frelimo's own ideology, and the circumstances of the collapse of the Portuguese empire which had enormously enhanced the party's self-esteem, made it unlikely that Frelimo would ever consider the Malawi or Botswana option of steering clear of the Rhodesia conflict in its own self-interest – as Britain's former Foreign Secretary David Owen later put it, 'If Mozambique had stood aside from the Rhodesian struggle it might have been possible for it to establish a relationship with South Africa.'[4] But ....

For Frelimo, the Rhodesian regime was not merely a privileged

---

[1] Christie, *Machel*, p. 109.

[2] Deon Geldenhuys, quoted in J Hanlon, *Mozambique: Who calls the Shots?*, London, 1991, p. 20.

[3] For the details of Frelimo's cooperation with ZANU see D. Martin and P. Johnson, *The Struggle for Zimbabwe*, and P. Pandya, 'Foreign Support to ZANU and Zanla during the Rhodesian War', *ISSUP Strategic Review*, November 1987, pp. 1-31.

[4] *The Times*, 21 October 1985.

ally of colonialism, but through its very nature as a rebel colony, it was a standing threat to the future security and independence of the territory. To fight against racist Rhodesia was also to fight against colonialism in Mozambique. The neutralisation of Rhodesian aggression was an imperative of national liberation in Mozambique itself.[5]

Mozambique could not live with a white-dominated Rhodesia which would inevitably become a natural haven for various anti-Frelimo elements, but within that constraint any kind of negotiation process was at least discussable.[6]

Although after the Lisbon coup Frelimo spokesmen made it clear that they would honour UN resolutions demanding the isolation of Rhodesia, their awareness of the costs to Mozambique's economy and fear of Rhodesian military reprisals meant that Frelimo maintained contact and open borders for almost nine months after independence. A contributing factor was the low level of guerrilla activity in late 1975 as ZANU was recovering from internal crises.[7] The move to close the border was made after close consultation with Presidents Nyerere of Tanzania, Kaunda of Zambia and Khama of Botswana at a mini-summit in Quelimane in February. Mozambique not only expected Western economic aid to sustain the cost of the sanctions but also believed that the determination of Britain and the United States would bring the Rhodesian crisis to a rapid conclusion, a view publicly expressed by Machel himself.[8] In the interim the decision to close the border was intended 'essentially...to destroy Ian Smith's economy'.[9] Mozambique's actions were not, however, limited to economic measures but included allowing ZANU to maintain large bases within the country, the deployment of small numbers of FPLM troops in Rhodesia, and giving ZANU some access to Soviet-bloc arms.[10]

[5] S. Vieira, 'Vectors of Foreign Policy of the Mozambique Liberation Front (1962-1975)' (Eduardo Mondlane University, seminar paper), p. 13.

[6] A point clearly made by Machel in his speech to the UN conference in Maputo on 16 May 1977; SWB ME/5515/B, 14-15.

[7] See Martin and Johnson, 'The Struggle for Zimbabwe, ch. 11.

[8] Interview, SWB ME/5398/B 4-6.

[9] Interview with Machel, *Observer*, 28 March 1976.

[10] *Observer*, 6 April 1980; Martin and Johnson, *The Struggle for Zimbabwe*, ch. 11; *Guardian*, 27 December 1979.

Origins and early development of Renamo

Whatever the virtues of such a stance, it would inevitably bring reprisals. The Rhodesian armed forces proved adept at making very damaging incursions into Mozambique and the FPLM not so adept at repelling them. But reprisals were not limited to overt actions carried out against ZANLA guerrilla bases; they included more covert responses of a kind familiar in counter-insurgency warfare elsewhere. An agreement to establish a clandestine 'pseudo-terrorist' movement in Mozambique had already been concluded between the Rhodesian Central Intelligence Organisation (CIO) and the Portuguese just before the April 1974 coup in Lisbon.[11] In fact Renamo was formed somewhat later from personnel of the élite black units of the Portuguese colonial forces, the GEs and the GEPs, who fled Mozambique before or immediately after independence. But some of the original core group from which Renamo was put together 'were members of the crack Flechas unit established by Portugal to fight Frelimo', a unit controlled by the Portuguese intelligence service rather than the military.[12] A key figure in these developments was Orlando Cristina, who had been associated with Jorge Jardim in the organisation of a system of self-defence for Niassa district, and later in the formation of the GEPs. A former DGS man who had been liaison officer in Tete with the CIO in the late 1960s, he was among those who fled to Rhodesia,[13] and brought with him files on the special groups used in the initial recruitment of the new force.[14] Early arrivals in Rhodesia were later supplemented from various sources, including inmates freed from Mozambican re-education camps near the border, often in helicopter-borne raids. Some of those released were former Frelimo soldiers imprisoned for corruption who also possessed military and guerrilla skills as well as grounds for personal resentment against the Frelimo government.

[11] The 'top secret' memo on the *flechas* and the formation of the Mozambican National Resistance reproduced in Flower, *Serving Secretly*, pp. 300-2, has given rise to confusion, since the implied continuity existed only in Flower's memory. This does not, however, call into question Flower's account of the CIO's role in establishing the organisation later.

[12] *To the Point*, (South Africa [here and subsequently]), 25 July 1980: 'Resistance to Frelimo regroups'.

[13] *To the Point*, 13 July 1979 carries a profile of Orlando Cristina, then fifty-one years old and head of Renamo's external affairs department.

[14] Martin and Johnson, 'Mozambique: To Nkomati and Beyond'. P. Fauvet and A. Gomes, 'The Mozambique National Resistance' (supplement to *AIM Information Bulletin*, no. 69); Paul Fauvet, 'Roots of Counter-Revolution; the Mozambican National Resistance', *Review of African Political Economy*, 29 (1984), pp. 108-21.

A radio station broadcasting propaganda into Mozambique actually pre-dated the establishment of the military force. Voz da Africa Livre (Voice of Free Africa) was set up by the CIO at Gwelo (now Gweru) and run by the Directorate of Psychological Warfare in the Ministry of Information. The Rhodesian government allowed Cristina and a handful of other refugees from Mozambique to begin broadcasting on 5 July 1976. As well as publicising the whereabouts and fate of Mozambican detainees, its output comprised a crude anti-Communism and insults directed at the Frelimo leadership mixed with exaltation of Eduardo Mondlane, of whom Renamo claimed to be the heirs. Claiming Mondlane as its ideological authority allowed Renamo to appeal to a broad nationalism and to dismiss Frelimo after his death as a movement that had fallen under the sway of Communist usurpers.[15]

The radio station therefore came first, and was followed by the establishment of a military unit which was to give substance to the propaganda. Cristina's main concern was with the broadcasts rather than operational military matters, which were firmly under Rhodesian control.[16] CIO officials suggest that as an operational unit the turning point came with the recruitment of André Matsangaíssa, a Frelimo officer arrested for theft and sent to a re-education camp from which he escaped in 1976. His leadership qualities led the Rhodesians to groom him for command of the unit. Serious military training of the group started at about the same time at a permanent training camp the CIO established for the purpose at Odzi, near Umtali (now Mutare). Joao Cabrita, who worked with Cristina on his clandestine radio station, claims that Matsangaíssa met Cristina in October 1976 in Rhodesia:

> He asked Cristina in a rather sarcastic manner whether he intended to change the political situation in Mozambique by shouting over the radio? Matsangaisse stated in no uncertain terms that the only viable way to bring about political change in Mozambique was through the barrel of a gun, and that he was willing to do just that. It was decided that Matsangaíssa would put his plans into practice shortly.[17]

---

[15] Andre E.A.M. Thomashausen, 'The Mozambique National Resistance' in C.J. Maritz (ed.), *Weerstandsbewegings in Suider-Afrika*, Potchefstroom University, 1987. See Paul Moorcraft, *African Nemesis: War and Revolution in Southern Africa, 1945-2010*, 1990, pp. 257-8, for a slightly different account.

[16] Martin and Johnson, 'Mozambique: To Nkomati and Beyond'.

[17] João Cabrita, court statement. This and a number of other statements referred to in this chapter were submitted in the case of *National Oil Company of Zimbabwe (Private) Ltd.* v. *Sturge* at which one of the present authors (Tom Young) appeared

A name and identity for the new group were provided at a meeting at Cristina's home in Salisbury (now Harare) in May 1977; that is, after it had been operational for some months.[18] After further military training, this original group acted as scouts for the Rhodesian army against the ZANLA presence over the border and as a fifth column inside Mozambique. Most of its early actions were also aimed at recruitment, such as its very first military operation in the Gorongosa mountains in February 1977 which resulted in the freeing of the inmates of a re-education camp.[19] Beginning, it is claimed, with just six men at the Umtali training camp, by December 1978 a total of 917 men were operating from within Rhodesia.[20] Acts of social banditry, and distribution of food and clothes from Rhodesia during the 1979 drought, bought the group a measure of support in central Mozambique, where Frelimo had established little effective presence.[21] Although most early Renamo recruitment was undoubtedly forced, some may have been voluntary – for example, in the Gorongosa game reserve in northern Sofala province, where Renamo seems to have struck a chord at an early date, allowing it to establish roots in an extensive area of mountain and plateau. A permanent Renamo camp, established at the end of 1977 in Gorongosa, came eventually under the personal control of Matsangaíssa, who had previously operated there as a Frelimo guerrilla. Difficult of access and supplied by air three or four times a week, it developed into Renamo's main base, and one from which it could threaten the important Maputo/Beira and Chimoio/Tete road links.[22]

As the war across Zimbabwe's eastern frontier and in its eastern districts escalated, the Rhodesians pushed Renamo further into Mozambique and set up permanent bases, but this implied little operational autonomy. In January 1979 the Rhodesian SAS began operating with Renamo, and later small *ad hoc* groups were attached to it in a training and advisory role. The first joint operation was a successful attack on a hydro-electric power station at Mavuze in which Renamo acted as guides and intelligence gatherers. It also provided cover for other SAS attacks into Mozambique, such as the March 1979 action against the Beira oil tanks, which was claimed

---

as an expert witness. For a report on the case see Financial Times, 12 March 1991.

[18] Martin and Johnson, 'Mozambique: To Nhomati and Beyond'.

[19] Jorge Correia, court statement.

[20] Thomashausen, 'The Mozambique National Resistance'.

[21] Joseph Hanlon, *Revolution*, pp. 229-31; *To the Point*, 13 July 1979.

[22] 'Gorongosa neutralizada agressão inimiga', *Tempo*, 474, 11 November 1979.

as a Renamo operation. However, the group was encouraged to develop its own *esprit de corps*, and designed its own flag and badges.[23] It also carried out own tentative attacks along the border zones of Manica and Tete provinces.

Despite these promising beginnings Renamo was facing severe problems by the end of 1979, and there was a real optimism in Maputo that its extinction was in sight. Matsangaíssa had been killed in an attack on Gorongosa town in October 1979, and soon afterwards Frelimo troops overran Renamo's encampment. Matsangaíssa's death precipitated a crisis and a contested transfer of command which culminated in a shoot-out at Chisumbanje in southern Zimbabwe (June 1980) with the supporters of Afonso Dhlakama emerging victorious. Above all, however, the Lancaster House settlement of December 1979 seemed to sound the death-knell of the organisation. With the resolution of the Rhodesian problem, the Frelimo leadership were convinced they could resume full progress towards their vision of socialism. The structures of political control were in place, an ambitious programme of economic development had been planned, and despite the batterings of the Rhodesians and of nature the way seemed open for rapid progress. The utter disintegration of that vision within a few years was due to three interconnected sets of factors: domestically, the relative collapse of Frelimo's effectiveness and legitimacy; regionally, the emergence of a more ruthless and determined leadership group in South Africa; and globally, a decisive shift in the balance of world power towards the United States.

South African strategy

Of these three factors the most important at the beginning of the 1980s was the South Africans, the precise determinants and objectives of whose foreign policy during this period remain obscure, although some of the more florid 'explanations' are hardly worthy of discussion. The idea that South Africa feared invidious comparison with Mozambique's 'successes' (an important part of Frelimo propaganda, endlessly repeated in the academic literature) seems bizarre, although this does not mean that Frelimo's victory did not have a symbolic value for young South African blacks.[24]

---

[23] Barbara Cole, *The Elite: The Story of the Rhodesian Special Air Service*, Transkei, 1984, p. 246.

[24] S. Ellis and Tsepo Sechaba, *Comrades against Apartheid: The ANC and the South African Communist Party in Exile*, London, 1992, p. 75. For events at the time see the *Guardian*, 25 September 1974.

But it seems unhelpful to attribute extremely general policy goals, e.g.:

> The South African regime, knowing that it was militarily and politically impossible to turn Mozambique into a Bantustan, tried to make the existence and functioning of any kind of organised society inviable. It defined its strategy as the devastation of Mozambique and of its capacity for later recovery.[25]

The reality was rather more prosaic.[26] Certainly the symbolic shifts in relations between the two states were thorough and swift. Three days before Mozambican independence the South African consul and his staff departed the capital, leaving behind a trade and visa office in a private house; the next day an ANC delegation led by Oliver Tambo arrived to an enthusiastic welcome.[27]

But such gestures were tempered by a realistic assessment of relations between the two countries. Frelimo had always made a distinction between the Rhodesian and South African cases, and it was aware of Mozambique's considerable dependence on its economic links with South Africa. Occasionally, it is true, Maputo (or rather Samora Machel) made public pronouncements about the liberation of 'our brothers' in Rhodesia and South Africa, and other statements (as in a speech to the Non-Aligned Movement in New Delhi that 'racial discrimination in South Africa calls for a war by the whole of humanity') that may have been tactically unwise.[28] But Mozambique generally stressed the legal nicety that South Africa, unlike Rhodesia, was a sovereign state recognised as such by the UN. Accordingly Mozambique was quick to assert that 'it is incorrect to make comparisons between the political situation which existed in Rhodesia and that which prevails in the Republic of South Africa. They differ in their political nature.'[29] For their part the South Africans reacted coolly but without much antagonism to an independent Frelimo-led Mozambique, convinced that the country's economic dependence would give them

---

[25] Vieira, Martin and Wallerstein (eds), *How Fast the Wind? Southern Africa, 1975-2000*, p. 216.

[26] For a balanced discussion see R. Jaster, *South Africa and its Neighbours: The Dynamics of Regional Conflict* (Adelphi Paper 209, 1986).

[27] See report by Stanley Uys in *New Statesman*, 4 July 1975.

[28] For the first see interview with Machel in *Afrique-Asie*, 217 (July 1980). For the second the speech *O Apartheid é o Nazismo da Nossa Época*, March 1983.

[29] Samora Machel interview, *Africa*, 107, July 1980. This was stressed privately to journalists. See for example Hennie Serfontein, *Rand Daily Mail*, 16 March 1988, *Le Monde*, 26 March 1980, and interview with Chissano, *Afrique-Asie*, 217 (July 1980).

considerable leverage.[30] In 1974-5 Prime Minister Vorster was still pursuing a détente policy with African states although there were already differences between him and his successor P.W. Botha who reportedly wanted to support the attempted coup in Lourenço Marques.[31]

For all the differences between Vorster and Botha, three issues would inevitably be central to relations between South Africa and Mozambique. First, like all regional powers, South Africa expected to be acknowledged by its neighbours – at least in the form of diplomatic recognition and ideally as a regional leader. What made this impossible was of course apartheid; and precisely because the regional states were economically and militarily so weak, symbolic disapproval was their most important weapon. However much the South Africans might appeal to the hitherto sacrosanct principle of non-interference in the domestic affairs of states, the intellectual and moral consensus in the world was simply that the enjoyment of this principle could be withheld from at least one country, namely South Africa.[32] The second issue concerned how much room for manoeuvre the ANC would have in neighbouring countries. The third set of issues, though for the South Africans always subject to overriding political considerations, concerned economic relations: specifically labour, gold and trade.

Thus South Africa's goals – to defeat the ANC and to secure some form of regional recognition – were not new, but the determination of the Botha regime to achieve them, and its willingness to use all forms of coercion, was. The first and more specific objective was to prevent the ANC from scoring successes in the armed struggle. The SADF had closely studied insurgencies and counter-insurgency methods worldwide, and 'in purely military terms, the generals knew just how difficult it is to defeat a guerrilla army once it has managed to set up a secure base and solid lines of supply.'[33] But the armed struggle waged by the ANC in South Africa was essentially symbolic, as the organisation could not serious-

---

[30] See comments by Vorster, *Financial Times*, 16 September 1974, and the *Observer*, 15 September. See D. Geldenhuys, 'South Africa's Regional Policy', pp. 142-3.

[31] See interviews referred to in G. Gunn, 'Learning from Adversity: The Mozambican Experience' in R.J. Bloomfield (ed.), *Regional Conflict and US Policy*, Ann Arbor, MI, 1988, pp. 134-85.

[32] The inconsistencies in this position were (and remain) intellectually interesting but politically irrelevant, and it was naive of South African policy-makers and commentators to think it could be otherwise. The penny finally dropped in February 1990.

[33] Ellis and Sechaba, *Comrades*, p. 95.

ly hope to defeat the South African government in a military sense. However, its symbolic nature did not preclude considerable determination on the part of the South African government to shield the country from ANC sabotage activity completely. An important part of the internal reform process introduced by P.W. Botha required that a 'firm hand' be shown towards 'terrorist' activity. Almost all of South Africa's direct and acknowledged incursions into Mozambique followed some form of armed action carried out in the Republic itself.

Secondly and rather more generally, there was the question of recognition of both the *de facto* and *de jure* kinds. The Botha regime was much more prepared to use its leverage to press other states in the region to accord South Africa some kind of recognition. Indeed Botha's first major policy initiative in the region, the 'constellation of states', while not wholly new, was given an unprecedented new emphasis and degree of detail during the first half of 1979.[34] It aspired to build some degree of political consensus in the region on the back of economic and technical cooperation; but as yet another attempt to secure some degree of regional and international legitimacy it was bound to fail. The black-ruled states maintained the Front-Line States structure which they had originally created to deal with the Rhodesian problem, and added to it the SADCC, an economic grouping intended to help those states reduce their dependence on South Africa. As a particularly vociferous protagonist of these initiatives and opponent of South Africa's proposals, Mozambique was bound to attract the hostility of a South African government that had invested so much in them. While the constellation idea failed, elements of it never disappeared from South African foreign policy – new elements such as non-aggression pacts were to emerge later.

The turning point

Aside from its general recognition that its economic dependence on South Africa constrained the possibilities of action, Frelimo did not read the signs very well. In fact, 'in the "anything is possible" euphoria surrounding the Lancaster House agreement, Machel began to "look the other way", and ANC infiltration into South Africa increased.'[35] The ANC in Maputo was heavily involved in the planning of attacks in South Africa for fairly obvious reasons

---

[34] Geldenhuys, 'South Africa's Regional Policy', pp. 148-51.

[35] G. Gunn, 'Learning from Adversity', p. 157.

– 'due to its proximity to South Africa's industrial heartland in
the Transvaal, it [Maputo] was considered the best site for an
Umkhonto we Sizwe forward base from which the infiltration of
South Africa would be masterminded.'[36] The somewhat guarded
circumlocutions of well-known pro-Frelimo spokesmen at the time
suggested that the routine Mozambican denials of ANC activity
were less than plausible (and in the light of later information
wholly incredible). Professor Isaacman suggested that 'although
the substantial escalation of military operations in the Transvaal
and other areas adjacent to Mozambique suggests that Frelimo
might be allowing guerrillas operating in small bands to pass through
its territory, this allegation is officially denied'.[37] More candid pro-
Frelimo observers were prepared to concede something rather
closer to the truth:

> Since independence in 1975, Mozambique has been one of the
> most important entry routes, not only for ANC guerrillas, but also
> for political cadres. Mozambique never allowed the ANC to have
> overt bases, but it turned a blind eye to people slipping over the
> border, usually to Swaziland and then South Africa. Even more
> important, it provided a route for people to come out again,
> keeping the exile leadership in close touch with events inside.[38]

Usually insurgents were put across the Mozambique/Swaziland
border after they had been issued with weapons in Swaziland. The
ANC operation in Maputo helped to plan and carry out some of
the group's more spectacular attacks in the early 1980s, including
that on Sasol facilities (1 June 1980), the Voortrekkerhoogte in
Pretoria (12 August 1981) and the car bomb outside the South
African Air Force headquarters (20 May 1983). When the South
Africans raided Maputo in January 1981, among those killed was
Motso Mokgabudi (also known as Obadi) who had led the attack
on the Sasol facilities. The South Africans also thought they had
killed the Communist Party leader Joe Slovo because a Portuguese
doctor who resembled him was killed by mistake.

The assumption of the premiership by P.W. Botha, who had
long been Minister of Defence, marked a new turn in South African
policy, notably a sharp expansion of its armed forces as well as a
new doctrine of 'total strategy'. These shifts in Pretoria were publicly

---

[36] Ellis and Sechaba, *Comrades*, pp. 77 and 125. Cf. the discussion in R. Kasrils,
Armed and Dangerous: My Undercover Struggle Against Apartheid, Oxford, 1993, ch. 13.

[37] A.F. and B. Isaacman, 'In Pursuit of Nonalignment', *Africa Report*, 28, 3 (May-
June 1983), pp. 47-54.

[38] Hanlon, *New Statesman*, 6 April 1984.

reflected in a war of words between the two countries, beginning in 1980 and continued with aggressive displays of military might by South Africa, which included one of the largest parades in South African military history.[39] As Defence Minister, Magnus Malan had emphasised that the Republic would fight its enemies 'even if it means we will have to support anti-communist movements....and allow them to act from our territory'.[40] The South African military and its military intelligence wing had certainly not ignored Renamo. A Major Breytenbach who had operated with the *flechas* in Mozambique in 1973, together with Colonel Charles van Niekerk, was appointed by the Department of Military Intelligence (DMI) to liaise with Renamo, and visited the Odzi training base on various occasions.[41] These contacts were invaluable in the transfer of Renamo fighters from Rhodesia to South Africa. After Robert Mugabe's election victory in Rhodesia (soon to be renamed Zimbabwe) in March 1980, some of Renamo's estimated 1,000 trained insurgents were sent directly from Odzi back into Mozambique. Cristina moved the radio station, Voz da Africa Livre, to the SADF special forces' base near Phalaborwa in the eastern Transvaal, and SADF transport planes also moved Renamo personnel and equipment there. Members of the Rhodesian SAS simply drove Renamo's South African-supplied vehicles in a convoy through the main Zimbabwe/ South African border post at Beitbridge. All this occurred under a prior agreement between the SADF commander and his Rhodesian counterpart, General Peter Walls, that in the event of a collapse of 'white' Rhodesia, units and individuals which could be subject to reprisals, such as the Selous Scouts and Renamo, would be transferred to South Africa. This transfer must have taken place with the knowledge and tacit acquiescence of at least some members of the British Governor's staff, though probably not of Lord Soames himself. Such was the situation in Zimbabwe at this time that there was probably little that could have been done in practical terms by the British to prevent it.[42]

In early 1981 Renamo guerrillas were transported into Mozambique

[39] For the verbal attacks see *Financial Times*, 20 February 1980, and *The Times*, 4 June 1980. For the parade see *Daily Telegraph*, 27 November 1980.

[40] *The Economist*, 16 July 1983, p. 19 (speech actually made in February). This was merely one of a number of bellicose speeches.

[41] Gulamo Tajú, 'Renamo. Os factos que conhecemos'; Martin and Johnson, 'Mozambique: To Nkomati and Beyond', mentions only van Niekerk (p. 13). See Flower, *Serving Secretly*, p. 262, for DMI's enthusiasm for their new charge.

[42] See the comments in Martin and Johnson, 'Mozambique: To Nkomati and Beyond', pp. 12-15; also Moorcraft, *African Nemesis*, p. 262.

in what Zimbabwean military observers described as 'an armada' of SADF helicopters.[43] A new base camp was established within Mozambique at Garagua, near the River Save, with a 2 km. perimeter and equipped with a helicopter strip. Initially Renamo continued to operate within familiar parts of the country, particularly Manica province along the Zimbabwe border and neighbouring Sofala. But by the latter half of 1981 a network of large, semi-permanent bases had been built up, from which attacks were mounted on small towns. A pattern of events began that was to be repeated elsewhere. In August 1981 an influx of Mozambican refugees from Espungabera district sought sanctuary and medical aid at Mount Selinda mission 1 km. inside Zimbabwe – the Frelimo members among them having been mutilated – and told tales of the destruction by Renamo of communal villages in Mozambique.[44] No attempt seems to have been made to replicate the early 'hearts and minds' campaign inside Mozambique, of which there is some evidence during the earlier period of operations out of Zimbabwe. The capture in December 1981 of Renamo's main base at Garagua was a military setback, which incidentally also resulted in the capture of a large quantity of documents illustrating the close links between Renamo and the South African military,[45] but Renamo was able to re-establish itself in Gorongosa, from where it had been ousted by the FPLM a year earlier. John Burlison, a British ecologist captured at Gorongosa and held hostage by Renamo from December 1981 until May 1982, estimated numbers there and in camps in northern Manica at perhaps 1,000 armed men in all, each with an automatic weapon, normally an AK 47. Renamo also had bazookas, two different calibres of mortar, both anti-vehicle and anti-personnel mines, plastic explosives, and some heavy machine guns.[46]

South African military intelligence encouraged a higher public profile for Renamo and a significant geographical expansion of its activities, particularly against the principal communication routes and the oil pipeline to Zimbabwe. With the independence of Zimbabwe and formation of the SADCC in 1980, anything which would sabotage efforts to reduce economic dependence was probably calculated as being in South Africa's interests. Support was provided by the South African Special Reconnaissance (Recce) Commandos,

---

[43] Collin Legum, 'The MNR', *CSIS Africa Notes*, 16 (15 July 1983).

[44] *Sunday Mail*, (Zimbabwe), 30 August 1981.

[45] Unlike the later 'Vaz' diaries, the Garagua documents were not published, and were dismissed by the South Africans at the time as forgeries. They formed the basis of an article in *Tempo*, 597 (21 March 1982).

[46] Interview broadcast on BBC World Service, 'The World Today', 22 June 1982.

which included former Rhodesian SAS men previously associated with Renamo. The 5th Recce Commando provided Renamo with a training base at Phalaborwa as well as its radio communications centre. Colonel Charles van Niekerk, who had been South Africa's military attaché in Nampula in the later stages of the colonial war, was established as the main contact between Pretoria and Renamo.[47] In particular, the South Africans wanted to open new fronts in Gaza and Inhambane provinces, in the latter case partly to make possible the delivery of supplies by sea rather than air, since air drops were both more expensive and more difficult to conceal. As before, Renamo was utilised as cover for sabotage attacks inside Mozambique. On 29 October 1981 South African units sabotaged the road and rail bridges over the Pungue river near Beira, and on 9 December 1982 they attacked the oil tank farm in Beira and Renamo attacked the Maputo-Zimbabwe rail link.[48]

During 1980-1 the important bases of Sitatonga and Garagua in central Mozambique relied heavily on logistical supplies from South Africa. This support came from the SADF bases of Phalaborwa and Skukuza in the eastern Transvaal and included such services as flying in standard rations.[49] After 1980 Renamo claimed to have defined its own main military targets, including the Beira corridor and the power lines from Cahora Bassa to South Africa.[50] Documents captured at the fall of the Garagua base show, however, that targets for future operations were discussed at meetings with the South Africans, as were the methods by which the SADF would supply and train Renamo.[51] For example, the minutes of a meeting involving Dhlakama, dated Zoabostad, 25 October 1980, state:

> Colonel van Niekerk, representative of the South African Government, began by referring himself to the objectives for the South African support to our struggle...saying that in the first phase, as we have completed the training of the soldiers evacuated from

[47] Moorcraft, *African Nemesis*, p. 261.

[48] Anthony R. Tucker, 'South Africa's War in Mozambique', *Armed Forces*, June 1989.

[49] A. Vines, ' "Hunger that Kills": Food Security and the Mozambican Peace Process', paper presented to Centre for Southern African Studies, Research Seminar series 1992, p. 7.

[50] Jorge Correia, court statement.

[51] Steven Metz, 'The Mozambique National Resistance and South African Foreign Policy', *African Affairs*, 85 (1986), pp. 491-507.

Zimbabwe, they will be moved to the interior. In this he stressed the opening of the fronts in Gaza and Inhambane and the closure of traffic on the railroad Beira-Umtali and the road Inchope-Vila Franca do Save.[52]

The Harare-Maputo railway line was attacked in December 1981 and regularly sabotaged thereafter. By the end of 1981 reports appeared of a Renamo base in Inhambane province, and at about the same time it became dangerous to use the Maputo-Beira road, the country's main highway. By 1982, a year of very significant expansion, Renamo already controlled the Gorongosa mountains, Maringue, and Garagua and Cavalo districts of Manica and Sofala provinces, and claimed that 20,000 people were living under its administration. The main base (shifted for security reasons every year or so) was firmly established in the Gorongosa area. By mid-year Renamo had moved south beyond Manica and Sofala into northern Inhambane and Gaza, and also north into southern Tete. Most significant for the future, however, was the shift across the Zambezi to absorb a small, independent guerrilla movement with local roots called Africa Livre, operating near the town of Milange on the Malawi border.[53] This allowed Renamo to open a new front in Zambézia and penetrate the populous and fertile Zambezi valley, Mozambique's most agriculturally productive province and the source of about 50% of its foreign exchange. But it also brought within reach the Nacala rail line, which carried the bulk of Malawi's exports to the sea. Renamo activity in the north increasingly aimed at strangling the traffic between Zimbabwe and Malawi to the Mozambican coastal ports. In September 1982 the group launched an assault on the border town of Milange, an important strategic target. From the springboard of Zambézia it was able to move north into Nampula and across towards the coast. Originally just a few hundred men, Renamo was estimated to have grown from perhaps 5,000 armed guerrillas in mid-1981 to a claimed 7,000-8,000 in 1983.[54]

The scale of operations also increased. Renamo began to attack and destroy small towns; it kidnapped foreign technicians and aid workers, sometimes killing them but more often holding them for ransom or exploiting them for propaganda purposes; and it

---

[52] Quoted in A. Nilsson, *Unmasking the bandits: The true face of the MNR*, London, 1990, p. 29.

[53] For more on 'Africa Livre', see Tajú, 'Renamo', p. 19.

[54] Frank, court statement.

carried out more spectacular operations against larger installations, notably the destruction of the oil pumping station at Maforga in October 1982.[55] The strategy, undoubtedly agreed with the South Africans and probably at their behest, appears to have been to concentrate on three kinds of target: the railways from Maputo and Beira to Zimbabwe, the pipeline from Beira to Mutare, and the main paved roads in the centre and along the coast of the country. Maps prepared by the Renamo military leadership in October 1982 divided Mozambique into six 'military regions', each subdivided into sectors. Within these were 'operational zones of permanent activity'. Priority targets included the Machipanda-Beira railway line; Manica-Vila Pery road; Espungabera road; Revué-Beira power lines; Umtali-Beira pipeline; and the Cahora Bassa transmission lines. The secondary targets included factories, the Revué dam and railway stations. In the period until the Nkomati Accord of March 1984 (see Chapter 6), Renamo also spread southwards, as encouraged by the South Africans, especially through Inhambane and towards the coast, presumably to facilitate resupply by sea. But there was also widespread destruction of the economic infrastructure and of development projects. According to official estimates, by 1982 Renamo had destroyed 840 schools, twelve health clinics, twenty-four maternity clinics, 174 health posts, two centres for the handicapped and 900 shops, while kidnapping fifty-two foreign technicians and killing twelve.[56]

Although South African support for Renamo could hardly be denied, the organisation maintained that at no time did South Africa direct its operations, qualifying even this by an admission that 'they shared strategic information about specific targets of Renamo'.[57] But the element of direction, at least in broader planning, was very strong. Renamo documents (the 'Vaz' diaries) captured at the Casa Banana headquarters in late 1985 set out under an entry for 24 February 1984 the following targets: 'Railways; Cahora Bassa; cooperantes, and other targets of an economic nature, SADCC'. These had presumably been agreed with the South Africans the previous day (23 February), when a meeting took place in Pretoria between Dhlakama and named officials of South African military intelligence. The diaries elsewhere note a 'General Plan no. 1 of 24 February 1984', namely:

---

[55] João Cabrita, court statement.

[56] Quoted in Metz, 'The Mozambique National Resistance', p. 479.

[57] Jorge Correia, court statement.

1. Destroy the Mozambican economy in the rural zones.
2. Destroy the communications routes to prevent exports and imports to and from abroad, and the movement of domestic produce.
3. Prevent the activities of foreigners (cooperantes) because they are the most dangerous in the recovery of the economy.

Although destruction was certainly the keynote, many aspects of Renamo activity superficially interpreted as externally directed destabilisation can also be viewed as normal guerrilla tactics aimed at isolating the rural areas and weakening the power of the centre. However, beyond the direct evidence that many decisions, for example to attack the Beira oil pipeline and the Beira-Malawi railway, originated with the South Africans and were imposed on an unwilling Dhlakama, who feared that the human losses would outweigh any tactical gains, the targeting of all the communication corridors at the same time was not an obvious military option for Renamo to choose in the early 1980s.[58] It may indeed have been indirectly responsible for some of Renamo's more unusual organisational features. Those corridors are spaced across the great length of Mozambique, from the Nacala line in the north, through the Beira corridor, to the Limpopo line in the south. To bring them all within operational range must have imposed an artificially wide theatre of action on the young movement, necessitating an equally artificial dynamic of growth. The important road artery to Zimbabwe and Malawi, running through Tete province, also stretched the organisation westwards. It is probably no coincidence that Renamo seems to have almost doubled in size in 1981-2, at a time when rail lines and ports in central and southern Mozambique (especially Beira) began to come under constant attack. Renamo's growth dynamic was sustainable only by forced recruitment, and this contributed to the use of extreme violence. Unlike other Southern African guerrilla movements, Renamo was not able to establish a firm territorial base and work out from there gradually, developing its own characteristic set of aims and beliefs and regional support base as it went. Left to itself, this might have occurred in central Mozambique, but Renamo's rapid expansion after its change of patron from Rhodesia to South Africa removed this possibility.

---

[58] *Domingo*, 16 December 1984. In their independence war against the Portuguese, Frelimo had never been so ambitious.

The structure, organisation and credo of Renamo

This dynamic did not preclude the development of a certain kind of politics. The Rhodesians had given Renamo no encouragement or opportunity to establish an independent political profile, continuing to publicise the activities of existing political groups in exile in Lisbon, even after Renamo's formation as a military unit in 1976.[59] By contrast the South Africans promoted the development of a political structure and image. A first European tour was arranged for Dhlakama in November 1980, taking in West Germany, Portugal and France, although no publicity was given to this visit at the time, and little is known of its content. A public political identity for Renamo was nurtured during 1981, with the initial establishment of a 'study group' headed by Cristina to draw up a political programme. A meeting chaired in 1981 by Dhlakama and attended by, among others, João Cabrita, Raul Domingos (then Dhlakama's secretary) and Zeca Calisto, who in 1982 became Renamo's commander in Zambézia province, made Dhlakama president and Cristina secretary-general.[60]

According to Constantino Reis (a Renamo defector), the pressure to develop a political leadership and programme came from the South Africans, who considered that Renamo required such appurtenances in order to attract national or international credibility.[61] However, even if at South African behest, it was a project which Cristina and others willingly supported by analogy with revolutionary Cuba, where an initially military revolt later created a leadership integrating elements of the guerrilla force with various political parties. But as a consequence of its origin in armed revolt by 'simple and uneducated' people, which initially occupied itself with assaults on re-education camps to free their inmates, Renamo lacked any similar leadership. Therefore, taking the limitations of the military commanders into account, it had been decided during a recent visit to Europe to restructure politically with the aim of transforming Renamo into a political party which, together with political figures and organisations already existing in exile, could form a single Front: 'My duties as Secretary General ... are precisely to follow up this decision emanating from the Military Commander, Afonso Dhlakama, after approval by the

---

[59] See 'End 'Immoral Frelimo' Call', *The Herald*, 21 August 1976; 'Opposition to Frelimo not co-ordinated', *The Herald*, 22 October 1976.

[60] Cabrita, court statement.

[61] Special supplement *AIM Bulletin*, 102 (January 1985).

National Council, which has a form similar to that of a Military Junta.'[62]

In fact the formation of a National Council did not occur until 1982. It comprised Afonso Dhlakama (president), Orlando Cristina (secretary-general) and several minor Mozambican political exiles, and was the result of a determined effort by Cristina and his collaborators to seek out members of the Mozambican exile community. During 1982 appeals were made to all anti-Frelimo groups (including the Frente Unida de Moçambique, or FUMO, led by João Khan since 1981, after the resignation of Domingos Arouca; the Movimento Nacionalista de Moçambique, or MONAMO, of Zeca Caliate; and Africa Livre) to unite their efforts. In March 1982, for example, Cabrita travelled to Nairobi to deliver a verbal message to exiles there.[63] Cristina himself went as far as the United States. The most important recruit was Gideon Fanuel Mahluza from Nairobi, who became a member of the National Council and for a while acted as foreign relations secretary, but who later left Renamo. He had been a founder member of Frelimo in 1962, but departed in its first split, a year later, and went on to become a leader of the Comité Revolucionário de Moçambique (COREMO), a small rival guerrilla movement to Frelimo which operated out of Zambia, and subsequently a leader of Africa Livre. Later that year Cristina also managed to recruit Artur Vilankulu, who had been COREMO representative in the United States.[64] However, other opposition politicians approached were reluctant to associate with a body so closely linked to South Africa. FUMO went so far as to denounce Renamo as 'a mixed force of Mozambicans, ex-PIDEs and mercenaries who were at first in the service of Smith's Rhodesia and are now in the service of South Africa'.[65]

The formation of the National Council therefore represented a move in 1982 to graft a political superstructure on to an existing military organisation; the impulse for this came both from the South Africans and from elements in Renamo under an obligation to them, but doubtless also with their own agenda. That military organisation had been set up and directed by Rhodesians, although it comprised Mozambicans, many of whom had either fought against Frelimo during the colonial war or had subsequently been incarcerated by it in re-education camps; their grievances against the

[62] Interview with Cristina, *Tempo Ilustrado*, 1981 (Johannesburg).

[63] Cabrita, court statement.

[64] Nilsson, *Unmasking the Bandits*, p. 37.

[65] *Star International Airmail Weekly*, 14 August 1982.

Maputo government were no doubt real. The establishment of the new structure did not arise organically out of the nature of the movement itself – indeed, they were incongruous. It was linked with the publication of Renamo's 'Manifesto and Programme', but was not responsible for drafting it: although this document purports to have been adopted by the National Council in August 1981 (when the National Council did not yet exist), the very first version, with an introductory section later dropped, seems only to have gone into circulation in Johannesburg in May or June 1982. The appearance of Renamo's Statutes and its Manifesto and Programme was noted in the Portuguese press just a few weeks later.[66] There is a real lack of evidence as to the status and role of the National Council during this period, although it did meet in South Africa after Cristina's murder at Walmerstad in 1983, in an attempt to end the internal struggle over who should succeed him as Secretary General, and selected Fernandes, the candidate favoured by South African Military Intelligence, with Dhlakama promoted to 'president and supreme commander'. Evo Fernandes later described the National Council as coming in third place in Renamo's political structure after the President and Secretary General, and comprising 'chiefs, military people, civilians and so on', who are 'proposed by the Secretary General and then nominated by the President'. This account enhanced the position of Secretary-General, still held at that time by Fernandes himself.[67] Other early meetings of the Council are said to have been held in West Germany in 1982-3. Possibly a description given in early 1984 gives an accurate indication of its then nature and competences: it was a 'very basic structure. Members do not have portfolios, but are given specific tasks by the President from time to time.'[68] As late as 1987, Renamo's political structure could still be described as basically a military command structure, headed by Dhlakama as Chairman of the National Council.[69]

The overwhelming predominance of the South Africans in Renamo's external relations did not preclude relationships with other political forces, and certain elements within Renamo clearly resented the excessive dependence on the South Africans. Renamo offices were established in Heidelberg, Lisbon and later also Nairobi

---

[66] *O Diabo*, 24 August 1982.

[67] In an interview published in *Defense and Diplomacy*, September 1985.

[68] E. Cain, 'Mozambique's Hidden War' in C. Moser (ed.), *Combat on Communist Territory*, Free Congress Foundation, Washington, DC, 1985.

[69] Thomashausen, 'The Mozambique National Resistance'.

and Washington. Until 1989 the external wing comprised semi-autonomous individuals who usually held their posts more because they had residence status in a particular country than because of any career structure determined by Renamo's central leadership:

> They are generally isolated and poorly informed on the situation within Mozambique. For this reason (and out of propaganda necessity), they issue communiqués and statements which are frequently divorced from what is actually happening in Mozambique and which often contradict the line taken by Renamo's internal leadership.[70]

The most important office was always the one in Portugal, where Renamo had representation from 1979. Until his murder in 1988, the dominant figure was Evo Fernandes, a lawyer of Goan descent. With South African backing, Fernandes became the major spokesman and contact figure for Renamo internationally, so that communications and most policy decisions came to be chanelled through him. Employment (also for Jorge Correia, the organisation's Lisbon representative in 1983-7) was provided by Manuel Bulhosa, former owner of the Maputo oil refinery nationalised by Frelimo, through his publishing house, Livraria Bertrand. Fernandes' long-standing personal friendship with André Thomashausen, a German academic educated in Lisbon, also brought him into contact with the University of Kiel, where Professor Kaltefleiter provided support (for example, making arrangements for meetings of Renamo representatives in West Germany). The early connections, then, were Portuguese, South African and West German, with a significant concentration of Mozambican exiles in Nairobi providing the basis for an office there. West German links date back to the first attempt to create a political identity for the movement in 1980. The second and third meetings of Renamo's National Council were held in West Germany in October 1982 and March 1983, after which a resident Renamo representative was appointed (João Rajabo da Costa). Professor Kaltefleiter (then an adviser to Chancellor Kohl) arranged a six-week visit by Dhlakama in November 1983, in which were included meetings with representatives of both the Hans Seidel and the Konrad Adenauer Foundations and with Franz-Josef Strauss, leader of the Christian Socialist Union (CSU) and Prime Minister of Bavaria. The CSU's links with Renamo were therefore of long standing, and independent of the involvement of other countries,

---

[70] Alex Vines, *Renamo: From Terrorism to Democracy in Mozambique?*, 2nd rev. edn, London, 1996, p. 32.

although they did also reflect the South African connections of Herr Strauss.

Just as in the early years its political structures remained somewhat hazy, much the same could be said of Renamo's 'ideology'. At the first meeting of the National Council in May 1982 (at Walmerstad near Pretoria where the Renamo leadership and radio staff were then based), a number of principles were agreed.[71] These included the creation of a government of national reconciliation which would establish a multi-party democracy within a maximum period of two years; a unitary but decentralised political system; a foreign policy based on non-interference in the domestic affairs of other countries; a mixed economy; the reintroduction of private and church-owned hospitals and schools; independent courts and private law clinics; an elected President who would appoint the Prime Minister, and whose government programme would be subject to approval by an elected National Assembly; reinstatement of traditional authority in line with the people's will; separation of church and state but the recognition by the latter of full religious freedom provided this was compatible with national interests; nationality based on birth in the national territory; and greater possibilities for acquiring nationality. These principles do not, in themselves, represent any agenda dictated by South African military interests; presumably the important thing for them was that Renamo should appear a convincing political entity to the outside world. However, they can be interpreted as bearing the influence (which has persisted) of ousted Portuguese interests (for example, on the question of Mozambican nationality). Yet it is significant that there was no mention of the return of nationalised property. The conclusion must be that the content was not actually dictated by any outside interest. According to a communiqué,[72] draft statutes and a programme (presumably the work of the study group set up the preceding year) were approved unanimously, and new heads of the departments of politics, external relations and information were appointed.

In July 1979 a party of journalists interviewed André Matsangaíssa inside Mozambique, and their accounts provide some insight into

[71] Reis, supplement to *AIM Bulletin*, 102 (January 1985). For an account of the link between Walmerstad and the SADF building at ZANZA House, Pretoria, see Nilsson, *Unmasking the bandits*, pp. 27-8. This event has sometimes been claimed as Renamo's first Congress, though often misrepresented as having taken place in Chimoio, Mozambique. Subsequently Renamo designated the June 1989 Congress in Gorongosa as the first.

[72] Annexed to Cabrita's court statement.

his aims and motivations during Renamo's Rhodesia-based period. Principal among these was to eliminate Communism in Mozambique and to attack the many re-education camps scattered across the country: policy-making could wait until later.[73] Suffice it here to note the gulf between Renamo's political aims as expressed in National Council papers and communiqués issued by the Lisbon office and the inarticulate rejectionism of its peasant soldiers. João Cabrita observed that all Mozambicans who defected from Mozambique to join Renamo during the early days in Rhodesia basically expressed alienation from a system imposed by Frelimo and speculated that this arose from the innate conservatism of the Mozambican peasantry.[74] A not dissimilar impression is created by the rare early interviews given by Dhlakama, himself the son of a former chief from Chibabava in Sofala province. In 1983 he described himself as a nationalist, whose only real responsibility was to rid his people of 'Communist oppression', and complained that Frelimo was worse than the Portuguese before them: 'The colonialists exploited us, but at least they didn't try to wipe out our traditions because they are so-called "reactionary".' He also spoke in general terms of introducing 'elections, real democracy and a mixed economy', and vouched that after his forces had won the war and guaranteed peace, they would allow the civilians and intellectuals to govern.[75] In a further interview in 1986 Dhlakama maintained that Renamo controlled the countryside while Frelimo 'hid in the cities'. Hinting at the possibility of a military coup by an exhausted Frelimo officer corps, he suggested that political reconciliation and a government of national unity could be an alternative to outright victory, but predicted that the latter could come in two years.[76]

The relative crudeness and vagueness, even internal contradictions of Renamo's formal political rhetoric may have exposed the organisation to ridicule. This was indeed a major feature of the campaign by the Frelimo government and its Western sympathisers to discredit Renamo – as Cahen put it, for Western observers there was no text to analyse.[77] Yet Renamo's primitive political campaign, albeit couched in crude anti-Marxist rhetoric, was not without

---

[73] *Daily Telegraph*, 5 July 1979; *The Herald* (Rhodesia), 4 July 1979.

[74] Cabrita, court statement.

[75] *International Herald Tribune*, 14 September 1983.

[76] P. Moorcraft, 'Mozambique's Long Civil War: RENAMO, puppets or patriots?', *International Defense Review*, 10 (1987), pp. 1313-16.

[77] Cahen, *Mozambique. Analyse politique de conjoncture*, Paris, 1990, p. 43.

popular appeal. It managed to voice the dissatisfactions of those who had been variously antagonised by Frelimo, with its policy of compulsory villagisation and attempts to collectivise agriculture, its assault on traditional practices and the removal of traditional chiefs, and its curbs on the Catholic Church. Thus Renamo drew on the sullen resentment felt by some people towards a government which could not meet their (extremely modest) material needs and was openly contemptuous of their traditions and beliefs. But for Renamo and its South African backers it would have remained largely sullen resentment. With Renamo, escape from the Frelimo government seemed possible – with all the tragic consequences that ensued from such an attempt.

6

A LUTA CONTINUA:
FRELIMO FIGHTS BACK

'South Africa is not going to attack and wage war on us. We shall stop in Pretoria [applause]. Do not fear, we shall teach these Boers a lesson [laughter and applause].'[1]

'His game was to acquire help for his collapsing country and leverage on his vastly more powerful neighbour. It was a case study of the diplomacy of weakness.'[2]

Although Renamo expanded its activities rapidly during 1982, Frelimo seems to have been relatively unaware until the middle of that year of the dangers that the group posed, and its response remained largely military, consisting of various 'mopping up' operations.[3] Despite a flurry of very high-level military exchanges with the Soviet Union in early 1982, which resulted in the announcement of increased military aid, Frelimo seemed reluctant to internationalise the conflict.[4] Nor were Mozambique's 'natural allies' prepared or able to provide the kind of assistance necessary. Relations with Mozambique appear to have been affected by shifts in Soviet understanding of world events and development issues even before the dramatic upheavals initiated by Mikhail Gorbachev in the mid-1980s. 'Overtures to the USSR for a Cuba-style special relation drew a rebuff even before Gorbachev came to power.'[5] In June Machel, flanked by the military leadership, addressed a

[1] Speech by Samora Machel, 4 April 1981, reported by Maputo home service SWB/ME/6694/B2.

[2] C. Crocker, *High Noon in Southern Africa*, New York, 1992, pp. 240-1.

[3] *Africa Confidential*, 23, 64 (August 1982). See also *African Business*, December 1983.

[4] *Guardian*, 4 June 1982. Crocker, *High Noon*, p. 243.

[5] R. Davies, 'Implications for Southern Africa of the current impasse in the peace process in Mozambique', Bellville: Centre for Southern African Studies, University of the Western Cape, working paper no. 9, 1991.

large rally of veterans of the anti-colonial struggle, suggesting a concern to rebuild political support but also a change in tactics against Renamo.[6] An important meeting of the Frelimo Central Committee in August came to the conclusion that military action was unlikely to be enough on its own to defeat it.[7] This meeting also seems to have marked a shift in Frelimo's approach. Certainly by mid-1982 Frelimo had embarked on a three-part strategy of rapprochement with the Western powers to isolate Renamo. This was to engage South Africa in direct negotiations, encourage the Western powers to put pressure on the Republic to do so, and continue to harry Renamo on the ground.[8]

The turn to the West

Mozambique's early foreign policy after independence was not geared to a strategy of conciliation with the West. Because it was a fighting anti-colonial movement Frelimo's 'foreign policy', at least initially, was quite open, driven as it was by the imperatives of waging armed struggle against the Portuguese. It thus sought aid from all quarters. Eduardo Mondlane had good American connections and for a while during the Kennedy presidency it looked as though sympathy in the United States for the lusophone anti-colonial movements might bear fruit. The Cuban missile crisis of October 1962 seems to have been important in shifting US official attitudes away from long-term strategies to lessen the appeal of Communism, towards confrontation with a perceived expansionist Soviet Union. The junior allies of the United States more or less followed its lead. Thus Frelimo was forced to take account of the contemporary geopolitical realities, especially as Portugal began to use the leverage within NATO offered by the base in the Azores. The Soviet bloc countries and China became the movement's arms suppliers, though some European countries, notably the Scandinavian ones, made important financial and moral contributions.[9] Thus by the time of its 2nd Congress Frelimo was already stressing the special position of the socialist countries. Later, within the context of Frelimo's own radicalisation, this special

---

[6] See *Tempo*, 610 (20 June 1982).

[7] *Tempo*, 620 (29 August 1982). See also *Notícias*, 17 March 1984.

[8] See Machel's later reference to this meeting in March 1984 SWB ME/7596/B 2-6.

[9] For an insider Frelimo account see S. Vieira, 'Vectors of Foreign Policy of the Mozambique Liberation Front'.

position became more than just acts of solidarity, referring rather
to common political goals, expressed in Frelimo's designation (in
its party programme) of the socialist countries as the 'liberated
zone of humanity'.

At Mozambique's inception as a sovereign state its foreign policy
was driven by the dual objective of completing the process of
decolonisation in its region and creating propitious conditions
for the construction of socialism within the country. Yet the Frelimo
leadership saw these tasks within a broader context of a more
general 'anti-imperialist' stance. There were domestic corollaries
to this – as, for example, the setting up of a Solidarity bank into
which Mozambican workers paid contributions to help in the struggles of other oppressed peoples. Within this context and continuing
a stance that pre-dated independence, 'Frelimo made early efforts
to maintain ties with the full set of socialist countries, while avoiding
identification as a camp-follower of any.'[10] Thus close relations
with the Soviet bloc countries were complemented by visits to
China and North Korea.[11] However, by 1980 Mozambique appeared
to be moving more and more definitely into the Soviet orbit.[12]
The reorganisation of its armed forces and security seemed to
rely increasingly on Soviet bloc support, and the country aligned
itself with that bloc at the United Nations, notably over Afghanistan
which the Soviets had invaded at the end of 1979. Maputo signalled
its closeness to the Soviet bloc by concluding the standard peace
and friendship treaties which conventionally contained three
security clauses: a pledge to consult in the event of a breach of
the peace; a prohibition against joining alliances aimed against
the other party; and a commitment to military cooperation to be
secured by other bilateral instruments. Mozambique concluded
such treaties with the Soviet Union (March 1977), Bulgaria (October 1978) and East Germany (February 1979), as well as one
with Romania (April 1979) which lacked such clauses. In formal
treaty terms at least, Mozambique was the Third World country
closest to the Soviet bloc. Its other international stances followed
a general 'progressive' orientation. It was non-aligned and expressed support for the Palestine Liberation Organisation, the opposition guerrillas in El Salvador, the Sandinistas in Nicaragua,
the Bishop regime in Grenada and Polisario in the Western Sahara.

[10] W. Minter, 'Major Themes in Mozambican Foreign Relations, 1975-77', *Issue*,
VIII (spring 1978), pp. 43-9, esp. 46.

[11] For relations with China see S. Jackson, 'China's Third World Foreign Policy:
The case of Lusophone Africa, 1961-1984' (unpubl. ms.).

[12] *Le Monde*, 25 November 1980.

It did not hesitate to recognise the 'Democratic Republic of East Timor' and to denounce Indonesian actions there. Aside from its relations with particular groups it adopted generally 'anti-imperialist' positions, including strong support for the demilitarisation of the Indian Ocean as well as progress towards a New International Economic Order.[13]

Regionally Mozambique grouped itself with the other black-ruled states in the region to create some sort of shield against South Africa, essentially in a political form as the Front-Line States and in an economic form as SADCC. With the first of these (originally formed by Zambia, Tanzania, Botswana and Mozambique and joined by Angola in 1976), the countries concerned hoped to maintain pressure on world opinion to force Pretoria to abandon apartheid; with the second they hoped to secure various forms of regional cooperation and to lessen their dependence on South Africa. The Front-Line States organisation, beyond the hyperbole, remained little more than a framework for the leaders of the black-ruled states in the region to consult regularly and to coordinate the continued pressure on the international community to bring South Africa to heel. Similarly SADCC, formed in the spring of 1980, was a rather skeletal organisation that did little to reduce its members' dependence on Pretoria or to increase cooperation among them, but was quite effective as a device to raise large sums of Western aid for various kinds of infrastructural projects. Given the geography of the region, Mozambique was of course a substantial beneficiary of such aid.

Thus initially Mozambique sustained a quite complex variety of relationships with the major Western states which were to a considerable extent a function of its transition to independence. Generally, relations with France and West Germany were hostile because both had been seen as supporters of the Portuguese colonial regime. As it consolidated its grip on power, much of Frelimo's routine diplomacy in pursuit of its non-aligned position consisted of the normalisation of relations with countries towards which it had initially been rather indifferent. Chissano worked diligently to improve relations with France, although relations with West Germany remained blighted by the status of West Berlin and the consequent veto on EEC aid.[14] Relations with Britain were rather more cordial, as there had been considerable coopera-

---

[13] See the speech on the latter by Chissano at the UN, *Notícias*, 29 August 1980.

[14] Such aid was conditional on recognition of West Berlin as an integral part of West Germany. See G. Winrow, *The Foreign Policy of the GDR in Africa*, Cambridge, 1990.

tion in resolving the Rhodesian crisis, and some British economic aid. The generally distant relations with Europe did not, however, preclude growing trade cooperation. Between 1978 and 1980 Mozambique signed loan and aid agreements with Britain, the Netherlands, Italy, France, Canada, Portugal and Greece; while even before this, at the time of independence, the EEC countries had collectively indicated their willingness to see Mozambique join the Lomé Convention, the trade agreement between the EEC and various African, Caribbean and Pacific stares.[15]

The Nordic countries constituted a special case, both because of their perceived independence from Cold War antagonisms and more specifically because of their concrete support for Frelimo during the anti-colonial war. Machel's April 1977 trip to the Scandinavian countries was his first official visit to the West and in November of that year the Nordic Five signed a $50 million agriculture agreement. For their own political and ideological reasons, the Scandinavian countries continued to be major supporters of Frelimo, particularly in the field of development aid.[16] Portugal also had a special position, though of a rather different kind. Relations with Lisbon remained volatile after independence, with provocations on both sides rooted in the material and psychological difficulties of facing up to the new situation.

Despite certain overtures having been made in 1974, relations with the United States were at best cool. Mozambique fell foul of Congressional initiatives to block aid (other than emergency food aid), but President Carter's less aggressive foreign policy and the effects of defeat in the Vietnam war meant that the United States was relatively uninterested in Southern Africa.[17] This changed with the Reagan presidency, which abandoned some of the previous hostility to South Africa, and under the terms of constructive engagement began to relax some of the restrictions on that country which had hitherto been in force. The general effects of this shift in US policy were also aggravated by a very specific dispute over Maputo's expulsion of alleged spies at the US embassy; it publicly charged that they had assisted the South Africans with intelligence for their first raid on the city. As a result the United States refused to appoint an ambassador and relations remained tense.[18]

---

[15] *Guardian*, 23 June 1975.

[16] For details see *Indian Ocean Newsletter*, 22 March 1986.

[17] For Congressional action see *International Herald Tribune*, 14 June 1976.

[18] The US government and many commentators remained curiously obsessed with Mozambique's voting record at the UN. See for example the comments of Melvin Laird in *International Herald Tribune*, 28 June 1985.

The new diplomacy thus began with some advantages but rather more disadvantages. Implementing it involved a hectic round of visits to and improvements in relations with various states. A major state visit by Machel to Western countries had been planned for June 1982 but was postponed until November 1983. Nevertheless, there were several visits of senior figures to the United States in 1982 as part of a strategy to pre-empt support there for Renamo. The most important was the meeting between Chissano and Secretary of State Shultz at the UN in October, which was followed by the despatch of a senior State Department official, Wisner, to Maputo in December 1982 for talks with Chissano and Machel.[19] In January Chester Crocker, the Assistant Secretary of State for African Affairs, had talks in Maputo with Machel and Veloso. His visit was closely followed by a group of five liberal Congressmen who favoured better relations with Mozambique.[20]

Chissano as Foreign Minister made the first official Mozambican visit to West Germany in June, meeting Foreign Minister Genscher and Economic Cooperation Minister Offergeld.[21] The issue of West Berlin was resolved in August 1982, which opened the way for West German aid and for Mozambique's membership of the Lomé Convention and thus receipt of EEC aid.[22] Non-official links with Italy pre-dated Mozambican independence. Frelimo delegations had attended conferences in Italy, and help was received (especially in the medical sphere) from the Communist council of Reggio Emilia. Solidarity shipments had been organised, and 'twinning' pacts began in July 1970 with one between Frelimo's central hospital in Cabo Delgado and that of Reggio Emilia; such pacts later continued in more orthodox local authority style (Reggio Emilia/-Pemba, 2 July 1975; Livorno/Beira in 1984).[23] Italian economic involvement in Mozambique also grew, as did Italian aid. By the mid-1980s Italy was Mozambique's main creditor and its most important trading partner, with projects in Mozambique valued at about $US 400 million.[24] They included the construction of two dams on the Sabie and Umbeluzi rivers (Corumane and Pequenos Libombos)

[19] *Indian Ocean Newsletter*, 18 December 1982.

[20] *Ibid.*, 22 January 1983.

[21] *Indian Ocean Newsletter* 26 June 1982.

[22] *Guardian*, 10 August 1982.

[23] *Tempo*, 904 and 905, 7 and 14 February 1988. Frelimo wounded had been sent for treatment to Reggio Emilia in October 1971, along with the first batch of nurses for training.

[24] MIO *News Review* 59 (5 September 1985).

largely financed by Italy, and carried out by an Italian consortium, COBOCO.[25] Furthermore, Italy was the principal Western source of bilateral aid to Mozambique.[26]

The British were seen as a way through to the Americans, and Prime Minister Margaret Thatcher as a useful influence on Reagan's attitude towards Mozambique. Mrs Thatcher took a personal interest in Mozambique which far outweighed its real importance to Britain, and this reflected both the good relationship with Mozambique which had developed through practical cooperation over the problem of Rhodesia and the good personal relationship which existed between the British Prime Minister and Machel. Machel admired the decisive effort made under Thatcher to assume Britain's constitutional responsibilities for Rhodesia, and he accordingly rendered decisive practical support for the Lancaster House settlement by leaning on ZANU at a crucial point in the settlement talks to accept the British plan.[27] Gratitude was thus due to Mozambique for helping Britain to rid itself of the Rhodesian albatross, and the opportunity was taken during Machel's 1983 visit to cancel debts incurred between 1976 and 1978 (some £22.5 million) and to promise modest amounts of new aid (primarily some £10 million to upgrade the Limpopo rail line), as well as food aid, although Mozambique was advised that further aid was dependent on its joining the IMF. Meetings with British businessmen were also a prominent part of Machel's visit.[28] In addition, discussions with the British government produced the promise of some limited British military assistance, initially in the form of a small number of places for officer training at Sandhurst.[29] The defence aspect of Anglo-Mozambican relations gained greater substance after the signing of a training agreement in July 1985, with the first forty-eight (Forças Armadas de Moçambique) officers completing their twelve-week course in May 1986. This was taught by British instructors at a separate complex within the Nyanga training area of the Zimbabwe National Army (ZNA) in eastern Zimbabwe. Thus, under Prime Minister Thatcher Mozambique enjoyed the distinction of becoming the only non-Commonwealth African state

---

[25] *Ibid.* 83 (5 September 1986).

[26] *Africa Research Bulletin*, 30 April 1987.

[27] See Michael Charlton, *The Last Colony in Africa: Diplomacy and the independence of Rhodesia*, Oxford, 1990.

[28] *Africa Economic Digest*, 28 October 1983.

[29] *Financial Times*, 22 October 1983.

to receive such military training assistance.[30] Official British defence assistance also included non-lethal equipment such as boots and uniforms, while a British company was associated with the provision of a £1.6 million package which included arms and training for a defence force for the Nacala line.

Relations with Portugal improved with the removal of various irritants between the two countries, including the freeing of some fifty Portuguese nationals at the end of 1979 and the dropping of all outstanding financial claims by Portugal in October 1980.[31] The resumption of something approaching normal relations came with a visit to Lisbon by Chissano in March 1981, followed by a state visit to Mozambique by Portuguese President Eanes in November. This was in turn followed by a visit by Portuguese Prime Minister Pinto Balsemão in June 1982, leading a largely economic delegation. There followed a rather emotional state visit to Portugal by Machel in October 1983 during which, despite the bonhomie, certain tensions were visible between different elements of the Portuguese government.[32] A number of agreements were concluded in the first 1982, including some modest military cooperation. Visits to Britain and Portugal formed part of a six-nation European tour which also took in Belgium, the Netherlands, France and Yugoslavia – a highly publicised initiative by the Mozambicans to establish their non-alignment as well as to attract investment and if possible military aid. Mozambique clearly signalled its intention to join the Lomé Convention and there was extensive lobbying of private business.[33] Publicly, at least, the delegates considered themselves pleased with the results, but these were finely judged and rather modest because there was little possibility that the major Western powers would make decisive military or economic contributions to the country.[34]

Despite all this, Moscow did not seek to punish or penalise

---

[30] Simon Baynham, 'British Military Training Assistance in Southern Africa: Lessons for South Africa?' *Africa Insight*, 22, 3 (1992), pp. 218-24.

[31] *Africa*, January 1982.

[32] On the visit see *Expresso*, 8 and 15 October 1983. For a detailed analysis of Portugal's relations with Mozambique see M. Cahen, 'Le Portugal et l'Afrique. Le cas de relations luso-mozambicaines, 1965-1985', *Afrique Contemporaine*, January-March 1986, pp. 3-55.

[33] See coverage in *West Africa*, 31 October 1983, *Africa Economic Digest*, 28 October 1983; *Guardian*, 21 October 1983, *Afrique-Asie*, 7 November 1983; *Indian Ocean Newsletter*, 22 October 1983; and an interview with Machel in *Le Monde*, 18 October 1983.

[34] See Council of Ministers communiqué, SWB ME/7486/B/1-3.

Mozambique as its opening to the West in 1982 gathered pace. High-level contacts continued and indeed intensified, and were cordial. In November 1982 Machel was in Moscow for the funeral of Leonid Brezhnev and met Ustinov, the Soviet Defence Minister. A new trade agreement was signed in January. Machel was in Moscow again in March 1983, accompanied by senior Frelimo leaders with economic responsibilities, including Mario Machungo and Sergio Vieira (planning and agriculture) and the Secretary of State for cotton. Indeed Soviet economic and food aid to Mozambique sharply increased after the 'opening to the West' had become irreversible.[35] In certain Frelimo circles at least the socialist countries remained a 'secure rearguard'.[36]

Nkomati and after

The strategy of 'turning to the West' was largely intended to intensify pressure on South Africa to negotiate directly, in line with Machel's dictum that Renamo was no more than a puppet of Pretoria. Despite (or perhaps because of) Renamo's rapid expansion, it seemed to many in Maputo that if its external support could be cut off at source, the organisation might collapse. In a regional context of increasingly aggressive South African actions, preliminary meetings took place between the two countries in December 1982 at Komatipoort followed by more formal talks in December 1983 at Mbabane.[37] Negotiations were held at ministerial level but it is clear that there had been talks through other channels before.[38] In February 1984 the announcement was made that the two countries intended to enter into a formal security arrangement.

The Nkomati Accord, signed on 16 March 1984 by Samora Machel and Prime Minister P.W. Botha of South Africa, bound each side to refrain from the use of force against the other and to prevent the use of their respective territories by any other 'state, government, foreign military forces, organisations or individuals which plan or prepare to commit acts of violence...directed against the other party'. As part of Mozambique's diplomatic strategy

---

[35] *Africa Confidential*, 15 August 1984. This point is rather ignored by Kuhne in his otherwise useful discussion 'What does the case of Mozambique tell us about Soviet ambivalence towards Africa?' in H. Kitchen (ed.), *Angola, Mozambique and the West*. See also US Department of State, *Mozambique: A Country in Transition*, Intelligence Research Report no. 175, June 1988, p. 9.

[36] Editorial in *Notícias*, 13 April 1984.

[37] *Daily Telegraph*, 20 December 1982; *Le Monde*, 20 December 1982.

[38] *Notícias*, 17 March 1984.

Nkomati was a success of a kind. Overt American hostility was modified, and this opened the way to ending the US ban on aid to the country and allowed for the stepping up of food aid, although some elements of the administration's proposals were blocked by a vociferous right-wing lobby in Congress. It was also true that after Nkomati various forms of direct South African support for Renamo did indeed cease. SADF advisers no longer made regular visits to Renamo bases, and air drops of supplies also stopped. Renamo's radio station, Voz da Africa Livre, ceased transmitting. The involvement of the United States in the negotiations as well as the enthusiasm of the South African Foreign Minister 'Pik' Botha for the Accord made that much necessary.[39]

But despite the brave face put on it, the Accord was expensive. Behind 'the extraordinary hoopla which accompanied the signing of the accord'[40] had been a highly secret process of negotiations about which neither the ANC nor the Frelimo Central Committee was informed until afterwards.[41] Mozambique's prestige as a regional political actor was severely damaged:

> For the ANC and the Communist party, the Nkomati Accord was a major disaster, especially since it coincided with the mutiny in the Angolan camps. It virtually shut down Mozambique as an infiltration route and took out of action probably the most useful of all the Frontline States from the military point of view.[42]

Much worse was the fact that on the eve of Nkomati, apparently on the orders of van der Westhuizen (head of South African Military Intelligence), the SADF had dropped several months' worth of arms supplies to Renamo and allowed 1,500 guerrillas to cross over into Mozambique with their weapons, before closing their camps in the Transvaal.[43] There was a considerable re-supply by

---

[39] For US involvement see *Expresso*, 4 February 1984.

[40] John Saul, 'Nkomati and After' in Saul (ed.), *A Difficult Road*, p. 401. For the 'hoopla' see reports in *West Africa*, 26 March 1984, and *Notícias*, 17 March 1984. The whole occasion was filmed by an East German film crew. *Notícias* 22 April 1984.

[41] Verschuur *et al.*, *Dix ans de solitude*, p. 17. For denials see interview with Chissano, *Afrique-Asie*, 2 July 1984. Frelimo's sensitivities come through very strongly in this interview.

[42] S. Ellis and Tsepo Sechaba, *Comrades*, p. 138. See also Kasrils, *Armed and Dangerous*, p. 211, and Stephen M. Davis, *Apartheid's Rebels*, New Haven, CT, 1987, p. 67. Davis suggests (pp. 128-9) that infiltration resumed from Mozambique in 1985. *Africa Confidential* also thought so (11 December 1985).

[43] Moorcraft, *African Nemesis*, pp. 272-3.

sea of Renamo units operating in the Beira area. Nor were any steps taken to demobilise Renamo members in camps in South Africa, and an extensive indirect network of front companies went into operation to supply Renamo both from South Africa and through third countries, Malawi in particular.

Continued Renamo activity quite soon led to demands from Maputo for some explanation, although initially the Mozambicans were careful not to accuse Pretoria directly, using such euphemisms as 'certain sectors' or 'elements'.[44] South African officials, including 'Pik' Botha himself, hotly denied any responsibility and throughout 1984 constantly asserted their commitment to Nkomati. South Africa's contradictory stance on Nkomati seems in part to have reflected real divisions among the policy-making élite. For the Department of Foreign Affairs, accustomed to the thankless struggle for international acceptance and legitimacy, a treaty between South Africa and the sovereign and neighbouring state of Mozambique represented a rare prize. For the DMI, by contrast, successful implementation would have marked a betrayal, not only of Renamo but of South Africa's strategic regional interests as it perceived them. As the demands of South Africa's counter-insurgency imperative were met, with Mozambique restricting the ANC presence to the minimum required to run its office in Maputo, the inference must be that the agenda of the State Security Council (SSC) required the continuing destabilisation of Mozambique and the paralysis of its transport corridors. The cumulative evidence suggests a cynical duplicity on the part of the DMI both before and after the signing of the Accord, even to the extent of sabotaging the proximity talks in Pretoria by bugging the negotiations between Foreign Minister 'Pik' Botha and the Frelimo delegation and passing on the information to Renamo's Lisbon office.[45] The degree of President P.W. Botha's actual awareness of these developments remains a matter of conjecture, but few serious official obstacles seem to have been put in the DMI's way, although support for Renamo was routed more deviously than before.

These differences and the determination of Frelimo to hang on to the Accord, however battered, ensured that both sides continued to assert their commitment to it and look for means to enforce it. Towards the end of 1984 the South Africans were offering their good offices in the search for a solution to the conflict which would involve negotiations with Renamo. 'Proximity talks' took

---

[44] *International Herald Tribune,* 12 June 1984.

[45] Nilsson, *Unmasking the Bandits,* p. 44.

place between the Mozambican government and Renamo in Pretoria during September/October 1984 but failed to achieve a cease-fire. At the eleventh hour a compromise seemed to emerge in the form of the Pretoria Declaration (3 October 1984), read out at a press conference by 'Pik' Botha with Veloso on one side and Fernandes on the other. The Declaration embodied four principles: Machel was to be recognised as President of Mozambique, all armed action had to stop, South Africa should play a role in the implementation of the Declaration, and a joint commission should be established to implement the agreement. In subsequent discussions it became clear that all three parties had rather different understandings of what had been agreed, and negotiations finally collapsed in mid-October.[46]

There was an important Portuguese dimension to these developments. Portugal itself had welcomed the Nkomati Accord and played an active diplomatic role in the process. It fitted well with a Portuguese policy initiative, evolving since at least early 1982, to promote the idea of 'trilateral cooperation', under which they hoped to provide experienced personnel for development schemes in Africa, financed by other Western states, that it was thought might help to weaken Soviet influence on Angola and Mozambique. At the same time, Portuguese links with Renamo persisted at various levels and were exploited by the DMI, with the large Portuguese community in South Africa providing cover and a convenient scapegoat for continued DMI involvement. The salience of Renamo's 'Portuguese component' was partly enhanced by the fact that it was this element, through South African subsidiaries and associates, that operated the front companies through which Renamo received most of its supplies.[47] The size of the support from Portuguese business finance was almost certainly exaggerated, with the Mozambican government itself an accomplice in this, since by emphasising the Portuguese connection it could avoid accusing the South Africans of duplicity – which in the initial months following Nkomati it was unwilling to do for tactical reasons.[48] Maputo went so far as to issue a communiqué charging

---

[46] *Africa Confidential*, 28 November 1984. For detailed reconstructions of events see Robert Davies, *South African Strategy towards Mozambique in the Post-Nkomati Period*, Scandinavian Institute of African Studies, Uppsala, research report 73, 1985, and Alex Vines, ' "No Democracy without Money": The Road to Peace in Mozambique, 1982-1992', CIIR, 1994. For possible Portuguese intrigues see *Expresso*, 20 October 1984.

[47] Robert Davies, *South African Strategy towards Mozambique*.

[48] See for example the interviews with Veloso, the chief negotiator of Nkomati

that 'the Portuguese component involved with armed banditry constitutes one of the major obstacles to the ending of violence in Mozambique'.[49] Highlighting the Portuguese role also allowed Maputo, hoping to split Renamo, to stress that the black Mozambicans fighting for Renamo were being used by their former masters.[50]

For the South Africans, stressing Portuguese involvement diverted attention to right-wing Portuguese in South Africa, Malawi and Portugal itself as supporters of Renamo, even suggesting that it was individual sympathisers in the SADF from the Portuguese community who were involved in completely unauthorised cross-border enterprises and personal initiatives. A prime example was provided by the 'top-level security investigation' by the South African police into the Portuguese community in South African and the SADF that was ordered by President Botha in early 1985, apparently at the urging of his Foreign Minister. In March 'Pik' Botha announced that the government had broken up a 'Mafia-type' crime and political syndicate in Johannesburg which, having enlisted the aid of Renamo sympathisers – former Mozambicans – in the SADF, had been engaged in various criminal activities on behalf of Renamo. Around a dozen active SADF members with Renamo connections had been identified, including combat soldiers and an interpreter at SADF headquarters. Some were dismissed from the service and the rest transferred away from bases near the border. To halt further activities on behalf of Renamo, presumably by any still-active remnants of the 'pro-Renamo group', South Africa installed a radar system to monitor cross-border flights.[51] Quite how much this was meant to achieve remains unclear, since aerial re-supply across the Mozambique-South Africa border was not a prominent accusation; rather, re-supply was alleged to be taking place by various land, sea and air routes, principally to northern Mozambique.[52]

When on 28 August 1985 Zimbabwean troops captured the diaries of Dhlakama's secretary, Joaquim Vaz, at Renamo's headquarters, this whole charade appeared hard to believe. These docu-

on the Mozambican side, SWB ME 7828 B2-5, 17 December 1984, and ME 7830 B1-4, 19 December 1984. For Mozambican press discussion of the 'Portuguese component' see *AIM Bulletin*, 31 December 1984.

[49] Text in *Notícias*, 3 November 1984.

[50] *Guardian*, 9 November 1984.

[51] R. Jaster, 'The Security Outlook in Mozambique', *Survival*, Nov./Dec. 1985, pp. 258-64.

[52] *Africa Confidential*, 17 July 1985.

ments (whose authenticity was never denied) revealed the extent
of SADF re-supply before Nkomati, and the clandestine visit to
Renamo's headquarters of the South African Deputy Minister of
Foreign Affairs, Louis Nel, without the knowledge of 'Pik' Botha
and in the company of named officials of DMI.[53] For a while

> ....the strains between foreign affairs and the SADF and their
> respective supporters in the cabinet and SSC reached breaking
> point. Viljoen and Pik Botha gave contradictory press conferen-
> ces.[...] Eventually a compromise line was formulated.... What
> Louis Nel had been trying to do was to set up a 'Camp David-style'
> settlement, but the army did not wish to tell Pik Botha in case the
> foreign minister would not let Nel go to the Renamo HQ as it
> would be too dangerous.[54]

By the end of 1985 the pretences which had sustained Nkomati
were becoming pointless. Leading members of the Mozambique
government publicly accused South Africa of complicity in various
forms of support for Renamo.[55] In October Mozambique formally
withdrew from the Joint Security Commission.

Economic crisis and reform

In the early 1980s Mozambique's vulnerable economy, damaged
by the Portuguese exodus and largely dislocated by Frelimo's attempts at whirlwind transformation, suffered external shocks which
it simply could not absorb. Most important, the massive spread
of Renamo activity throughout the provinces brought direct destruction not merely of productive economic assets (state farms, rural
shops) but of the transport infrastructure (road and rail) that
were so important in the marketing of goods, as well as sowing
general fear and insecurity which were inimical to economic activity
of any kind. In addition the drought of 1982 was the worst in
fifty years with no rain in the south of the country between mid
1982 and the end of 1983.[56] Facing a projected cereals deficit of
670,000 tons, the government began an increasingly desperate

---

[53] See the bizarre interview with General Constand Viljoen, SWB ME/8080/B3-7.

[54] Moorcraft, *African Nemesis*, p. 276.

[55] Chissano at a meeting of non-aligned ministers in Luanda in September, and
Machel himself at the United Nations, 25 September 1985. See *AIM Bulletin* 111
(supplement).

[56] For effects of the drought see *Tanzania Daily News*, 30 January 1983, and *Morning
Star*, 6 January 1984.

series of appeals for international assistance from the beginning of 1983 onwards.[57] By the end of the year some 600,000 to 700,00 people were starving in Gaza and Inhambane.[58] Not for the first time in Mozambique, this phase of the drought ended with torrential rains at the beginning of 1984, destroying crops and damaging irrigation systems. These recurred first in Tete province and then in the southern part of the country.[59] Relief efforts were plagued by Renamo attacks. Finally, all these factors, along with the damaging effects of a hostile international economic environment (sharp oil price rises and falling sugar prices), combined to produce a collapse in production and in internal and external trade.

The sheer rapidity of the worsening of Mozambique's economic crisis forced the government's hand, particularly in the matter of rescheduling debt. By February the country had no option but to approach its creditors.[60] Thus the intimate links between a controlled turn to the West and renewed relations with Pretoria with the purpose of containing South African hostility were almost precisely replicated in the economic sphere. Yet at this stage Frelimo appears to have opted for a strategy of partial closer integration into the Western capitalist world and its multilateral institutions – and in that context a reactivation, indeed a deepening, of economic relationships with South Africa – while seeking to retain its political freedom of action and in some sense its socialist strategy as the leadership understood it. It may have calculated also that closer economic relations with South Africa would induce or sharpen differences within Pretoria's policy-making élite and make destabilisation a less attractive option.

This shift in economic policy formed part of a complete reassessment of economic and development policies at Frelimo's 4th Congress in April 1983. Although considerable emphasis was placed on the external sources of economic difficulties, it was accepted that these had accentuated structural problems in the management of the whole economy. The core problem was seen to be that the concentration of resources in the state sector had both been badly managed and had 'crowded out' other forms of economic activity

[57] *Notícias*, 13 January and 29 July 1983. For the argument that delays in relief were politically engineered as part of a campaign against Mozambique, see *New Statesman*, 3 March and 19 October 1984. The aid agencies claimed the situation had only recently become apparent. See *Guardian*, 30 November 1983.

[58] *The Times*, 30 November 1983.

[59] *Guardian*, 1 February 1984.

[60] *Notícias*, 4 February 1984. See also *Africa Economic Digest*, 28 October 1983.

to the detriment of production. There were several aspects of this. First, it was proving extremely difficult to administer the state sector itself and to secure a return on investment, given the forms of planning adopted and the severe shortages of appropriately trained personnel. Secondly, the accumulating inefficiencies of the state sector and their funding by bank credit was undermining financial equilibrium in the economy. Thirdly, the state and planned part of the economy was losing its grip on the parallel or privately-owned economic activity – as shown by the decline in the official marketing of cash crops and the appearance of parallel markets characterised by speculation and rampant inflation.[61]

It followed in principle that the solutions to these problems was to secure greater efficiency in the state sector, to allow greater scope for the non-state sector and to permit a larger scope for the operation of market forces and price signals. The specific measures that were taken to implement these solutions naturally varied. Securing greater efficiency in the state sector was seen largely as a matter of discipline and decentralisation of decision-making. Discipline came to be seen increasingly as a function of management and control, to be achieved by means of incentives and professional training.[62] Decentralisation of decision-making took a number of forms, the most dramatic involving the dispersal of people round the country and the redeployment of senior cadres of the regime.[63] Other measures included giving greater powers to provincial governments and more autonomy to state farm managers.

The Central Committee report also emphasised the need to establish or re-establish functioning markets in rural areas. The role of the private sector in marketing was to be promoted. Prices were to be set to provide incomes for peasant producers and encourage investment. Rural terms of trade were to be used as a criterion in price setting. Controls were removed from a number of commodities, while those official prices that remained were sharply increased. Finally, resources were to be channelled to those who could produce most efficiently. Expansion of the state farm sector was to cease and that sector was to be 'consolidated'. Some

---

[61] See M. Mackintosh, 'Economic Policy Context and Adjustment Options in Mozambique', *Development and Change*, 17 (1986); M. Wuyts, 'Mozambique: Economic Management and Adjustment Policies' in D. Ghai (ed.), *The IMF and the South*, London, 1991, pp. 215-35.

[62] See Final Resolution, 3rd session of Central Committee, SWB ME 7627 B5/8, 26 April 1984.

[63] *Domingo*, 29 May 1983.

of the bigger state farms were broken up and their land distributed to private farmers. State structures were to provide much greater support for the non-state sectors.[64]

These internal measures were complemented by others seeking to ensure some degree of external equilibrium, both in relation to the capitalist world in general and to South Africa in particular. The country's immediate problem was the rescheduling of its debt: part of the price of this was joining the IMF/World Bank system. Mozambique attended the IMF as an observer in September 1983 and secured full membership in September 1984. Debt rescheduling was agreed in November 1984. A new investment law promised compensation for nationalisation and repatriation of profits.[65]

As noted, economic relations with South Africa constituted an important if secondary part of negotiations both before and after the Nkomati Accord. The Cahora Bassa dam, the port of Maputo and migrant labour continued to link the two countries, though all were easily subject to political manipulation. Clearly sharing the Department of Foreign Affairs perspective, South African state agencies made vigorous attempts to orchestrate some economic benefits for Mozambique. During 1984 there were high-level meetings dealing with trade credits, labour matters, tourism and fishing rights.[66] In some areas the South African state could directly offer rewards. In the field of labour a joint economic working group was set up which met in May and heard Mozambican demands for increased mine labour. Subsequently there were several meetings between Mozambican officials and the Chamber of Mines, in which the Mozambicans offered the removal of all restrictions on recruiting labour, including geographical scope and age. As a result the number of Mozambicans going to work in South African mines rose by about 12,000.[67] South Africa continued to express interest in Maputo port and to offer some funds for its rehabilitation. The government also encouraged private business to develop

---

[64] For some details on the effects of these measures in one important area see O. Roesch, 'Rural Mozambique since the Frelimo Party Fourth Congress: The situation in the Baixo Limpopo', *Review of African Political Economy*, 41 (September 1988), pp. 73-91.

[65] Text in *Notícias*, 23 August 1984.

[66] See Mozambique Information Office News Review, 43 (29 November 1984) for details. For useful commentary see Davies, *South African strategy towards Mozambique* and 'South African Strategy towards Mozambique since Nkomati', *Transformation*, 3 (1987), pp. 4-30.

[67] See, for example, meeting of labour delegations, November 1984, SWB ME/7794 B8-9.

relations with Mozambique. Business opinion was indeed initially enthusiastic (a large number of South African business people had attended the Nkomati ceremony). But, rhetoric aside, this interest was limited to certain sectors (trade, tourism) and even this was shortly to be choked off by the escalating conflict in Mozambique as it became clear that Nkomati was failing to produce the promised effects. The economic benefits of Nkomati proved to be as meagre as the political and military ones.

Given the country's appalling circumstances the imperatives of production at any price were apparent in these measures. But even in extreme circumstances politics never works in a conceptual vacuum, and the nature of the solutions proposed for the country's economic problems speaks volumes about Frelimo's Marxism. While much of the formal language of Marxism-Leninism was retained, its irrelevance now began to be clearly visible, as the method of implementation of many of the reforms suggested. CAIL, the largest state farm entity, 'was quietly dismantled...without a word appearing in the Mozambican press'.[68] It was announced that no new cooperatives would be formed, as they would take too long to produce results.[69] It is of course true that, 'although the Fourth Congress asserted that the agrarian question was the central issue confronting Mozambique at that time, the balance of class forces was never subjected to an analysis that could aid in formulating a socialist strategy', but this is because Frelimo had never had much use for such analysis.[70] And while doubtless there were disagreements within Frelimo between those who saw the new economic measures as a temporary retreat and those who saw them as a new departure and a way forward, these differences meant little in Marxist terms and had everything to do with competing visions of the way to catch up with progress. Thus the solutions proposed for the country's economic difficulties, namely the securing of greater efficiency in the state sector and allowing market forces greater room for manoeuvre – in themselves compatible with many kinds of political practice – betokened the begin-

---

[68] Fauvet, 'Alarming Decline means end of State Farm', *Africa Now,* January 1984; cf. Bowen, 'Let's Build Agricultural Producer Cooperatives', p. 157.

[69] Hanlon, *Revolution,* p. 118. For the collapse of cooperatives in Gaza see O. Roesch, 'Rural Mozambique since the Frelimo Party Fourth Congress: The Situation in the Baixo Limpopo', *Review of African Political Economy,* 41 (September 1988), pp. 73-91.

[70] Wuyts, *Money and Planning for Socialist Transition: The Mozambican Experience,* Aldershot, 1989, p. 69.

nings of a shift among the Frelimo leadership from a socialist to a liberal vision of modernity.

Back to the front?

Frelimo's dramatic shifts in its international and regional diplomacy, and to some extent its economic policies, did not signal a lack of political activity in the battle against Renamo. Politically there was a two-pronged response. On the one hand the state armed itself with a number of new penalties to deal with crime and public order offences. These included the death penalty for certain economic offences and the reintroduction of public flogging (abolished in 1975). Such penalties were first used in April 1983 when two black marketeers were sentenced to death.[71] Measures had already been taken to secure greater control over the movement of population by the implementation of systems of residents' cards, at first in Maputo (June 1982) and then in other major urban centres. On the other hand Frelimo also moved, if not towards the abandonment of the vanguard party concept, at least towards some of the old characteristics of a 'front' emphasising patriotic virtues rather than the 'class enemy'. It abandoned much of its '*marxisant*' truculence towards organised religion in the wake of a meeting with church leaders in December 1982, where demands were voiced for the restoration of church buildings, and the right to train religious personnel and to import or produce religious material.[72] In 1983, as requested by almost all the religious delegations to the meeting, a Department of Religious Affairs was created in the Ministry of Justice, removing such matters from the hands of militants. Further small symbolic concessions were made such as reinstating Christmas Day as 'Family Day'.[73] Also significant was the rehabilitation of collaborators and 'enemies of the revolution' (these included members of the ANP, PIDE, the special élite units of the Portuguese army and members of so-called puppet organisations) all of whom had hitherto been identified at workplaces as 'those who compromised with colonialism'. At the end of 1981 it was announced that these practices would cease and at a meeting called in May-June 1982 to which about 1,000 former collaborators were summoned they (as well as any others in the country) were

[71] *Indian Ocean Newsletter*, 9 April 1983.

[72] See *AIM Bulletin*, 78, supplement on meeting with representatives of religious organisations.

[73] Decree 11/82 Permanent Commission People's Assembly.

pardoned.[74] Simultaneously hundreds of people were released from re-education camps.

The primary purpose of Frelimo's 4th Congress was to integrate and legitimate these various shifts in policy and tactics. It had been delayed for a year, in part because of pressing diplomatic business but also because the leadership clearly considered that the party needed considerable revitalisation. 'Dynamising' the party was of course a perennial task, though by 1982 the organisation had perhaps reached new depths of lethargy.[75] In October 1982 the Central Committee noted massive inactivity among party branches within enterprises and the state sector.[76] There was thus a concentrated build-up to the 4th congress, within both the party and the country at large. After two sessions of the Central Committee Frelimo held its first national conference in mid-March.[77] This drew up the theses for the 4th Congress which were approved by the Central Committee in August and made the object of a national seminar in September.[78] Considerable efforts were made to publicise the theses, including members of the senior leadership holding meetings all over the country, with extensive media coverage. Attempts were made to inject a certain element of razzamatazz and fiesta to the proceedings, itself an indication of the degree to which Frelimo felt it had lost touch with 'the masses'. Within the rather severe limitations of Frelimo's notion of fun these included cultural events, tree-planting, a national voluntary work day and a fuel-saving day.[79] The OMM even organised a home improvement campaign.[80]

Although the main themes of the Congress had been prepared in advance and there was no doubt that they would be agreed, the discussion was remarkably open and critical. The leadership clearly sought to draw on the *poder popular* dimension of its political practice and to encourage criticism by 'the masses'. The Congress theses had foreshadowed such themes as 'mobilising' religious believers, drawing on the skills of the veterans of the armed struggle, penalising bad work, restoring commercial networks and praising

---

[74] *Tempo*, 609, 13 June 1982. For detailed (if rather fulsome) accounts see *Morning Star*, 29 June 1982, and *Zimbabwe Herald*, 25 August 1982.

[75] *Indian Ocean Newsletter*, October 1982; *Guardian*, 14 December 1982.

[76] *Tempo*, 626 (10 October 1982).

[77] *Tempo*, 598 (28 March 1982).

[78] For the text of the theses see *Tempo*, 624 (26 September 1982).

[79] See Frelimo *Relatorio sobre a Preparaçã do 4 Congresso*.

[80] For some politically correct remarks on this see *Guardian*, 24 September 1982.

small projects – in other words, generally emphasising the mobilisation of 'own resources' rather than the implementation of grand
plans. Congress delegates were encouraged from the platform to
be critical and many were. But the party retained the full litany
of 'Marxism-Leninism' (even in minor ways, for example the adoption of the term 'politburo' for the ruling party body), standardising
it with the Soviet bloc model. No substantial changes were made
in the party documents between the 3rd and 4th Congresses, and
it seems likely that the consensus among the leadership was that
only some tactical adjustments were necessary.

Following the Congress, and in response to criticisms that the
body was excessively dominated by officials, the Central Committee
was enlarged to include 130 members (though few of the original
members were removed) and sought to make the Party itself rather
more open. Many of the new members were veterans of the anti-
colonial struggle, not a few of whom had previously fallen foul
of Frelimo's periodic bouts of puritanism. These shifts in the party
were reinforced by reshuffles in state structures in line with the
need to deploy people more effectively and to decentralise. Several
senior figures (Dos Santos, Machungo, Chipande) were named
as provincial governors and many others were deployed to the
rural areas.[81] The imperatives were not only to increase production
but also to restore relationships with the peasantry. Public rhetoric
to the contrary, Frelimo could not but be aware that in some
areas of the country Renamo had met with at least sullen acquiescence rather than active opposition.

Revitalised to some extent, the Frelimo leadership saw no need
to slacken the military effort against Renamo. The Congress had
fully backed Frelimo's 'policy of peace', which included a new
offer of amnesty to Renamo. However, in the government reshuffle
that had followed the Congress, Machel had taken personal charge
of defence; although Chipande retained the title of minister, he
was named also as Governor of Cabo Delgado (the area least
affected by the Renamo insurgency).[82] During tours of Inhambane
and Gaza provinces Machel announced a stronger role for the
military, including newly-created positions of provincial military
governors. Part of the move to bring back the veterans was to
help in training local militias and defence units. There had been
a well-publicised hand-out of weapons to crowds in Maputo in

---

[81] For details see *Africa Economic Digest*, 3 June 1983; *Domingo*, 29 May 1983.
[82] *The Times*, 30 May 1983.

mid-1982. But much of this was rather symbolic – Renamo would not be defeated by old men clutching old guns.

Despite a determined government response in Manica province, Renamo had continued to expand its theatre of operations and to approach closer and closer to Maputo. It was operating in Gaza province by 1983, and succeeded in creating its own momentum in that drought-wracked year. Around the time of Nkomati, hundreds of Renamo guerrillas moved into Maputo province (some doubtless from military camps over the South African border), and refugees crossed into South Africa and Swaziland.[83] Road and rail transport came under attack in the south, especially after late 1985, which saw repeated attacks on the rail lines from Maputo to Swaziland and South Africa, and on the powerlines in Maputo Province.[84] But in Inhambane province the government forces successfully recaptured a string of Renamo bases during 1983-4 (perhaps they were no longer viable due to the drought and, later, to restrictions on SADF support activities post-Nkomati). Renamo's main base for all the southern provinces at Tome in Massinga district fell in August 1983. Yet the overall picture in the south was one of increasing disruption and insecurity.

What made the situation throughout the country increasingly uncertain, however, was intensification of the war in Zambézia, which stretched government forces and provided a springboard for Renamo expansion northwards. Renamo guerrillas first appeared here in late 1982. They launched attacks along the Malawi border at Milange and Morrumbala, pushed southwards to the north bank of the Zambezi and swept eastwards towards the coast. They halted 35 km. short of Quelimane, having destroyed tea and cotton plantations in their path.[85] Though this advance was subsequently checked, Renamo revived the Zambézia front in August 1983, capturing twenty-four Soviet technicians in the Morrua mining area. Shortly after the Nkomati Accord was signed Renamo succeeded in surrounding Nampula city and in cutting the Nacala rail line. In July 1984 it began operating in Cabo Delgado, and at the end of the year attacked Lichinga, capital of Niassa.[86] During 1985-6, it pushed deep into Zambézia, taking the sugar town of Luabo in the Zambezi valley in July 1985, destroying the sugar

[83] *Sunday Star*, 15 September 1985.

[84] *AIM Bulletin*, 115, February 1986.

[85] J. Legrand, 'Logique de guerre et dynamique de la violence en Zambézia, 1976-1991', *Politique Africaine*, 50 (June 1993), pp. 88-104.

[86] *Sunday Star*, 15 September 1985.

factory and holding the town for two months.[87] Sugar production (one of the few remaining export earners) was brought to a complete halt in the region on 9 January 1986, when Renamo took Marromeu (recaptured by the Zimbabweans on 26 January).[88] By February 1986 the agricultural marketing network in Milange district was completely wrecked.

There was therefore a military logic to Renamo's concentration on Zambézia, but the shift was also encouraged by Zimbabwean intervention just to the south. Limited numbers of Zimbabwean soldiers had moved into Mozambique in late 1982 to guard the Beira road/rail-line and also the Beira-Mutare oil pipeline, which carried almost all of Zimbabwe's petroleum imports.[89] During 1984 the ZNA was drawn in further by Renamo ambushes of trucks carrying essential maize supplies from Malawi to Zimbabwe along the highway crossing Tete province. Machel met Zimbabwe's President Mugabe in Harare on 11 June 1985 to discuss the worsening security situation and the possibility of military assistance; in August Mugabe announced in Parliament that preserving Zimbabwe's access to the sea through Mozambique was worth any price, even a commitment of '20,000-30,000 men'. Later that month about eleven ZNA battalions comprising more than 10,000 soldiers were committed to the area of Tete, Manica and Sofala. The ZNA offensive in 1985-6 included the use of paratroops and the capture of Renamo's Casa Banana headquarters at Gorongosa (twice).

Such offensives in Renamo's Sofala heartland probably provided the prime cause for Renamo's further concentration away northwards and towards the Malawi border, though this was also encouraged by the South African military in the run-up to, and following, the Nkomati Accord, since Malawi offered a route for continued SADF support. Yet the motivation for Malawi's involvement in the Renamo insurgency remains a puzzle, given the country's evident interest in the continued functioning of crucial communication corridors through Mozambique, something that was imperilled by Renamo action. It has been suggested that Malawi's relationship with anti-Frelimo forces dates back to the early 1960s, when it accommodated several of the nationalist groups that would coalesce into, and then break with, a radicalised

---

[87] *Domingo*, 2 August 1992.

[88] Anthony R. Tucker, 'South Africa's War in Mozambique', *Armed Forces*, June 1989.

[89] Following a high-level meeting between Machel and Mugabe. See *Indian Ocean Newsletter*, 23 October and 13 November 1982.

Frelimo.[90] One of the individuals associated with Renamo in the early Rhodesia-based days (or at least the radio station) was Jorge Jardim, known for his association with President Banda and the Malawi Congress Party which helped found the separatist Uniao Nacional Africana de Zambézia based in Blantyre, acting as a splinter group designed to counter Frelimo activities in northern Mozambique. This particular group may have reappeared after Mozambican independence in western Zambézia near the border, in the form of the group colloquially known as Africa Livre. Initially quite separate from Renamo, this was incorporated into the larger group in 1982. Furthermore, Orlando Cristina had also established close links with the Banda regime after some personal involvement in training the Malawi Young Pioneers.[91]

After 1981 Malawi became an important conduit for Renamo incursions into Zambézia and Niassa provinces, collaborating with forces whose targets for sabotage included the Cuamba-Entre Lagos section of the Nacala railway. The ambiguity of Malawi's stance arose precisely from the fact that Banda preferred to run with both the hare and the hounds, trying both to placate protagonists in the Mozambican war and to allow as much covert support for Renamo from Malawi as he could get away with without a strong reaction from Maputo. It was Malawi's continued turning of a blind eye to Renamo operations that precipitated the biggest crisis of late 1986 when in September Renamo units routed poorly supplied government positions, especially near Mutarara in the southeast corner of Tete province (site of the crucial rail bridge over the Zambezi) and the Zambézian town of Milange. During a short visit to Blantyre Machel, leading an almost entirely military delegation, and accompanied by Presidents Mugabe and Kaunda, threatened Malawi with the closure of its borders and even military attack if it did not cease supporting Renamo.[92] He accused Malawi at the highest level of direct participation in the destabilisation of Mozambique, blaming this on racial inferiority complexes though in other speeches he exonerated Banda personally.[93]

Through a series of leadership meetings during 1986, Frelimo struggled to redeploy its resources with something approaching desperation. A crisis session of the Politburo in March, lasting

[90] See D. Hedges, 'Apontamento sobre as relações entre Malawi e Moçambique 1961-1987', *Cadernos de Historia*, 6 (1987), pp. 5-28.

[91] Gunn, *Cuba and Mozambique*, 1987.

[92] MIO, *News Review*, 19 September 1986.

[93] *Tempo* 832, 21 September 1986.

some two weeks (also attended by first secretaries of provincial party structures), clearly foreshadowed changes that gradually emerged in the following months. In a formal statement the party leadership portrayed the key issue as the reassertion of the party over the state, though now in terms of efficiency rather than talking of rooting out a class enemy.[94] Concretely this led to the appointment of key figures in the leadership as 'super ministers' supervising groups of ministries. Thus Machungo took control of most economic ministries except agriculture, and Rebelo of all ideological and social spheres, while Chipande was restored as overlord of security and military matters.[95] There was a further reshuffle in April, though it amounted to little more than moving familiar faces round. An eight-day meeting of the Central Committee in July – followed by a special meting of the Politburo, the Standing Commission of the People's Assembly, the Council of Ministers, and the leaderships of the mass democratic organisations – led to the announcement of further changes. The long-recognised over-centralisation of the regime led to the appointment of a Prime Minister in July (Mario Machungo) to run the government while Machel 'concentrated his efforts on defence leadership'.[96] As result Machel surrendered the chairmanship of the Council of Ministers and of the People's Assembly.

At more or less the same time Frelimo's Central Committee announced its determination to proceed with new elections for all the People's Assemblies. The electoral process had been suspended for a total of four years on the grounds of the insecurity within the country due to the activities of Renamo, and given that the security situation in 1986 was the worst ever, it is reasonable to assume that the decision to hold elections was an attempt to restore confidence by demonstrating the government's presence on the ground and its ability to mobilise public support. It is likely too that it was intended to signal to Western countries that Frelimo had real support, especially to the United States, where a pro-Renamo lobby demanding free elections had gained influence. These elections saw a modest extension of democratic practice as conventionally defined. Provincial assemblies themselves were responsible for choosing deputies to the national legislature (whereas in 1977 the 'election' of deputies had been for a single

[94] Full text of communiqué in *Notícias*, 6 March 1986. English text: supplement to AIM, *Mozambique News*, 117.

[95] *Notícias*, 29 March 1986.

[96] Communiqué, 17 July 1986; SWB ME/8315/B7-8.

list of candidates chosen by the Frelimo Central Committee) and the secret ballot was to be used in the National Assembly poll, as well as at the provincial, urban and district levels. At the local level, choice of candidates continued to be conducted by show of hands, after the candidates had answered questions from electors at public meetings.

These gestures notwithstanding, events had moved far beyond Frelimo's ability to control or even to cleave to a socialist strategy of any kind. Despite a determined diplomacy and some military successes, Frelimo continued to lose its grip while Renamo expanded its operations: it temporarily recaptured the Gorongosa headquarters in February 1986 from the Mozambican troops garrisoned there, and had once more to be ousted by the Zimbabweans. In late September, thousands of Renamo guerrillas crossed over from Malawi into the Upper Zambezi valley, taking Zumbo, Milange and Mutarara – apparently pushed across the border by a rattled Malawian government.[97] The bridge at Tete city was the sole transport link across the Zambezi left intact.[98] Operating in groups of 350-600, Renamo within three weeks attacked the district capitals of Namarroi, Milange and Alto Molocue.[99] Towns throughout the central region fell and elections for the People's Assemblies in Tete and Zambézia provinces were badly disrupted. Then, to crown a traumatic year, in late October 1986 Samora Machel was killed when his aircraft crashed just inside South Africa. He was returning from a summit meeting of front-line leaders in Zambia which followed the confrontation with Banda the previous month. By the time of his death the country was virtually broken, sustained only by the imperatives of the contemporary world order and Renamo's inability to seize and hold major urban areas. How had this obscure organisation, once widely regarded as 'more than a nuisance, less than a threat',[100] been able to prostrate the country in less than four years?

---

[97] *Notícias*, 3 October 1986; *Observer*, 12 October 1986.

[98] Africa Watch, *Conspicuous Destruction*.

[99] MIO, *News Review*, 28 November 1986.

[100] A Western diplomat quoted in the *Financial Times*, 17 December 1980.

7

MOZAMBIQUE AT WAR WITH ITSELF

'We didn't realise how influential the traditional authorities were, even without formal power. ...We are obviously going to have to harmonize traditional beliefs with our political project. Otherwise, we are going against things that the vast majority of our people believe – we will be like foreigners in our own country. I think we are gathering the courage to say so aloud. We will have to restore some of the traditional structures that at the beginning of our independence we simply smashed, thinking that we were doing a good and important thing.'[1]

'Traditional spirit mediums and diviners, sometimes Ndau but more often local specialists, also play a pivotal role in regulating daily life on Renamo bases. No major decisions,...are ever undertaken without a prior consultation with the spirits.[...] Diviners and spirit mediums are also kept busy magically protecting Renamo bases, making them invisible to Frelimo soldiers, 'vaccinating' Renamo combatants to make them bullet-proof, identifying witches amongst the civilian population and captives contemplating flight. All residents on Renamo bases are obliged to participate on a regular basis in such religious ceremonies – ceremonies in which the ancestral spirits ideologically legitimate Renamo's war against Frelimo.'[2]

As we have shown, Frelimo understood its war of liberation as part of a process of building a nation out of diverse groups kept separated and divided by colonialism. Although the anti-colonial revolts of the nineteenth and early twentieth centuries (and even the earlier pre-colonial wars) marked the beginnings of drawing together some of the ethnic and regional threads, even if in temporary and geographically limited alliances against the enemy, Portuguese colonialism finally triumphed because Mozambicans

[1] Luis Honwana, one-time Minister of Culture, quoted in Finnegan, *A Complicated War*, p. 125.

[2] Otto Roesch, 'Renamo and the Peasantry in Southern Mozambique: A view from Gaza Province', *Canadian Journal of African Studies*, 26 March (1992), pp. 472-3.

had failed to unite. Frelimo's armed struggle had overcome these divisions, thereby providing a base for the construction of the new nation. As the political process became more radicalised, a second theme of social progress was added to national freedom. 'Liberation' came also to mean, negatively, the defeat of 'feudalism' as incarnated by Nkavandame and the social strata he represented; positively, it meant the prospect of both development and social emancipation. For a considerable period these political beliefs shaped Frelimo's understanding of Renamo's war: as little more than an attack on Frelimo's nation-building and development project. This was an attack, moreover, largely if not wholly directed by hostile external forces, utilising Mozambican collaborators, either former stooges of the colonial regime or Frelimo's own traitors and defectors. This combination of elements in turn accounted for Renamo's tactics, especially the extreme violence visited on civilians along with the deliberate destruction of development projects and the economic infrastructure.

This account of Renamo as a violent apolitical movement whose only rationale must be that it operated on behalf of some malevolent outside interests was assiduously cultivated by the Mozambican government and its academic and journalistic publicists with considerable skill and success.[3] Nor was it wholly false. Renamo's persistent assaults on the transport infrastructure serving Mozambique's neighbour states was the most unambiguously South African-inspired aspect of Renamo's war. It directly damaged the Mozambican economy as well as further internationalising the conflict by drawing in other actors in defence of their own interests. The destruction of the development infrastructure and the national transportation network was also, in part at least, clearly inspired by South African destabilisation strategies.[4] South African support for Renamo, while often exaggerated, remained important. The organisation was not afforded substantial rear-base or sanctuary facilities inside South Africa, and although re-supply continued by devious routes after the Nkomati Accord (the need for restraint and subterfuge having become paramount), the South African military pursued a 'minimalist' strategy of ensuring Renamo's survival by providing intelligence

---

[3] For some discussions of this aspect see T. Young, 'From MNR to Renamo: Making Sense of an African Counter-Revolutionary Movement' in P. Rich (ed.), *The Dynamics of Change in Southern Africa*.

[4] See especially P. Johnson and D. Martin, *Apartheid terrorism: The destabilization report*, for the Commonwealth Committee of Foreign Ministers on Southern Africa, London, 1989.

and arms when it seemed in danger of defeat.[5] Thus re-supply was not lavish, and had to be supplemented by what Renamo managed to obtain by capture from the Mozambican army.

Waging war

The niggardliness of suppliers and the absence of a secure rear sanctuary meant that the war remained one fought at a low level of military technology, and that Renamo had to adapt to living off the land – in practice off the peasantry. The main weapon on both sides was the AK-47 assault rifle. Renamo also habitually employed knives and machetes, especially in the north and centre of the country, but it also had an ill-assorted array of weaponry as well as a few SAM-7s, which the group was unable to operate.[6] But the low level of military technology favoured mobility and guerrilla tactics over conventional forces; and although areas of established Renamo operation certainly existed, bases within them usually remained mobile, although perhaps less so in Zambézia than elsewhere. Even the largest and most important bases, including Dhlakama's headquarters (normally situated in or near the Gorongosa), shifted periodically in response to the threat or reality of government or Zimbabwean assaults. Renamo had the ability to concentrate forces for offensives, but was not equipped for anything beyond hit-and-run tactics and sabotage on a sustained basis. Thus persistent destruction of the development infrastructure and anything representative of the Frelimo state continued to guide its day-to-day operations.

These particular features of its military situation (including, as we have suggested, Renamo's need to extend its theatre of operations extremely widely, and extremely fast, throughout Mozambique), in part account for the widespread intentional use of extreme violence against civilian populations.[7] The 'Gersony Report' found

---

[5] Unorthodox methods and ivory smuggling were resorted to. See A. Vines, 'Change and the Military in Mozambique', paper given at a US Defense Intelligence College Conference on Change and the Military in Africa, Alconbury, England, 6-7 May 1993. On DMI/Renamo involvement in poaching and the illegal ivory trade, see 'Under Fire: Elephants in the Front Line', a Environmental Investigation Agency, London, 1992. See also the claims of Colonel Jan Breytenbach, *Observer*, 18 April, 1993.

[6] Moorcraft, *African Nemesis*, p. 280.

[7] Renamo has periodically argued that atrocities attributed to it were part of a propaganda campaign organised by President Chissano. But such atrocities had

that by far the most important reason for the massive increase in Mozambican refugee numbers in neighbouring countries was the violence perpetrated by Renamo. The author of this report assessed that Renamo had been directly responsible for at least 100,000 civilian deaths, as well as for systematic and coordinated violence against civilians in all parts of the country. He observed:

> The level of violence reported to be conducted by Renamo against the civilian population of rural Mozambique is extraordinarily high. That the accounts are so strikingly similar by refugees who have fled from northern, central and southern Mozambique suggests that the violence is systematic and coordinated and not a series of spontaneous, isolated incidents by undisciplined combatants.[8]

Among the implications of Gersony's findings were that Renamo found it necessary to extract food and labour from the peasantry on the spot, while trying to prevent the escape of manpower from areas under its control, and that it used the toughest of methods to do so. Gersony identified three notional areas of Renamo operation: in ascending order of oppression, these were 'tax', 'control' and 'destruction' zones. The last category is self-explanatory. 'Control' areas near Renamo bases experienced extreme degrees of forced labour, especially involving porterage duties, and other abuses. The inhabitants of the more sparsely populated 'tax' areas escaped more lightly.

While it may be that Gersony's three-zone typology creates the impression of something closer to the Khmer Rouge system of slave camps in Cambodia in the 1970s and 1980s than to the more haphazard and far less fanatically ordered African reality, its broad outline remains plausible.[9] Despite the conventional wis-

---

been reported from a much earlier date (see *The Herald*, 15 June 1982), and in the press of countries not notably hostile (e.g. *Malawi News*, 27 May-2 June 1989).

[8] Robert Gersony, *Summary of Mozambican Refugee Accounts of Principally Conflict-related Experience in Mozambique*, Washington, DC: Department of State, Bureau for Refugee Programs, 1988, p. 25. The findings were based on 196 individual interviews with refugees in twenty-five locations, in five countries. The author, Robert Gersony, was an experienced academic who had previously conducted refugee surveys for the State Department.

[9] Finnegan, *A Complicated War*, p. 80; although certain deficiencies of methodology have been highlighted – e.g. Gersony's acceptance that interviewees spoke entirely freely when they attributed 94% of all murders to Renamo and only 3% to Frelimo. Gersony may have been naive in this because, e.g., in Zimbabwe refugee opinion was monitored by the authorities for evidence of pro-Renamo sympathies which might identify Renamo infiltrators, and to this extent refugees there may well have

dom about guerrilla movements, extreme brutality appears to have
played a part in Renamo's rapid spread throughout Mozambique
after 1980 (even if it later proved counter-productive in the attempt
to achieve international support and recognition).[10] This violence
had two purposes. The first and more significant was the attack
on the Frelimo state. Government and party officials were the
priority targets here. In rural areas their physical elimination served
to isolate communities and remove them from the authority of
the central power, and it thus complemented the destruction of
the economic infrastructure and the severing of communications.
Essentially, it worked to disarticulate the state. Secondly, violence
was exemplary, intended 'to instill a paralysing and incapacitating
fear into the wider population...by conjuring a vision of inhumanity
and maniacal devotion to the infliction of suffering, that sets them
outside of the realm of social beings and hence beyond social
control and even resistance'.[11]

K.B. Wilson imputed to Renamo a 'cult of violence' distinguished
from other violent activity naturally associated with warfare by
ritualistic elements which the perpetrators believed imbued the
activity with value or power. He distinguished between Renamo's
numerous massacres, especially in the south, where large numbers
were despatched in order to destroy local morale, and killings
with ritualistic or symbolic elements. The numbers involved in
what he termed 'ritualised violence' designed to terrify and impress
need not be great, as his own researches in Zambézia suggested,
but the spectacle of gruesome public killings was designed to have
psychological impact over a wide area. Within rural communities
isolated and reordered to support a semi-permanent Renamo
presence, exemplary killings served to cow the population and
maintain control. The effect of this violence may have been to
induce passivity and a sense of fear, anxiety and helplessness.[12]

The argument that the violence directed against civilians was

---

learned to be self-censoring in their comments.

[10] We remain sceptical about the degree to which, as Clarence-Smith puts it, 'it
seems axiomatic that a guerrilla force has to be "like a fish in the water"' (correspondence in the *Southern African Review of Books*, June/July 1989, p. 22). Dhlakama
himself has occasionally invoked this metaphor: see *Die Welt*, 6 January 1989.

[11] K.B. Wilson, 'Cults of Violence and Counter-Violence in Mozambique', *Journal
of Southern African Studies*, 18, 3 (September 1992), pp. 527-82.

[12] An impressionistic report on both sides of the line, published in *Der Spiegel*,
47/87, tends to suggest this in Renamo-held Mozambique. See also Cole P. Dodge
and Magne Raundalen, *Reaching Children in War: Sudan, Uganda and Mozambique*,
Bergen, 1991.

indeed purposeful and instrumental was supported by in an apparent lessening of such activity in areas where the local Frelimo influence and presence had been eliminated and Renamo was relatively well established. Such situations did prevail in central and northern Mozambique in some localities and certainly where some base of popular support existed, grounded in ethnic or regional factors. In the Gorongosa region there was reasonably good and cooperative coexistence with the civilian population and little apparent fear.[13] The Renamo presence in Zambézia seemed at this time to have been less brutal and better organised than its first arrival in the area had been.[14] But in southern Mozambique, where Frelimo had a strong base, and where by virtue of the numbers involved the elimination of its supporters could not be achieved by simply picking off a handful of local party officials, there was a significantly high incidence of atrocities.[15] This probably also explains why it was above all in the south where Renamo resorted to the widespread use of child-soldiers.

Induction into Renamo's own ranks was also draconian, perhaps reflecting its Rhodesian and South Africa training during the organisation's formative period. Forced recruitment was widespread, certainly from the early 1980s onwards.[16] A variety of control mechanisms deterred escape; principal among these was the fear of execution, while the practice of transferring captives away from their home area was also significant. Recruits were kept in separate training bases attached to, but not integrated with, operational bases, and underwent two or three months' military instruction. In certain cases the harshness of the treatment meted out to new recruits was in itself a disincentive to volunteer. Renamo's recruitment process in Nampula province centred on incarcerating all recruits, whether volunteer or captives, in a cage or chicken coop, called a *jaula*, for long periods during which they were subjected

---

[13] Nicholas della Casa, held by Renamo for eighteen months, mainly in Gorongosa, and released at the end of 1988, likened the local civilian attitude to Renamo to that of Dorset villagers towards NATO troops in their area – some grumbling, but no real complaints. *Sunday Telegraph*, 18 December 1988.

[14] *Guardian*, 6 October 1982.

[15] Lina Magaia's harrowing collection of tales of atrocities is set in southern Mozambique although her Introduction is at pains to point out that atrocities had occurred throughout the country. Lina Magaia, *Dumba Nengue: Run for Your Life*, Trenton, NJ, 1988.

[16] W. Minter, 'The Mozambican National Resistance (RENAMO) as described by ex-participants', Washington, DC, 1989, puts it at over 90%.

to various forms of deprivation and trauma in order to break them psychologically before formal military training began.[17]

Alongside harsh internal discipline and forced recruitment, however, some foreign captives held at Renamo bases observed high morale, and although many recruits were press-ganged, others appeared to have joined voluntarily out of boredom or because of hunger and poverty.[18] Even when recruits were originally press-ganged, the excitement they experienced – compared to the dull, impoverished life in the countryside – was enough to induce some to stay willingly.[19] While most recruitment in Gaza province, where Renamo had no natural base, was forced (including the recruitment of children), there was also some voluntary enlistment on the part of marginalised youths. Despite the harshness and danger of life in Renamo ranks, it held the attractions of excitement and access to luxury items and women, as well as providing a means for settling old scores with neighbours and local authorities in their home areas.[20]

Violence seems to have been a crucial rite of passage for forced recruits. John Burlison, held prisoner by Renamo for several months in 1982, reported seeing hundreds of recruits kept under armed guard until they committed their first attacks, after which they were warned that if they fled and were captured by government troops, they would be executed as terrorists.[21] There are reports of Renamo recruits who were compelled to kill fellow villagers or even relatives, to bind them to the movement through guilt and fear of retribution, and plentiful evidence exists of the gradual induction of children into the art of slaughter (by killing first animals and then people). The more extreme acts of exemplary violence, especially those involving young guerrillas, were clearly used as part of a battle-hardening technique.[22] Renamo's young peasant abductees in Inhambane province were initially ill-treated, humiliated and beaten, and then exposed to short periods of kindness and understanding, as an inducement to wholehearted involvement in training and then participation in Renamo's military

---

[17] Roesch, correspondence in the *Southern African Review of Books*, December 1989/ January 1990.

[18] Moorcraft, 'Mozambique's long civil war' *International Defense Review*, October 1987, pp. 1313-16.

[19] Hanlon, *Revolution*, p. 229.

[20] Otto Roesch, 'Renamo and the Peasantry', p. 478.

[21] Cited by Allen Isaacman in his preface to Magaia, *Dumba Nengue*, p. 12.

[22] Finnegan, *A Complicated War*, pp. 25-6.

activities. Those who could not stand this treatment sought to run away, sooner or later, despite the dangers if they were caught. (Among a group of forty-eight former Renamo recruits the average period spent as an active guerrilla before escape was found to be a surprisingly short twelve months.)[23] In practice, reliance on such methods as these was dictated by the size of Renamo's field of operations, and the narrowness of its support base. In the absence of any rewards in the leadership's gift – other than the guerrillas' access to a gun, loot and a relatively well-organised system of first aid – violence was probably the most effective and cheapest means of obtaining obedience both within the ranks and outside them.[24]

None of this, of course, precluded the existence of semi-formal military structures. Indeed until the late 1980s Renamo arguably remained an almost purely military organisation; there were few attempts at building political structures in Renamo-held areas, or at political teaching within the military itself, save for rare instances of political commissars (in Tete and Manica) who had gone through a course of Frelimo political education.[25] The reality was that Renamo retained all the features of an army. In 1985 Renamo's then secretary-general, Evo Fernandes, described a fairly conventional military structure:

'We have the President, Afonso Dhlakama, who is also commander in chief. Then we have generals. The generals have military commanders under them. The regional commanders have sector commanders. The sector commanders have zone commanders under them. Then there are battalions and platoons and so on.'[26]

A somewhat later version was more elaborate: Renamo's military council was said to consist of fifteen generals: three chiefs of staff, ten provincial commanders, and Afonso Dhlakama's personal staff. The chiefs of staff were in command in three operational areas: north (from the Rovuma to the Zambezi rivers); centre (the Zambezi to the Sabié rivers); and the south (from the Sabié river to the South African border). The ten generals, each in command

---

[23] Anders Nilsson, 'From Pseudo-Terrorists to Pseudo-Guerrillas: the MNR in Mozambique', *Review of African Political Economy*, 58 (1993), pp. 35-42.

[24] The point about economy is made in the Introduction to D. Riches (ed.), *The Anthropology of Violence*, Oxford, 1986.

[25] Georgi Derlugyan, 'Mozambique: a tight knot of problems', *International Affairs* 3, (March 1990), pp. 103-11.

[26] Interview in *Defense and Diplomacy*, 3 September 1985.

of all the forces deployed in any one province, were all technically subordinate to the chiefs of staff in their respective operational areas. Below this level the organisation became less clear.[27] Renamo statutes merely stipulated the existence of a military council comprising regional commanders and military service directors, which assisted the commander-in-chief in military issues. A slightly different version of the military hierarchy published in mid-1986 spoke of twelve generals (one for each province and two from Dhlakama's general staff), plus the operational commanders.[28]

This army had an effective system of command and control under strict military discipline based upon a formal rank structure.[29] A German hostage held at a Renamo base for a month in 1986 noted that the officers sat according to rank in the officers' hut at the centre of the village. They adhered to a rigid military etiquette, asking permission of their superiors before every stage in the proceedings: entering the hut, washing, drinking water, serving, smoking and leaving the table. Rank was colour-coded. The 'general' in command of the 200-strong Angónia company (part of the Matenje regiment) wore a dark red necklace as an insignia of rank. The platoon leaders beneath him, each in charge of forty to fifty men, wore blue cravats on duty and signalled their authority by the use of whistles. Group leaders commanding twelve to fifteen men wore pink cravats and, like their platoon leaders, used whistles for issuing orders. Leaders of specialist units (radio operators, mine-layers or grenade-throwers) had yellow cravats.[30]

Renamo also possessed an efficient radio communications system (superior to that of the Mozambican army), donated by the South Africans, which played an important part in its mobility and effectiveness as a guerrilla force. This gave it the ability to mass large numbers of small units for attacks and to disperse them rapidly for strategic retreats.[31] This military hierarchy and centralised coordination coexisted with regional variations in tactics. Child guerrillas were active with Renamo units in the south but not in the north. In some parts of the country, small Renamo

[27] André Thomashausen, 'The Mozambican National Resistance Movement'.

[28] *Africa Confidencial*, 9 (June 1986).

[29] Minter, 'The Mozambican National Resistance' and Paul Moorcraft, 'Mozambique's long civil war'.

[30] N. Baron, 'The Struggle Continues: Diary of a Kidnapping in Mozambique by Robert Rosskamp: An Analysis' in A. Vines and K.B. Wilson (eds), *War in Mozambique: Local Perspectives* (forthcoming).

[31] Finnegan, *A Complicated War*, p. 58; Alex Vines, *Renamo: From Terrorism to Democracy in Mozambique?*, London, rev. edn, 1996, p. 82-3.

gangs engaged in hit-and-run tactics, while in Zambézia in particular they operated at battalion strength, taking towns and holding the areas around them for substantial periods, although evacuating the town itself. Their communications network allowed for this regional variation within an overall coherence of military strategy and purpose. It made possible a change in tactics in most areas, moving towards smaller and more mobile bases. This followed the loss of Casa Banana in the latter part of 1986, a decrease in logistical aid reaching Renamo from South Africa, and the loss of Malawi sanctuaries.[32] The radio net linked Renamo's shifting headquarters in central Mozambique to subordinate bases throughout the country (though smaller outposts might still need to rely on runners or motorcycle messengers).

A final characteristic of its military organisation which gave Renamo organisational coherence was the domination of its military leadership by Shona-speakers from central Mozambique, especially the Ndau subgroup to which Dhlakama himself belongs.[33] This appears to have been not a matter of policy but an accident of the organisation's own history and early operations out of Rhodesia and into Manica and Sofala provinces, although it may also have been an effect of the leadership struggle following the death of André Matsangaíssa in 1978.[34] At the middle levels the picture is mixed, with significant regional variation. In Zambézia almost all the officers were local. In general, however, a large majority of the military commanders were Shona-speaking 'veterans', although the rank and file include men from all ethnic groups.[35] This held good for most parts of Mozambique. In Nampula in the late 1980s, those of sergeant-major level and below in Renamo were said to be local Macua who had been captured, while those of officer rank above them were all Ndau from central Mozambique.[36] Doubtless this reflected both Renamo's recent rapid spread throughout Mozambique and its practice of compulsory local recruitment. In

[32] Vines, *Renamo*, p. 86; Zambézia was the exception.

[33] Mozambique's 1980 census results for home language by province suggests Shona-speakers form only about 8-9% of the total population, the great majority being in Manica and Sofala provinces. The Ndau are the largest Shona-speaking group inside Mozambique and, like the Manyika, straddle the border with Zimbabwe, where they form an estimated 6% of the much larger Shona population of that country.

[34] Roesch, 'Renamo and the Peasantry in Southern Mozambique'. See also Vines, *Renamo*, pp. 83-5.

[35] Minter, 'The Mozambican National Resistance', p. 12.

[36] Information given in interview.

one area of Gaza province, for instance, the composition of Renamo bands reportedly changed over the years – by the end of the 1980s many of the troops were local but the commanders were still all Ndau-speakers from further north.[37] Yet some battalions were known to be all-Ndau, such as the crack Grupa Limpa, which was used to spearhead offensives and attracted a reputation for toughness and effectiveness.[38]

Even at the topmost level of the command pyramid there were non-Ndau who had risen through ability; for example Raul Domingos, a Sena from Zambézia who was southern commander before promotion to Foreign Affairs Secretary, and then Secretary for Organisation. There appears to have been no ethnic bar to such internal promotion. There is, however, a sense in which the Ndau set their stamp on Renamo's military, with others required to adapt or acculturate to their pattern. Accusations were made of Shona linguistic hegemony. Constantino Reis claimed that his problems at Gorongosa headquarters arose 'because I didn't speak Ndau, only Shangaan. And when I spoke Portuguese, they said I was showing contempt for the national languages.'[39] Conversely, Minter observes from his interviews that while the majority of Renamo commanders were Shona-speakers, the language used in any particular Renamo unit depended on the ratio of different ethnic groups represented in its ranks.[40] However, Ndau does seem to have developed as Renamo's military lingua franca and the language of its radio communications. Renamo even made reference to 'initiation schools' at which both military skills and the Ndau language were taught to specialist grades, such as radio operators, and those destined for promotion into the officer corps. That such linguistic training was overlaid with supernatural associations – initiates acquiring power from learning the 'language of the spirits' – did little to make the Renamo military less opaque to outsiders.[41] In Gaza province, not only were the Ndau dominant at both officer and rank-and-file level in the Renamo military, but

---

[37] Finnegan, *A Complicated War*, p. 210.

[38] Vines, *Renamo*, p. 85. Cf. Jovito Nunes, 'Peasants and Survival: The social consequences of displacement – Mocuba, Zambezia', draft paper, April 1992.

[39] Interview, *AIM Bulletin* supplement, January 1985.

[40] He also observes that only interviewees from central Mozambique differentiate between Shona dialects, the tendency elsewhere being to lump all Shona-speakers together as 'Ndau'. See also Vines, *Renamo*, pp. 83-5.

[41] See Alex Vines, 'Diary', *Southern African Review of Books*, 4, 4 and 5, issue 20/21, (July/October 1991).

Renamo was widely perceived to be a Ndau political project.[42]

The war of the spirits

Despite occasional references to health, education and economic officials, Renamo appears to have lacked a comprehensive system of direct administration for civilian areas. However, it did make efforts where possible to provide some basic services – establishing schools, for example, as well as destroying them, notably in Manica, Sofala and Zambézia provinces. Evidence for these and for the medical treatment of civilians by Renamo male nurses and first-aid orderlies appears to have come especially from the Gorongosa region.[43] Apart from a vestigial provision of education and health care, Renamo generally relied on a system of indirect administration. A significant Renamo-eye view of the guerrilla-civilian relationship was provided by Secretary-General Fernandes in 1985:

> Administration doesn't have anything to do with the military. We are based on the traditional system: the administrative system depends on the area the chieftain has. There are the lower chieftains, but we also have what we call *mujeebas.* [...] What happens then if a military unit needs new bases? We ask the chieftains where we can settle a base in their area. Then they say such and such a place is better because there is water there, and a nice, thick forest. The *mujeeba* is our representative at the village level. He knows everybody in his village. Nobody can come without being known. Then nobody also can betray us because he surveys the area. He has a weapon – not an automatic weapon but a Mauser or something...these chieftains, if they don't live too far away from military units, are in mobile connection with us because they are involved in some military activities. For instance, if we need to haul captured ammunition from a cache, we call people to come and carry it. And we have specific bases only for receiving food from the people. They come to give it to us every time, and nobody forces them.[44]

This form of indirect rule allowed for alliances to be struck with local representatives of traditional power, and provided the basis

---

[42] Roesch, 'Renamo and the Peasantry', p. 469.

[43] Minter, 'The Mozambican National Resistance', p. 8. Constantino Reis, for example, helped to build a primary school in Gorongosa in 1983 and taught there for several months.

[44] In *Defense and Diplomacy*, 3 September 1985.

for elements of a cultural revival. It was well adapted to the mobility of guerrilla war, so that once forced to shift base, a Renamo company or platoon could remake its previous relationship with a new civilian population. It was also simple and effective, ensuring local provision of food and labour by the simple expedient of using and resuscitating the very traditional mechanisms which Frelimo had been trying, often ineffectually, to suppress. *Mujibas* (usually young civilian collaborators of the guerrillas, who provided auxiliary services) were appointed to police the system and formed an effective spy and surveillance network.[45] They existed as part of a usually strict social and spatial division between Renamo military structures and the civilian population. Normally this was expressed in the layout of the base. In the case of the highly mobile Renamo camps in Gaza, which depended on a semi-military life of pillage and for sustenance on bovine meat, it was defined rather by means of a rigid physical and hierarchical allotment of separate areas for combatants, and civilian living and sleeping quarters.[46]

At the Renamo base at Mariri in Nampula the civilian-military relationship was rigidly compartmentalised.[47] The only civilians to be found inside its confines were actually imprisoned there (wives and child-servants of soldiers), or else were temporary captives (male recruits taken locally and held pending intensive military training and transfer to another base elsewhere, often hundreds of kilometres away). Any contact between soldiers at the base and the civilian world outside (including the chiefs) was effected at the control-post on its periphery. Within its confines all important military infrastructures (such as the armoury) were situated at the core, near the huts of the officers and within what – figuratively speaking – seems to have been a series of concentric circles of increasing authority and power whose secrets were guarded against outsiders (*mujibas*, for example, were completely excluded from the base). Near the centre, too, was the radio transmission point, which permitted officers to communicate with the national headquarters in Gorongosa, 1,000 km. away, as well as with each other when out on operation in the bush.

Right up till the 1990s Renamo was widely described as crudely anti-Communist and anti-Frelimo, with no political programme as such. It has already been suggested that the 'ideology' Renamo

---

[45] *Mujibas* were a feature of ZANLA's campaign in Zimbabwe, and appear to have been copied by Renamo from them. The word itself was first coined by ZANLA.

[46] Roesch, 'Renamo and the Peasantry', p. 471.

[47] Christian Geffray, *La Cause des Armes au Mozambique*, Paris, 1990.

presented to the outside world was very much for international consumption. However, the remarkable tenacity and expansion of the organisation have to be explained, and the difficulties involved in doing this are compounded by analytical assumptions that all Western observers tend to make that politics presupposes programmes, ideological beliefs, calculations of political support from different kinds of groups and so on – so that, in the absence of these, what does exist must be 'social banditry' or 'destabilisation' inspired by 'traditional animist superstition [which] has replaced political mobilisation'.[48] Yet Renamo's widely reported practice of consulting the local land chief before setting up a new base, in order to obtain the support of the legitimate owners of the land (that chief's ancestral spirits), can surely be seen as a political statement of sorts, albeit one couched in symbolic language that is obscure to outsiders.

The elaboration of a symbolic language drawing on religious idioms seems largely to have occupied the space left void by the dearth of Renamo policies as such. Elsewhere in Africa, peasant concerns have often been channelled into a religious idiom. Traditional forms of belief particularly lend themselves to protest in this form, because of the usually strong association between the spiritual realm and the land. It was therefore natural that Renamo's peasant-soldiers should articulate grievances related to forced villagisation in this mode. This accompanied the destruction of communal villages and the slaughter of Frelimo officials running them, while the evacuation of their inhabitants to their former more dispersed settlements, under the restored authority of chiefs, brought the civilian population into Renamo's system of indirect rule. But this seems also to have gone hand in hand with enormous religious eclecticism and an exaggerated respect paid to the outward symbols of religious observance. The local church or mosque was often the only building left undamaged in a Renamo attack on a settlement.[49] Captives of Renamo and other observers have remarked on their habit of carrying bibles, and their approving and enthusiastic attitude to religion – any religion, it sometimes appears. At one large base, 'religion was much in evidence: pictures of Jesus, bibles in huts, an Islamic mosque, and churches for Ethiopian Copts, Seventh Day Adventists and Catholics.'[50] The

[48] Paul Fauvet and Alves Gomes, 'The Mozambique National Resistance'.

[49] *Tempo* 947, 4 December 1988, p. 29.

[50] J. Wheeler, 'From Rovuma to Maputo: Mozambique's guerrilla war', *Reason*, December 1985. An ostentatious display of bibles may well have impressed certain missionary sects who assisted Renamo. See, for example, *Southscan*, 4, 34 (15 Sep-

most intimate connection, however, seems to have been with traditional systems of belief, although Renamo bases also hosted religious
healers from African Christian churches, especially Zionists, who
like their non-Christian colleagues practise spirit possession and
exorcism and had been subject to state repression for this reason.[51]

It seems clear that some local chiefs as well as traditional healers
and magicians provided support for Renamo, at least in some
parts of the county.[52] Disgruntled traditional healers, who retained
their status and importance for the peasantry, proved an ideologically compatible instrument for Renamo in fostering its insurgency.[53] In the Shona-speaking areas of central Mozambique where
Renamo originally operated and recruited, spirit mediums are of
social and potentially also political importance, as they are in neighbouring Zimbabwe. Some have certainly been associated with
Renamo bases in Manica and Sofala – at Casa Banana, for example,
and at other bases in the Gorongosa area. Renamo's first military
commander, André Matsangaíssa, died in late 1979 in an attempt
to retake Gorongosa town, having been assured of victory by a
spirit medium.[54] Ranger suggests there were residual elements of
organisational methods based by Renamo's early Rhodesian tutors
on those used by ZANLA:

> Interpreting the most recent evidence on Mozambique some-
> what freely one can construct the following picture. The MNR
> was begun by the Rhodesians as an ironic tribute to ZANLA; it
> was taught by its Rhodesian mentors to operate like ZANLA; to
> sing *chimurenga* songs; to make use of spirit mediums. It was sent
> in first of all to Shona-speaking areas in Mozambique and was
> provided with gifts to win over the people, whom it was taught to
> seek to persuade rather than to terrorise. Of course, since then
> the MNR has lost its Rhodesian and gained South African back-
> ers; it has spread far beyond the Shona zones of Mozambique;
> and it has notoriously had recourse to appalling terror. Neverthe-
> less, there remain traces of that parody ZANLA origin.[55]

Renamo of necessity drew on religious idioms outside of Shona

tember 1989), pp. 262-3.

[51] Roesch, 'Renamo and the Peasantry', pp. 473-4.

[52] Minter, 'The Mozambican National Resistance', p. 8.

[53] Roesch, 'Renamo and the Peasantry', p. 475.

[54] *Tempo* 780, 22 September 1985.

[55] T.O. Ranger, 'The meaning of violence in Zimbabwe', paper delivered at a
conference in Cambridge on violence and decolonisation in Africa, April 1991.

culture, and sought to adapt itself to local practices. Indeed, the proportion of Shona-speakers in the Mozambican population is so small, and Renamo's geographical spread was so wide, that it could hardly do otherwise. Yet Renamo is known to have carried with it elements from the belief systems of central Mozambique, which it introduced into new areas of military expansion. The protective presence of 'lion' spirits to accompany and guard Renamo soldiers has, for example, been claimed by Renamo members themselves in some fairly remote and unlikely places.[56] In parts of Zambézia and northern Tete, Renamo tried to extend the role of 'lion spirit' mediums of Shona conception into non-Shona areas through a systematic hierarchy of mediums attached to its bases. One such medium (a Ndau brought in from central Mozambique) at the important Maqueringa base of northern Zambézia during the 1985-90 period, on the one hand, received regular instructions and medicaments from the provincial base of Alfa Zema; on the other, he interacted with local religious powers by displaying an essentially Zambézian pattern of possession and holding rituals in a local graveyard.[57] In Tete, Renamo detachments operating in the valley of the Zambezi typically practised traditional local cults, while Renamo political commissars in southern Tete and in Manica existed alongside much more numerous 'witch doctors and sorcerers who have their strong psychological influence on the rank-and-file'.[58]

There were also military advantages in the reputations that Renamo fighters, and especially the Ndau, had for supernatural powers. Renamo recruits in Tete adopted Ndau as their language of communication, linking it with a popular belief in such powers, and particularly that the Ndau had special powers of vengeance after death.[59] The language implicitly derived symbolic power from this belief, so that in drawing on this existing resource Renamo may have been able to reinforce what Wilson would term the 'cultic' aspects of violence. Ndau has elsewhere been called 'the language of the spirits' by Renamo officials, and in southern Mozambique it is a language employed in exorcisms.[60] Finally, beneath

---

[56] See the *Southern African Review of Books*, July/October 1991, where in the 'Diary' Alex vines relates the claim by two Renamo representatives in Lisbon that Lion and Snake spirits protected them from the interference of Portuguese police.

[57] K.B. Wilson, 'Cults of Violence and Counter-Violence in Mozambique'.

[58] Derlugyan, 'Mozambique: A tight knot of problems'.

[59] Magaia, interview, *Race and Class*, 30 April 1989.

[60] See Alex Vines, 'Diary'.

the externally-oriented claims that Frelimo had betrayed and abandoned the political heritage of Eduardo Mondlane by adopting
un-Christian and un-African 'Communist' ways, it was common
on Renamo bases for the claim to be made that a 'war of the
spirits' was being waged by Renamo to return Mozambique to its
ancestral and traditional ways.

Explaining the conflict

These general features of the conflict in Mozambique made possible
a wide variety of local dynamics in different parts of the country
which still elude comprehensive analysis. In Érati district of Nampula province Frelimo policies, particularly villagisation, proved
alienating and divisive to the point where a number of local (Macua)
chiefs organised wholesale support for Renamo among sections
of peasant society when it entered the area in the mid-1980s. Local
Macua patterns of land tenure gave the advantage to the lineage
which controlled the land on which the communal village was
built, creating serious contradictions between different traditional
political and kinship groupings which Renamo was able to exploit.
As well as 'loser' lineages, alienated rural youths initially joined
in the war, made possible by the incursion of Renamo arms and
military organisation, with 'joy'.[61] Beyond the impact of communal
villages Frelimo's suppression of key Macua cultural and religious
practices, along with the marginalisation of traditional authorities,
had elicited considerable antagonism. Under Renamo's system of
indirect rule, traditional chiefs were able to return their followers
to something resembling their traditional way of life. Yet only
some populations in Érati rallied to Renamo, the pattern of pro-
and anti-government allegiances following pre-existing lines of conflict between historically opposed rival ethnic groupings. In the
no-man's land between the Macuane (who supported Renamo)
and the Érati (who clung to the protection of the government
forces) people did their best to survive by placating both sides.
And where Renamo had established itself, it did not develop into
anything resembling a political movement but, on the contrary,
remained a military machine largely reliant on capturing men
from Government-held areas for the recruitment of its soldiers.
Economically, it remained predatory towards the peasantry. Chiefs
played a key role, helping to recruit a corps of local police respon-

---

[61] C. Geffray, *La cause des armes*. See also C. Geffray and M. Pedersen, 'Nampula
en guerre', *Politique Africaine*, 29 (1988), pp. 18-40.

sible for collecting a tax in food to sustain the Renamo base, and
also *mujiba* auxiliaries.

Arguably Nampula represented a 'worst case', where forced
resettlement into communal villages after 1980, but most especially
after 1984, created widespread popular disaffection which Renamo
was able to turn to its advantage. Moreover, the province had
other peculiarities, notably that traditional authorities enjoyed an
unusual degree of respect and popular prestige, since the colonial
pattern of forced peasant cash cropping which had prevailed in
Nampula and elsewhere in the north permitted the survival of
pre-colonial political institutions to a much larger extent than in
the more developed economies of the centre and south. These
authorities had been instrumental in providing Renamo with recruits,
intelligence and logistical support, while their political and kinship
networks provided Renamo with an important avenue of penetration into new areas of the province.[62] This meant that although
in the conventional sense Renamo had no extensive social base
for waging guerrilla war, it was able to count on the widespread
neutrality of the peasantry, who in no real sense supported Frelimo.[63]

Yet such adaptive strategies had their limitations, especially in
relation to the south of the country. Frelimo's villagisation policy
was not a comparable factor in Gaza, with its dependence on
migration for wage labour, since it never posed the serious threat
to subsistence that it did for the largely cash-cropping peasantry
of the north; nor was the involvement of traditional authorities
with Renamo (which were in any case very weak in this part of
Mozambique) of significance. In the densely populated southern
third of the province, where the flood plain of the Limpopo favours
agriculture, villagisation had been accepted, if not welcomed. (Most
communal villages in Gaza were created in the south of the province,
and in the wake of floods which devastated the Limpopo valley
in early 1977.) However, Renamo succeeded in establishing its
major bases in the dry hinterland of the province, from where it
mounted incursions against existing communal villages in the river
valley areas. Villagisation might have been perceived as an economic
threat to the extensive cultivators and cattle-herders of the dry
northern hinterland, yet few communal villages were established
here, and the more obvious explanation for Renamo penetration

[62] *SARoB*, December 1989/January 1990.

[63] For a critical review of Geffray, emphasising the contribution made by desta-
bilisation to the crucial discontents of the countryside, see Bridget O'Laughlin,
'Interpretations Matter: Evaluating the War in Mozambique', *Southern Africa Report*,
January 1992, pp. 23-33.

relates to the area's remoteness from large centres of population. Nonetheless Renamo had little local support in Gaza as a whole, where it was viewed as very much a Ndau political project. Virtually all Renamo commanders and most of the trained combatants were Ndau speakers from central Mozambique. Local recruits (the vast majority of them were initially captives) were integrated into logistical and procurement units, engaging in combat only if attacked. They were expected to learn Ndau, which served as the official language of the base. Widespread use was made of children, inducted into military training at about eight or nine years of age.[64]

The Ndau military commanders actively propagated a 'neo-traditionalist culture of insurgency'. Base commanders drew upon the symbolism used in religious ceremonies and healing practices in southern Mozambique. They frequently dressed in the symbolic garb of the spirit world; wearing, for example, two sashes crossed over their chests: the black sash symbolic of the *munguni* spirit used for divining purposes by southern Mozambican religious specialists, and the white sash symbolic of the *mandau* spirit used for exorcisms. This duality refers back to the nineteenth-century Nguni migration from Zululand and the subjugation of the Ndau, who were incorporated into the regiments of the Nguni Gaza empire. Today most traditional healers in southern Mozambique utilise both Nguni and Ndau spirits when treating patients. Indeed, the two spirits coexist in the person of the Nyamasoro, who simultaneously exercises the functions of diviner and healer, and they aid him or her in those functions.[65] But this practice is peculiar to southern Mozambique, and does not extend north into the Shona-speaking areas of the centre from which the Ndau commanders came. It therefore represents a Renamo adaptation of its symbolic message to the culture of the south, albeit one with limited persuasive power there. Thus while Renamo's religion-based propaganda had found resonance among the rural population of Gaza, it was not translated into popular support, for essentially cultural and ethnic reasons. Fear and mistrust were displayed in Gaza towards the Ndau,

> ....who are renowned for their custom of taking a particular medication when alive that enables their spirit to return from the dead to persecute and bring misfortune upon those people who wronged them...and the Ndau are believed to have the power to transform themselves into such a spirit after death.[...] It is

---

[64] Roesch, 'Renamo and the Peasantry', p. 469.

[65] We are grateful to Alcinda Honwana for this explanation.

significant that virtually all Ndau Renamo combatants are said to have taken this medication as a way of obtaining revenge on those who might kill them or wrong them in some way.[66]

But ethnic reasons were perhaps paramount. Many Frelimo leaders come from Gaza, a province where the party has always had real support, so that forced to choose 'between the ideologically appealing – but foreign – traditionalism of the Ndau, and the ethnically familiar but sometimes socially disruptive policies of Frelimo, the people of southern Mozambique have tended to come down on the side of Frelimo'.[67]

Clearly, there was no simple correlation between the level of villagisation in a province and the intensity of Renamo activity; Cabo Delgado amply demonstrates this, as the province least affected by the insurgency but where villagisation was most vigorously pursued. No doubt the strong tradition of support for Frelimo in some areas, as well as its remoteness from the main theatres of conflict and lack of enticing strategic targets, were all relevant. Nonetheless, peasant discontent with the communal villages had been manifest even here and in Mueda district, the historical cradle of Frelimo's struggle for Mozambican independence. The Makonde peasants of Ngapa near the Tanzanian border withdrew from communal villages to set up autonomous villages of their own, but they did not turn towards Renamo.[68] Conversely, Zambézia province, with very few communal villages, was profoundly involved in Renamo's war. Indeed, sporadic anti-government guerrilla and bandit activities occurred after independence even before Renamo made its presence felt in August 1982. Other factors at work have undoubtedly included the military effort Renamo was willing to make because of the position and natural fertility of this area (and probably also because of its ease of access from Malawi), as well as the way these considerations interacted with the region's special traditions and idiosyncratic social and cultural fabric. Probably also significant was the absorption of Africa Livre by Renamo in 1982, giving it some structure, support-base and local political legitimacy in western Zambézia. Moreover, Zambézia is a deeply socially divided society, in which the old *patronato* system has proved resilient enough to absorb Frelimo officials, mainly those of *assimilado* background. Nor did the province ever really support Frelimo, either

[66] Roesch, 'Renamo and the Peasantry', pp. 476-7.

[67] Ibid., p. 472.

[68] Rudebeck, 'Conditions of People's Development in Postcolonial Africa', unpubl. paper, 1988/9.

before or after independence, as Samora Machel himself recognised.[69] Ordinary people often welcomed the looting of captured
commercial centres in late 1986 even where there was little dis
tribution of goods, while many *comerciantes* were also looted by
their own employees and dependants under cover of Renamo
banditry.[70]

It was in Zambézia that the Renamo administration attained
its most organised form. In 1986-7 Renamo established a food
production system in many areas, based on taxation and labour
on special fields, as organised by former chiefs, for example in
the district around Milange.[71] Even after the area was retaken by
the Mozambican army in mid-1988, Renamo still retained important
bases in the south of the district, and in areas under its control
cultivation continued, some health care was provided (there was
even a maternity unit at Renamo's 'district hospital') and attempts
were made at elementary political mobilisation.[72] However, all the
Zambézian towns taken by Renamo had their populations
evacuated. At Gilé, controlled by Renamo from October 1986 until
july 1988, surrounding villages were put under the authority of
the chiefs, who had the task of organising food, recruits and
porterage.[73] Morrumbala in southern Zambézia was deserted for
the whole nineteen months of Renamo occupation, the entire
population of the town having been marched off into the bush. All
subsequent dealings with them were effected through the medium
of *régulos* and *mujibas*. Food produced at Morrumbala was distributed
to Renamo bases in Manica and Sofala to the south.[74] The 'war of
the spirits' also took a different form here; one that was more
akin to a cult of magical protection and competitive spiritual
prowess associated with attainments by specific military leaders in
accordance with Zambézia's more 'individualistic' traditions.[75] As
elsewhere in the country, Renamo cultivated local spirit mediums

---

[69] K.B. Wilson, personal communication. See also the comments in Vail and White, *Capitalism and Colonialism in Mozambique*, ch. 9.

[70] K.B. Wilson, 'War, Displacement, Social Change and the Re-Creation of Community: an exploratory study in Zambezia, Mozambique', preliminary report of a field study in Milange district, March-April 1991. Refugee Studies Programme May 1991.

[71] *Notícias*, 13 July 1988.

[72] K.B. Wilson, 'War, Displacement, Social Change'.

[73] *Mozambique File*, January 1989.

[74] Information from Oxfam fieldworker.

[75] K.B. Wilson, 'Cults of Violence and Counter-Violence'.

and healers, whose increase in numbers and influence also reflected the social strains and anomie induced by the war.[76] The history of the war at Derre in Morrumbala district illustrates how Renamo became a Zambézian phenomenon. In the initial stages of the war (1982-4) most ordinary people had an indifferent or mildly positive attitude towards Renamo. Although conditions deteriorated during the following two years, it began to use the Zambezi valley and local auxiliaries, who behaved less unpredictably and harshly than expected. By now Renamo-supporting chiefdoms also existed where conditions had stabilised. Derre fell to Renamo in 1986 for a second time, and during an initial period after the capture the population went into hiding in camouflaged pits called *camblinha* (a traditional resort in threatening and dangerous conditions). But a *modus vivendi* was eventually attained. Until the army counter-offensive in the area in late 1990, Renamo operated an administrative regime which was neither particularly intrusive nor violent, and which provided very basic health and educational services and allowed for some market activity. The key to this relatively benign state of affairs (in relation to other parts of the country) was probably the ease with which an agricultural surplus could be produced locally to support the Renamo soldiers, and the existence of a social base which allowed for voluntary local recruitment. After 1986 new troops, mostly of Zambézian origin, were moved in, and more were recruited locally. They created a more civil-based administration which tried to mobilise the support of the people. The level of food tax collected by the chiefs for Renamo was not onerous, and tribute labour on Renamo-managed fields engaged only one adult household member per household for two days a week.[77]

Fragmentation and disorganisation

Clearly, widely varying local circumstances in Mozambique, and Renamo's tactics in dealing with them, suggest that Frelimo's understanding of the conflict was limited and that it became rooted in structures and practices that proved much more resistant to eradication than Frelimo's leaders had ever imagined. Material factors were not unimportant, and had indeed previously con-

---

[76] See Jovito Nunes, 'Peasants and Survival'.

[77] K.B. Wilson, 'The Socio-Economic Impact of War and Flight in Posto Derre, Morrumbala District, Zambezia', January 1992 (described in the Archivo Histórico de Moçambique as forthcoming).

strained the colonial regime. The country's size and shape alone make effective control difficult, and these difficulties are compounded by the lack of north-south communications (the important arteries bisect the country laterally), and by the existence of several natural regional centres, while all power is concentrated in the capital, 1,900 km. from Mozambique's northernmost border but only 102 km. from South Africa. Colonial rule failed to integrate the country economically or indeed administratively until late in the day, so that a marked legacy of the colonial past has been Mozambique's fragmented economic development. Historically, the country comprised corridors of communication linking Central and Southern Africa to the coast, so that there is no major rail line which both begins and ends inside Mozambique.[78] This economic legacy dovetailed with considerable regional and ethnic diversity, which Frelimo did not manage to overcome.

With independence in 1975, coming after a long guerrilla war but actually precipitated by the collapse of the metropolitan power in Lisbon, Frelimo had still to establish a presence over large areas of this elongated country, but the conflict in neighbouring Rhodesia meant that in much of central Mozambique it had little opportunity to do so. Indeed, in as much as Renamo can be said to have developed a regional base during the war, it was located in Manica and Sofala, where the insurgency began and where Renamo was able to count on some support, if only tacit, from the peasantry. During the early 1980s Renamo was able to attract some voluntary recruits from the area by claiming that Frelimo was southern-dominated.[79] In particular Gorongosa in northern Sofala was long the main area of its shifting headquarters, regarded as a centre of support for Renamo, as well as being an area where the connection between it and the Shona spirit cult was particularly strong and close.[80] Some commentators in Mozambique have even claimed to discern underlying elements of the past in the conflict: the 'people of Monomotapa' versus the Gaza empire established by Soshangane.

In addition to the difficulties of integration associated with geographical and cultural diversity, Mozambique under Frelimo displayed all the structural weaknesses of the African state to an extreme degree, with an acute lack of qualified cadres, weak

---

[78] M. Newitt, 'Towards a history of modern Moçambique', *Rhodesian History*, 7, 5, pp. 33-47.

[79] Joseph Hanlon, *Mozambique: The revolution under fire*, p. 229.

[80] *Tempo* 780, 22 September 1985, pp. 10-12.

infrastructure and hence poor administrative control. These factors interacted with, and reinforced, the regional and ethnic fragmentation. They also severely affected the military capacities of the state; Renamo faced an army which was 'under-trained, underequipped, underpaid, and underfed'.[81] Military logistics suffered *inter alia* from Renamo assaults on the transportation system, so that more than one garrison is known to have been driven to forage for its food. Morale was widely recognised to be poor, and during the war there were plenty of rumours of troops illicitly collaborating with, or even spying for, Renamo. Logistical problems aside, the army was encumbered by a post-independence over-emphasis on conventional weapons that was inappropriate to countering a rural guerrilla insurgency.[82]

Contingent factors also had their effects. In the early 1980s an unusually severe drought affected much of central and southern Mozambique, and there were many deaths in Tete as a result of famine. In Gaza and Inhambane provinces, where Renamo activities were most intense, people had lost much of their remaining foodstocks and cattle to Renamo forces and were running out of roots and berries in the bush.[83] Their suffering was greatly exacerbated by Renamo tactics, which in Inhambane not only targeted relief vehicles for attack, but also focused on starving peasants seeking to make their way to government feeding stations. An estimated 25% of the normally marketed grain overall was lost due to Renamo action, compounding rural hardship just as the distribution and commercialisation networks were disappearing throughout rural Mozambique. In circular fashion, this provided further fertile ground for Renamo expansion. In so expanding, Renamo was destroying the development infrastructure linked to the communal villages which Frelimo had created (health posts and schools).[84]

These structural and contingent factors did much to shape the war into a confusing patchwork of shifting local engagements. Yet to make sense of Renamo it is essential to bear in mind three elements: the nature of the indigenous African societies; the policies pursued by the Frelimo government in the first phase of its rule;

---

[81] Finnegan, *A Complicated War*, p. 56.

[82] See Herb Howe, 'Mozambique at a Standstill' in *Defence Africa and the Middle East*, 11, 2 (March 1985), pp. 14-15. See also *Indian Ocean Newsletter*, 5 November 1983, pp. 7-10, on the state of the armed forces, and ION, 25 September 1993.

[83] Conspicuous Destruction (*Africa Watch* report, 1992).

[84] See Glenda Morgan, 'Violence in Mozambique: Towards an Understanding of Renamo', *Journal of Modern African Studies*, 28, April (1990), pp. 603-19.

and the South African involvement. Many of Frelimo's policies antagonised sections of the population. Its more or less open door policy for the ANC antagonised Pretoria. The South Africans were able to capitalise on these discontents to shape a force whose main *raison d'être* was the destruction of economic targets and of the skeletal framework of political and administrative control that Frelimo had been able to set up in the rural areas. It is not clear whether Renamo ever had any meaningful political goals as such. It was able to exploit a deteriorating social and economic situation and maintain in the field a fairly large body of armed men effectively living off the countryside. It acquired a momentum of its own by exploiting the prevailing social crisis and economic collapse in the rural areas. Geffray's comment perhaps summarises as well as anything a very complex series of truths: 'The responsibility for the development of the war can be divided as a follows: only the South African intervention can account for the beginning of the war – that country has a major responsibility for the conflict – while the political choices made by Frelimo in building its power in the countryside can explain the fact that this war was grounded in the social fabric of rural Mozambique.'[85]

[85] Geffray, *La Cause des Armes au Mozambique*, pp. 3-4.

8

THE RETREAT FROM SOCIALISM

'We see no need to negotiate with terrorists. It is possible to defeat them militarily.'[1]

'On the harsh return journey, we stay at camps where no sentries are posted. The camps lack basic defence perimeters, which even a lowly SADF corporal would insist upon. The Viet Cong would have made mincemeat of this lot, we think. We conclude that Renamo guerrillas are doing so well militarily, not because they are any good, but because Frelimo is so bad.'[2]

Following the trauma of Machel's death in 1986, the Frelimo leadership drew on its greatest political strength – the coherence of its ruling group. The choice of Chissano as the new leader was virtually inevitable. Frelimo's multiracial rhetoric notwithstanding, it was inconceivable that the leading figure would not be an African, and the considerable racial heterogeneity of the Politburo reduced the number of plausible contenders to very few. There were inevitably obvious changes of style. Chissano could not hope to replicate Machel's presence and showmanship, and his instincts were more collegial and less impulsive – as he put it himself, 'President Machel was more dynamic than I am. I need a lot more support to make decisions than he did.'[3] He also had considerably greater administrative experience. Nonetheless, from the beginning the new government stressed the continuity of policy on all essential issues. In his first public speeches as leader, Chissano identified economic reform (including reducing bureaucracy), reorganisation of the armed forces, reinforcement of the party structures and better 'mobilisation' of the people as his central objectives,

---

[1] Interview with Joaquim Chissano, *Le Monde*, 11 December 1986.

[2] Paul L. Moorcraft, *African Nemesis*, p. 284.

[3] The *Independent*, 2 March 1987. For background on Chissano see *Domingo*, 14 July 1991.

loyally crediting Samora Machel with having taken the key initiatives in all these areas.[4]

While this stress on continuity had a basis in reality (much of the government's new thinking had been precipitated by the disasters of 1986), it almost certainly disguised a distinct shift of pace and the preparation of dramatic new departures. It seems likely that Chissano's assessment of the country's situation was rather more radical than he could publicly admit. Tentatively at least he had come to the view that the war was unwinnable in a military sense and that somehow Renamo had to be brought to negotiate. However, this involved not only considerable domestic economic and political change (including substantial shifts in Frelimo's understanding of socialism, at least as defined since the 3rd Congress) but also vigorous diplomacy abroad, both to maintain pressure on South Africa to cut or at least reduce its links with Renamo and to isolate Renamo from possible wider international support – so making negotiation the only attractive option for the 'armed bandits'.

The fight goes on: The regional and international settings

At the time of Chissano's assumption of office the military situation was extremely bleak. It seemed that Renamo might capture Quelimane, cutting the country in two and providing an opportunity to set up an alternative government (as well providing the possibility of re-supply by sea). That at least was the fear in Maputo and the task to which Chissano immediately devoted his energies, appealing to regional allies for assistance.[5] The idea of negotiations with Renamo was dismissed on the oft-repeated grounds that there was no-one to negotiate with.[6] Rather the first order of business was relations with regional neighbours. Pressure was maintained on Malawi to act on terrorism.[7] On 19 December the two countries signed a joint security pact which formalised the principles already

[4] See *Le Monde*, 11 December 1986; and opening speech to the 6th session Central Committee *Notícias*, 7 January 1987.

[5] MIO *News Review*, 26 February 1987. Chissano suggested this publicly during a visit to Zimbabwe *AfricAsia*, 40 (April 1987) and later in the People's Assembly *Tempo*, 887 (11 October 1987).

[6] *Notícias*, 9 December 1986.

[7] See Chissano's speech to the Diplomatic Corps – *Notícias*, 14 November 1986 – and to the nation – *Notícias* 1 January 1987. The Mozambican press prominently displayed the (plentiful) evidence of Malawian complicity in Renamo operations. See *Notícias*, 16, 18 and 22 December 1986.

agreed by a joint security commission (set up in October at the time of Machel's visit to Malawi) meeting earlier in the month.[8] In line with its new commitments Malawi was persuaded to contribute a military force of some 500 to guard the Nacala line.[9] Chissano's first overseas visit as head of state was to Tanzania, where he secured promises of additional military assistance. A January visit to Zimbabwe included senior military figures in the Mozambican delegation.[10] President Mugabe had already repeated Zimbabwe's unquestioned support against the Renamo bandits, and thus elicited a Renamo 'declaration of war' against Zimbabwe.[11]

With such help, a major government counter-offensive got under way in early 1987 during which the army was able progressively to recover territory along the north bank of the Zambezi, with the aid of some 2,000-3,000 Tanzanian troops in defensive positions in the Zambezi valley to garrison re-captured towns. The army captured the Mutarara bridge and retook five key towns while a Tanzanian force garrisoned the provincial capital of Quelimane. Simultaneously Zimbabwean paratroopers spearheaded a parallel offensive in Manica and Sofala, in order to pin Renamo down at the Malawi border. Frelimo's rather better performance on the battlefield owed something to increased British and Zimbabwean training for FAM officers as well as to the reorganisation of the army, a process started by Machel that Chissano sought to carry forward. In a major reshuffle of senior positions in the armed forces, Generals Hama Thai, Tobias Dai and Domingos Fondo, all associated with successful campaigns, were made chief of staff, army chief and commander of the frontier guards respectively.[12] In response Renamo shifted its main operations southwards towards Gaza and Inhambane – partly, it would seem, in an attempt to isolate Maputo. Renamo had always had much less appeal in the south of the country and this seems to have inclined the organisation towards a more overt terrorism involving numerous incidents of the slaughter of civilian populations, notably at Homoine and Manjacaz. Convoys and trains were attacked and their passengers killed. Small towns and villages near the capital were attacked and wrecked.

The successes of the government counter-offensive up to mid-

[8] It first met in Nampula in December See *Notícias*, 5 and 20 December 1986.

[9] *Guardian*, 30 December 1986.

[10] *Tempo*, 850 (25 January 1987).

[11] *Independent*, 8 November 1986; *International Herald Tribune*, 21 November 1986.

[12] *Notícias*, 22 June 1987, and A. Isaacman, 'Chissano's Friends and Enemies', *Africa Report*, September-October 1987, pp. 48-51.

1987 created a space for active diplomacy, to which the energies of the senior leadership were largely devoted from May 1987 onwards. In May Chissano made his first visit outside Africa as head of state, visiting Britain and Italy, the two European states with which Mozambique had the best relations. Despite the range and intensity of this diplomatic activity, it was supplementary (aside from the routine appeals for aid and investment) to Mozambique's main effort, which was aimed at the United States. South African support for Renamo, however extensive and however clandestine, had been increasingly contested by right-wing elements in the United States who, resenting the constraints of the policy of 'constructive engagement' pursued by Assistant Secretary of State Chester Crocker, saw aid to Renamo as the best way of furthering the policy of 'rolling back' Communism throughout the world.[13] In Mozambique and indeed elsewhere, with the active encouragement of intelligence agencies (notably the CIA, whose head William Casey introduced the technique of 'sub-conflict' operations to ensure 'plausible deniability'[14]), such organisations increasingly pursued a 'privatised' foreign 'policy' that might be at odds with the official one.

The main stimulus for the emergence of an active Renamo presence in the United States was Machel's visit to Washington in 1985, to which opposition was mobilised by an organisation called the 'Conservative Caucus'. Although it failed in its immediate objective, the campaign created an interest in Renamo among a wider group of American right-wing organisations. This network comprised well-funded institutes conducting policy analysis, including the Heritage Foundation and its less analytically-minded offshoots such as the International Freedom Foundation and Freedom Incorporated; leading religious figures such as Pat Robertson and Jimmy Swaggart; and other, more obscure and shadowy groups coalescing around such organisations as the World Anti-Communist League, the mercenary magazine *Soldier of Fortune*, and Free the Eagle.[15] Some of these groups formed associations and branches in Europe – particularly in Britain – and in South Africa.[16]

By far the most important of these pro-Renamo advocates was the Heritage Foundation, which both published its own position papers and briefings on various foreign policy issues and acted

[13] See useful background in *Washington Post*, 15 February 1987.

[14] *Africa Confidential*, 9 September and 2 December 1988.

[15] P. Nesbitt, 'Terminators, Crusaders and Gladiators: Western (private and public) support for Renamo and Unita', *Review of African Political Economy*, 43 (1988), pp. 111-24.

[16] *Observer*, 9 October and 13 November 1988.

as a kind of financial conduit for other more 'specialist' right-wing groups in the United States and abroad. Heritage's own position on US policy towards Mozambique in the 1986-8 period reflected right-wing dismay over the decision of the Reagan administration – in the light of Frelimo's reforming dynamic and its distancing from Moscow – to increase its 'humanitarian' aid budget for the war-torn and drought-stricken country. Heritage and its cohorts were convinced that the Reagan team (in particular those in the State Department who were diluting the US position in Southern Africa) were being 'hoodwinked' by the diplomatic charm of a 'totalitarian' regime.

By 1987 the pro-Renamo lobby had become extremely active, with supporters in politically significant positions, the most important of whom was Senator Jesse Helms of North Carolina, a member of the Senate Foreign Affairs Committee. A Mozambique Research Center was established in Washington by the evangelist Tom Schaaf, who had become a key figure in the nexus of organisations supporting Renamo and who was also strongly rumoured to have connections with the CIA. United States-based assistance and propaganda increasingly used Malawi as a conduit. An important element was the activity of Evangelical Christian missionaries in the Malawi/Mozambique border area who had links with Schaaf in the United States.[17] American attempts to influence Renamo from 1986 onwards were reflected in divisions within the external wing which centred on Evo Fernandes, his racial origins, and his close South African and Portuguese connections. In August 1986 pressures from the United States right wing demanding greater black representation in Renamo succeeded in securing the abolition of the post of secretary-general and demoting Fernandes to head a 'Department of Studies'.

Thus Mozambique's efforts were focused on two objectives. The first was to deprive Renamo of any further support from the conservative sections of Congress. Elsewhere in the world, especially in Angola, they had persuaded the Reagan administration to support 'freedom fighters' against governments who either were, or were thought to be, within the Soviet orbit. The second was to persuade the United States administration itself to pave the way for Mozambique's access to various kinds of multilateral bodies, regarded by the Frelimo leadership as essential to pull the country out of the crisis it faced. High-level contacts with the United States and other Western countries continued throughout 1987. Maputo

---

[17] See especially Steve Askin, 'Mission to RENAMO: the militarization of the religious right', *Issue*, 18, 2, 1990, pp. 29-33.

sought to contact a wide range of political forces in the United States, from State Department officials to Republican presidential advisers.[10] A key figure in the regime, Armando Guebuza, spent two weeks in the United States in May. The appointment of the new American ambassador, Melissa Wells, was finally confirmed in September (her Senate ratification had been held up for months by Senator Helms). This increased tempo of contacts culminated in an important visit to Washington in October during which Chissano met Reagan as well as Congressmen, Senators and the Congressional Black Caucus. The US government announced that it would be prepared to mediate between the two parties to the Mozambican conflict and the Mozambicans clearly agreed.[19] The Reagan administration's policy remained in considerable disarray, however, threatening to become a major cause of dissension within the Republican party.[20] The State Department firmly opposed any support for Renamo, and as part of its battle against other elements within the administration it released the Gersony Report, in part to discredit the organisation and its US supporters. Pro-Renamo forces faced increasing opposition as this and other evidence of Renamo massacres – particularly that at Homoine – attracted worldwide publicity and condemnation. Support for Renamo continued among the more woodenly 'anti-Communist' sectors of the US right wing, but after Gersony Renamo was fundamentally discredited in mainstream conservative circles.

The regional complement to Mozambique's global diplomacy remained the application of world pressure on South Africa over apartheid, to achieve the immediate objective of cutting off support for Renamo. Despite its virtual worthlessness Mozambique had never repudiated the Nkomati Accord, although it had abandoned its provisions for a joint security commission in the face of overwhelming evidence that South Africa was ignoring its obligations under it. Relations between the two countries, which had reached a fever pitch of mutual insult in the months before Machel's death, remained venomous and were additionally soured by the complexities of the Machel plane crash and the apparent duplicity of the South Africans in handling the inquiry into the exact cir-

---

[18] *Notícias*, 7 and 10 August 1987.

[19] *Southscan*, 7 October 1987; *International Herald Tribune*, 12 November 1987. Crocker suggests that Chissano realised there was no military solution to the conflict; see *High Noon*, p. 249. The Mozambican press offered only bland accounts of this meeting. *Notícias*, 6 October 1987.

[20] J. Stephen Morrison, 'The Battle for Mozambique', *Africa Report*, September-October 1987, pp. 44-47.

cumstances.[21] The war of words continued through late 1986 and into 1987 even though low-level technical cooperation (for example, in relation to Maputo harbour and the Cahora Bassa dam). In January South Africa demanded further expulsions of ANC people (including the deputy chief of military intelligence) from Maputo, and the Mozambicans complied.[22] In May South African commandos killed three people in attacks on separate targets in Maputo (though the Republic refused to confirm or deny the actions). In June Defence Minister Malan suggested that South Africa might have to consider supporting Renamo.[23]

The Mozambicans perhaps had little choice but to cling to the tail of the tiger. Even the horrors of the Homoine massacre in July 1987, which brought accusations (angrily rebutted) of South African complicity, were turned to advantage, starting with a joint liaison committee to investigate it. Persistent efforts by Veloso produced a summit meeting between Chissano and Botha at Songo in September 1988, with the great Cahora Bassa dam as a backdrop and symbol of renewed cooperation. Both sides pledged to revive Nkomati, to rebuild and defend Cahora Bassa, and to step up economic cooperation in other fields; both expressed determination to rebuild the powerlines. Indeed, on 28 November the vessel *Drakensberg* unloaded an estimated 10 million rand worth of 'non-lethal' military equipment at Beira destined for use by a special unit of the Mozambican army being created to guard these lines. Renamo sabotage continued, however. The blowing up of 674 pylons between April 1988 and the beginning of 1989 brought the total number destroyed by Renamo since 1983 to about 1,200.[24] It may be that the SADF, which had shown little interest in the success of such projects in the past, continued to provide Renamo – despite its apparent independence – with the resources to disrupt any imminent agreement to restore production from the dam.[25] It may also be that Pretoria's apparent desire to provide security assistance for the transmission lines stemmed from the adoption of a 'corridor approach' to Mozambique; that is, securing for itself

---

[21] The issues were highly technical, and opinion was split between those who blamed the crash on pilot error and those who suggested that the plane had been diverted by some sort of decoy beam.

[22] Full list in Ellis and Sechaba, *Comrades against Apartheid*, p. 169.

[23] *Guardian*, 29 June 1987.

[24] *Mozambiquefile*, January 1989.

[25] Vines, *Renamo*, p. 29.

corridors of economic utility such as Cahora Bassa and Maputo harbour, while continuing to sponsor destruction elsewhere.

Further economic reform and Western aid

Second only to the intensification of Frelimo's battle against Renamo came action attempting to reverse the massive decline of the Mozambican economy, a decline which had become desperate during 1986. The bare economic facts could hardly be disputed. Between 1981 and 1985 GDP fell by about 8% a year. Marketed production of the main agricultural crops in 1986 was only about 25% of the 1980 level. Industrial production fell by about half. The balance of payments deteriorated yearly, international reserves were exhausted and payment arrears had reached US $1.2 billion. The government's budgetary position had worsened, with the current account deficit in 1986 reaching 50% of current expenditure.[26] It was with these issues that the leadership confronted the first new People's Assembly, the full economic team dominating the speeches and debates, painting a bleak picture of the economy and demanding a new sense of 'realism' in order that the search for a solution to the economic problems should have a chance to succeed.[27]

The leadership's answer to these problems, the Programme of Economic Rehabilitation (PRE), was presented as unavoidable, though there was little real debate on its merits. The Programme was a rolling comprehensive set of measures whose central purposes, at least as presented to the People's Assembly, were the revaluation of the currency and the boosting of the agricultural sector with the aim of restoring 1981 production levels by 1990. By the end of January 1987 some twenty-five new laws and other administrative measures (clearly drafted some time previously) had been announced. They can be more or less divided into four.[28] First came the devaluation of the metical, to be achieved in two stages. An initial devaluation of 80% in January was followed by a further 50% in June. Secondly, and again in a series of stages, price controls were to be lifted from most food crops, except basic grains, as well as from most other consumer goods. Thirdly, a determined attempt was to be made to reduce the state budget deficit by

[26] Report by Prime Minister Machungo Consultative Group for Mozambique, 9-10 July 1987.

[27] For the proceedings of the People's Assembly *Notícias*, 15-21 January 1987.

[28] *Notícias*, 31 January 1987.

cutting subsidies and limiting the losses of state firms. Fiscal and pricing reforms aimed at broadening the tax-base were to be implemented. These included changes in rent laws, shifting from forms of rent control that linked rents with incomes to a system based on the value of the property. Finally, there was to be a continuing programme of decentralisation of economic management, to be assisted by privatising state sector assets. Managers were to have greater freedom to dismiss surplus workers and provide incentives to others.

These measures, ostensibly at least, formed the basis for negotiations and subsequent agreement with the IMF and the World Bank. An agreement signed with the Fund in March released a $51 million structural adjustment facility, and was closely followed by $106 million from the Bank in balance-of-payments support. This in turn made possible meetings of foreign donors and creditors to arrange debt rescheduling. In May the Club of London agreed to reschedule $279 million of commercial debt. Mozambique's public debt of $453 million was rescheduled over an unprecedented period of twenty years (with a ten-year grace period).[29] The Consultative Group meeting in Paris (9-10 July) produced bilateral aid of some $700 million, targeted to allow a doubling of imports by 1990. Paralleling these efforts to keep the Mozambican economy afloat were aid pledges. As the 1986 harvest had been the worst on record, the country was desperately short of all foodstuffs, and needed some 700,000 tonnes of food aid for the 1987/8 season. At a meeting of donors and non-governmental organisations (NGOs) held under UN auspices, Mozambique appealed for $245 million in emergency aid.[30] This and successive donor conferences became a regular feature of the Mozambican situation with net aid disbursements averaging some $760 million a year between 1986 and 1989.

The Frelimo leadership was keen to emphasise that the PRE was the result of a long internal debate dating back at least to the 4th Congress, although the emphasis was usually placed on measures decided by the Central Committee in 1986.[31] The PRE was also presented by the leadership very much in terms of solving the short-term crises, especially the budget deficit, and as reflecting the principle of a war economy. But the gaping contradictions

---

[29] *Financial Times*, 18 June 1987.

[30] *Notícias*, 2 April 1987.

[31] Mozambique Briefing Economic Recovery Programme. See interview with Machungo, *Notícias*, 9 April 1987.

between the new realities and the increasingly threadbare remnants of Frelimo's old economic rhetoric, as well as the country's growing dependence, made this account rather implausible.[32] The PRE was largely sponsored by the IMF and the World Bank, and indeed much like structural adjustment programmes (SAPS) imposed elsewhere on African states (a point whose political significance we return to below). The public (and private) documentation makes it clear that these measures had long been expected. The delay was partly a consequence of arguments about the rates of devaluation and concerns that Mozambique lacked the manpower to set up a structural adjustment programme and required assistance to do so.[33] Comiche, the Central Bank governor, reported to the Assembly that there had been twenty-two World Bank and five IMF missions to the country in the period 1985-6.[34] Frelimo's claims that the PRE was a national effort were intended partly to sustain its own prestige and partly followed from IMF/World Bank requirements that SAPs be presented as wholly 'voluntary'. It is doubtful if anyone was deceived by these poses:

> In private conversations with foreign delegations, senior government leaders are prepared to admit quite candidly that the membership [of the IMF] became a necessity, with all western nations ganging up behind the IMF and refusing to allow any flow of credit until Mozambique accepted a structural adjustment exercise within the classic IMF framework.[35]

The demands of the IMF/World Bank were indeed largely supported by other aid agencies and Western states which were happy to leave details of policy formulation and a coordinating role to the Bank.[36]

Whatever the final verdict on the policy, politically it involved the massive subordination of the Mozambican state and indeed the whole country to outside agencies. An undue stress on the continuity with earlier Frelimo reformism overlooks the extent to which the PRE and post-PRE policies constituted the wholesale

---

[32] The 5th Congress Economic and Social Directives managed to avoid even mentioning the PRE!

[33] Internal World Bank documentation, and interview with UNDP economist in Maputo, 28 July 1988.

[34] *Notícias*, 17 January 1987.

[35] J. Marshall, 'Structural adjustment and Social Policy in Mozambique', *Review of African Political Economy* 47 (1990), pp. 28-43.

[36] For some evidence see V. Tickner, 'Structural Adjustment and Agricultural Pricing in Mozambique', pp. 25-42.

handover of the economy to international agencies, a process exacerbated to be sure by the parlous circumstances of much of the Mozambican population. Given prevailing assumptions in those circles and agencies, any sense of restructuring the Mozambican economy in terms of either its production structure or its economic relations was unthinkable. Finally, the World Bank view that the PRE would 'establish the conditions for more rapid and more efficient economic growth in the medium and longer term when the security situation and other exogenous constraints have eased' was wholly disingenuous if not downright mendacious.[37] The fact that the PRE was much like any other structural adjustment programme certainly showed the absurdity of calling the war 'exogenous' (a point made by many observers), but the clear implication was that if the forms of economic management were essentially sound, then it was the 'exogenous' features that would have to change. At a time when the tattered remnants of sovereignty still required a certain deferential politesse towards Third World countries, the 'international community' could not make it much clearer that it expected political change to accompany economic reform.[38]

Political and constitutional change: the liberal option?

It has already been suggested that Chissano contemplated greater political change than his early statements indicated, although there were signs in late 1985 and in 1986 that Machel himself may have been moving in the same direction. Certain things were clear right from the beginning. Changes in the personnel of the regime indicate a policy of Africanising the government and thus making it more 'national'. The notable developments here were the dropping of Sergio Vieira (widely held responsible, perhaps unfairly, for neglecting Machel's security) and the sidelining of Marcelino dos Santos to the prestigious but politically almost irrelevant presidency of the People's Assembly (though this had already been signalled before Machel's death). Beyond these rather obvious gestures involving major figures there was a continual but gradual process (for example, in government reshuffles in January and May 1987 and in January 1989) of replacing whites and Asians with Africans.

In addition to these developments, the postponement of

---

[37] World Bank, *Economic Policy Framework*, 1987-9.

[38] The first World Bank report on Mozambique had suggested that 'The main sticking point seems to be the Government of Mozambique's refusal to share power with the armed bands'. World Bank, *Mozambique Economic Report: An Introductory Economic Survey*, 1985, p. 14.

important decisions (particularly those pertaining to constitutional reform), certain shifts in the party structures and its practices, and in the tone and rhetoric of the Frelimo leadership all indicated that change was in the air. The 4th Congress had already signalled a revival of Frelimo as a broad front, although it had retained the ideological commitments of the vanguard party period. Chissano's instincts were to push this strategy further. First, Frelimo had to be more inclusive in its recruitment policy and therefore, more participatory in its approach; or at least it had to broaden its appeal. Secondly, in order to make itself a more mass-oriented and national party, Frelimo had to tolerate and even, within limits, encourage a greater degree of autonomous action on the part of groups and bodies outside Frelimo itself. Indeed, the internal changes were argued for in terms of the abandonment of a dependency complex which could not but have implications for non-party organisations.[39] Inevitably, political language that seemed unnecessarily provocative from the point of view of a broader front was likely to be dispensed with. It is likely that Chissano himself had never been very comfortable with the more stridently 'Marxist-Leninist' language of the Frelimo regime. Certainly in his public speeches from the time he first became leader it became clear that a new rhetoric was being adopted, stressing Frelimo's comprehensive national appeal and frequently referring to Mozambicans 'of all classes'. There also gradually developed a more self-critical tone that went beyond concealing real problems behind the ritual repetition of 'democratic centralist' clichés. Clearly, reading these signals, the Mozambican press began subtly to reflect these shifts, and increasingly voiced coded or allusive criticisms of past practices and echoed the leadership's demand for realism.[40]

Decisions on these matters were implemented quickly, as often by the quiet abandonment of previous norms as by formal decisions or procedural changes. The most conspicuous example of the new tolerance was the mending of fences with the churches, particularly the Catholic Church. At an early meeting with the three archbishops Chissano called on them to adopt 'national positions'.[41] Although more important for its change of tone than for any matters of substance, this encounter was part of a process which continued with a gradual restoration of some kind of social legitimacy to religious bodies of all kinds. In some provinces by

[39] *Notícias*, 22 August 1987.

[40] This is noticeable in editorial comments. See e.g. *Tempo*, 852 (8 January 1987).

[41] *Notícias*, 8 December 1986.

May 1987 previously confiscated church property was being quietly returned, while in June 1988 a more formal announcement was made concerning the return of church buildings, including schools and hospitals and the Matola seminary.[42] Church organisations were also to be allowed access to printing and distribution facilities. All members of the government began to show almost exaggerated deference to church organisations, including foreign ones.[43]

Similarly, within Frelimo itself signals were used to promote change as much as formal alterations of the rules. Considerable attention was devoted to internal party matters during 1987 and 1988, a succession of ordinary and special meetings of party bodies began not only to deploy the new style of internal Frelimo practices but to prepare the way for a public registration of the shifts contemplated at the next congress. The first session of the Central Committee after Chissano's accession (6-10 January 1987) postponed that congress to 1989 and devoted much discussion to party and membership matters, including the revival of political education. At its 7th session (7-12 August 1987) the Central Committee approved new norms for the involvement of party members in economic activity, allowing anything but 'speculative' businesses. Moreover, it announced that the party's mass organisations were permitted, indeed encouraged, to engage in profit-making activities and to increase the size of their memberships. It also elected a commission to begin preparing for the party's 5th Congress.

During the 8th session of the Central Committee (3-9 March 1988) there was a 2nd extraordinary session at which Chissano suggested that Frelimo aspired to 'a society where every citizen advances along with the advancement of our Fatherland, and a society where the people will benefit from the wealth generated by the work and intelligence of the Mozambican people. This is the meaning of our ideal in building socialism.'[44] At the 2nd national conference (19-24 July 1988), at which the party leadership had called for the fullest critical discussion, previously taboo subjects began to be raised, notably regional favouritism and the use of vernacular languages, as well as the performance of the armed

---

[42] *AIM News Bulletin*, 144 (July 1988). This return of properly had apparently been promised at the 1986 meeting. See also *Africa Confidencial* (17 May 1987). Crocker suggests that one of the promises made to the Americans in October 1987 was the restoration of religious freedoms and the return of church property. See Crocker, *High Noon*, p. 249.

[43] See e.g. Chissano's reception for visiting American Methodists; *Tempo*, 964 (2 April 1989).

[44] SWB ME/0092 B/3.

forces. An increasingly critical tone became normal, with frequent references to the weakness of Frelimo itself as an organisation, Chissano himself suggested that 'after 13 years of independence, and despite all our efforts, results in terms of cadre training are not very visible'.[45] This intense Frelimo effort during 1988 was geared to producing the theses for the Congress, which were finally released in November. By the time this Congress took place, it was clear that substantial ideological changes would be adopted. Not for the first time the leadership had used greater openness of discussion in the party to move in the direction it wanted to go. The provincial congresses preceding the national one were outspoken, and continually denounced the performance of the armed forces. Simply by raising the possibility of negotiations with Renamo it began to legitimise the idea.[46]

These various tendencies, encouraged by the leadership, finally culminated in the 5th Congress held in July 1989, the documents of which signalled the first major ideological shifts since the 3rd Congress. Although the particular combination of deletions and insertions (which appears to have been carried out in a rather bureaucratic fashion) produced somewhat incoherent texts, as well as inconsistencies between the programme, the statutes and the report of the Central Committee, the general thrust of the changes was clear. All references to Marxism-Leninism and the Soviet bloc countries were carefully removed, along with any associated phrases such as 'proletarian internationalism' and 'scientific socialism'. To a large extent references to class (including the working class, worker-peasant alliances and notions of a vanguard) and internal enemies were also removed, although one or two references remained in the statutes. The new elements adopted by Frelimo were less clear, partly because many of them verged on the vacuous (for example, 'democratic society of general well-being') but in so far as they shared a common theme, this was free association, including a wholly new emphasis on citizens' rights, minority groups and decentralisation of government functions and such values as tolerance and tranquillity. The Central Committee report in particular openly discussed such matters as racial and regional inequalities.

What attracted attention (and this was almost certainly intentional) was the 'abandonment of Marxism', and it was of course true that Frelimo's nation-building project was being disengaged from the

---

[45] The Frelimo National Conference (Frelimo Information Department, 1988), p. 6.

[46] See reports of such meetings in *Tempo*, 964 (2 April 1989).

Marxist formulas in which it had been originally expressed.[47] But the abandonment of Marxist jargon presented no great difficulties – we have already suggested that it had never served any analytical purpose for the Frelimo leadership. Nor is there any evidence that it occasioned any resistance or indeed much interest among the party membership.[48] What Chissano did not at this stage intend to surrender was Frelimo's 'directing role'. Utilising familiar Marxist phrases about the need for the 'creative application' of socialist principles, and retaining much of its traditional understanding of democratic centralism and the leading role of the party, Frelimo now sought to present itself as playing that role on behalf of all 'social groups' – a sort of one-party social democracy.

Paralleling this process of dramatic party change was a process of constitutional change. The reforms covered a wide area of legal and related matters, but in substance they clearly amounted to the adoption of a liberal understanding of the state. The legal apparatus itself was restructured and civilianised, a process completed with the abolition of the Revolutionary Military Tribunal and the release of some 1,000 prisoners held in connection with it.[49] Other vestiges of the period of revolutionary legality, such as flogging, were abolished. In 1988 Mozambique ratified the African Charter on Human Rights, and consultations were begun with religious groups on a new religious freedom law.[50] The vicissitudes of constitutional reform are indeed among the clearest evidence that Chissano almost from the beginning was preparing to embark on dramatic changes. Although the text produced by the original constitutional revision process was approved by the Central Committee in August 1987 and (by acclamation) at the second session of the People's Assembly in September 1987, it was not acceptable to Chissano and was returned to the Commission for Revising the Constitution for further work.[51] On the grounds of further public debate, the decision was put off by the 10th session of the Central Committee and postponed yet again by the September 1989 Assembly.

The dramatic shift in the proposals for constitutional reform

---

[47] For a clear example see Chissano's speech to the Central Committee; *Notícias*, 18 August 1987.

[48] *Africa* (Lisbon), no. 114. One Frelimo tradition appeared to remain intact. The Central Committee report took twelve hours to read.

[49] *Notícias*, 17 April 1989.

[50] *Notícias*, 14 July 1989.

[51] *Notícias*, 21 August and 24 September 1987.

are the clearest evidence that at some point after the July Congress the front strategy was abandoned and the decision made to take a new direction. A combination of internal and global factors seems to have brought this about. Despite periodic counter-offensives by the government (and these remained important even during the process of negotiations), it became clear that Renamo could neither defeat the FAM nor be defeated. Chissano's reforms of the armed forces, though not without effect, did not produce the results hoped for (though the reasons for this remain obscure). The war had settled into a confusing patchwork of shifting local engagements, without fixed fronts and identifiable front lines; apart from major offensives, when it might take temporary control of sizeable areas, Renamo more typically held numerous pockets which existed alongside government-held zones. Although areas of established Renamo operation certainly existed, bases within them remained mobile. Even the largest and most important, including Dhlakama's headquarters (normally situated in or near the Gorongosa), shifted periodically in response to the threat or reality of FAM or ZNA assaults.

In June 1989 Mozambique announced that within two years the Soviet Union would withdraw its military advisers and reduce its supply of military equipment. Any idea of a military victory, if it had ever been plausible, was rapidly fading. The country's desperate economic weakness gave its major creditors and the multilateral institutions enormous leverage, and pressure was increasingly brought to bear on Maputo to negotiate. Even among those countries and agencies less concerned to exert political leverage, 'donor fatigue' was making its appearance – by September 1989, out of a total of 916,000 tonnes of food aid sought for the period 1989/90, only 297,000 tonnes had been pledged; whereas at the same point in 1988/9 donors had already promised some 51% of requirements.[52]

These dramatic international developments impacted on more local regional ones. The Tanzanians withdrew their forces at the end of 1988; also, for some time Zimbabwe had been reassessing its role in the conflict as discontent at the costs, within both the ZNA and the country at large, increased. Some Zimbabwean parliamentarians began questioning their country's involvement in Mozambique and it seems likely that Zimbabwean intelligence had come to the view that the war was unwinnable.[53] The most important

[52] *South Scan*, 1 September and 10 November 1989.

[53] See *West Africa*, 6-12 March 1989, and the useful discussion in Vines, *Renamo*, pp. 61-5.

shift, however, came from the South Africans. The military reverses in Angola, the developing peace process in relation to Angola/Namibia, and the political demise of P.W. Botha seemed to offer new opportunities.[54] F.W. De Klerk's first overseas visit in Africa as leader of the National Party was to Maputo, where he stated that 'Renamo should, according to our view, stop violence, and become part of the efforts for peaceful development in Mozambique.'[55] In a second visit later in the year De Klerk, now State President, stated emphatically that the South African government was not assisting Renamo.

Finally, the clear-cut indications from preliminary soundings of Renamo (from early 1989) that Frelimo would not be able simply to absorb the rebels into existing structures, together with the increasing unavoidability of doing a deal with the organisation, combined to push the Frelimo leadership towards the achievement of a single task – ending the war on almost any conditions. Henceforth, despite attempts by Frelimo to suggest that they were the result of some new political maturity, the processes of party change, constitutional reform and peace negotiations were inextricably linked to that single task.

The beginning of the end: dealing with Renamo

Frelimo's strategy, while maintaining the existing principle of continuing to isolate Renamo internationally, now took on two further dimensions. Its military weakness and extreme dependence on outside forces compelled Frelimo to find a way to negotiate with an organisation not hitherto noted for its 'modern' political skills. The government's repeated denunciations of Renamo as armed bandits without a political programme was not purely propaganda – there were genuine difficulties in making contact with such an organisation, particularly one whose external 'representatives' were out of touch with realities in Mozambique. But in these new circumstances the abandonment first of 'Marxism-Leninism' and subsequently of the party's 'leading role' made it possible to shift the political terrain in more dramatic ways and to use those shifts to continue keeping Renamo off-guard and disadvantaged – to draw Renamo on to a different kind of political terrain, which maximised

---

[54] P.W. Botha's ill-tempered departure from the South African political scene was in part connected with differences about regional politics. See *The Star*, 22 August 1989.

[55] *Independent*, 20 July 1989.

Frelimo's (political) advantages and minimised Renamo's (military) ones. The idea (and possible the fact) of negotiations, however vehemently denied by Frelimo spokesmen, clearly pre-dated mid-1989, when Chissano first publicly announced that overtures were being made.[56] Before that the government had instituted a legally entrenched amnesty for Renamo guerrillas in December 1987, extended for a further year at the end of 1988. It was acknowledged at the December Peoples Assembly that the government was aware that 'people of goodwill' were trying to make contact with Renamo, though at this stage only with the intention of persuading them to mend their ways. Chissano himself used presidential visits to the provinces both to legitimise the idea of negotiations and to begin the process of de-demonising Renamo. In presidential visits to the provinces, crowds were rhetorically asked whether there should be dialogue with the 'armed bandits' (occasionally the word 'Renamo' was used instead), even if only with a view to their integration. Despite the ritual negative responses, the question was repeatedly asked.[57]

But negotiations between such bitter political enemies required mediation. They were still greatly complicated by the asymmetry, as perceived by Frelimo, between on the one hand a universally recognised government, in control of the national and provincial capitals, and on the other an essentially military force characterised not only by a low degree of political legitimacy but also by a shadowy and elusive leadership with an ill-defined political stance. In this context Frelimo's new rapprochement with the churches proved useful. The Catholic Church had already been calling for reconciliation from 1986 onwards, and a pastoral letter read in all churches on 17 May 1987 called for talks between all parties. This followed shortly after Chissano's official visit to the Vatican, at which the Pope was invited to visit Mozambique – Chissano also

[56] There were periodically rumours of talks much earlier. See *Indian Ocean Newsletter*, 227, and *Africa Confidencial*, 13 (December 1986). Foreign Minister Mocumbi was reported as saying in Lisbon in July 1987 that there had been informal contacts with Renamo. See *Sunday Times* (SA), 16 August 1987. Jacinto Veloso, a key figure in the regime, suggested (let slip?) in an interview that 'We believe in a military solution in the medium term.' *Indian Ocean Newsletter*, special report, 28 February 1987. Government spokesmen continued to deny the reality of talks even while they were going on. For routine denials see *Mozambique News Review*, 123 (18 February 1988) and *AIM Bulletin*, 145 (August 1988). For a discussion of the history of these contacts see A. Vines and K. Wilson, 'Churches and the peace process in Mozambique' in P. Gifford (ed.), *The Christian Churches and the Democratisation of Africa*, Leiden, 1995, pp. 130-47.

[57] Rally in Nampula *Mozambiquefile* no. 149 November 1988. Rally in Maputo province *Tempo*, 968 (30 April 1989) and *Mozambiquefile*, 154 (May 1989).

expressed a wish to open diplomatic relations with the Holy See and assured the papacy there would be no obstacles to the building of a Catholic seminary in the country.[58] A papal visit followed in September 1988 (part of a five-country Southern African tour), during which the Pope called for an end to the war and, at a mass in Maputo on the last day of his visit, appeared to urge talks.

Although the Protestant churches had generally been less confrontational towards the government, they too were keen to enjoy the fruits of greater official tolerance as well as taking part in any 'talks about talks'. In the event it was they who took the lead. Much behind-the-scenes activity bore fruit first in indirect contacts with Renamo and then in direct meetings in Nairobi between delegatious from the Mozambican Council of Churches and Renamo in December 1988 and February 1989. The church delegation asked to meet Dhlakama himself. As part of this process Frelimo had drawn up a twelve-point paper to be delivered to Renamo which was circulated to embassies in late June 1989 and later publicly revealed just before the 5th Congress.[59] While the efforts of the churches were undoubtedly important and continued to be so, the process was also greatly assisted by pressure from more mundane political forces. The first half of 1989 saw a veritable flurry of diplomatic activity. On his return from an overseas visit in April, Chissano had meetings with 'Pik' Botha (his second visit in three months) and the Soviet deputy Foreign Minister, Adamishin. Botha and Adamishin met for consultations too. Chissano also met Prime Minister Margaret Thatcher at the British military training base in Zimbabwe, and although there was no hint of it in the press, she was known to favour negotiations with Renamo.[60] At a press conference in Beira on 23 June, Chissano held out the possibility of 'dialogue' provided that acts of violence ceased. Shortly afterwards the US Assistant Secretary of State was in Maputo for talks.

Much of this activity was designed to find mutually acceptable mediators. In early July Chissano asked President Mugabe at a private meeting to act as mediator and also, apparently, to discuss the implications of a cease-fire.[61] But the long-standing good relations between the ZANU and Frelimo leaders, coupled with the

[58] *Africa Confidencial,* 17 (May 1987); *International Herald Tribune,* 6 May 1987; *Noticias,* 6 May 1987.

[59] *Southscan,* 5 July 1989.

[60] See *Tempo,* 965 (9 April 1989).

[61] *Independent,* 17 July 1989.

previous strong hostility between ZANU and Renamo, required a
mediator who would be acceptable to the other side. It was this
that brought Kenya into the picture. For some time Kenya had
not only allowed a Renamo office in Nairobi but had provided
the organisation with a transmitter and travel documents. Frelimo's
contacts with Kenya had begun some time earlier. In 1988 President
Moi's chief foreign policy adviser, Bethwell Kiplagat, had discussions
with Chissano which were followed by a visit to celebrate ten years
of Moi's rule.[62] Kenyan officials had been present at both meetings
between the Mozambican church leaders and Renamo delegations.
So Chissano now requested Kenyan mediation, which was agreed
and announced at the end of a two-day visit to Maputo by Moi
in late July 1988.

The churchmen finally met a Renamo delegation headed by
Dhlakama in August. Although Frelimo's twelve-point document
was rejected by Renamo, which presented its own sixteen-point
statement, the process had at least begun – however haltingly.
Renamo's demands included the withdrawal of Zimbabwean troops
and a commitment to multi-partyism, but its leaders were in fact
prepared to be flexible on such issues. The real difficulty was
mutual political recognition, with Dhlakama demanding recognition of Renamo as a political party and the government insisting
on the legitimacy of the existing institutions.[63] Reluctant to make
further concessions, Chissano dismissed Renamo's sixteen points
as 'meaningless'. Two further rounds of meetings chaired by
Mugabe and Moi in September and December, failed to break
the deadlock, and the two presidents issued a call for direct talks
between the two sides.

Through this period Chissano kept up the pressure on Renamo
by maintaining a rapid pace of domestic change. A revised draft
constitution was prepared, following a decision of the People's
Assembly in September 1989.[64] The new constitution was to dis-
mantle the developmentalist party-state and replace it with a conventional 'democratic' structure, with the government accountable
to the public via elections in which citizens of all political persuasions could participate. Apart from introducing an extensive
section on the role of the courts and protection for human rights,
it proposed direct elections for a fixed-term presidency (the Presi-

---

[62] *Notícias*, 11 and 14 October 1988.

[63] *Southscan*, 8 September 1989.

[64] Partido Frelimo Anteprojecto de Revisão da Constituição. Also in *Tempo*, 1006
(21 January 1990).

dent would no longer be identical with the president of Frelimo) and for the legislature, and was carefully phrased so as to be compatible with either a single- or a multi-party system. The presidential powers remained formidable and the grey areas of the constitution (such as the structure of regional government) all pointed to considerable presidential discretion. But this Constitution was able to play its part in a strategy of undermining Renamo; first by removing that organisation's few shreds of international respectability by simply conceding the substance of its demands' and secondly by maintaining Frelimo's presence as a national party in a new kind of (electoral) political game.

But Chissano too was under pressure to make a key concession. The United States had already become publicly involved in finding common ground between Frelimo's twelve points and Renamo's sixteen points, reducing them to seven points.[65] In January 1990 Mozambique was removed from the State Department's list of 'Marxist' countries, completing its symbolic turn to the West as well as opening up the possibility of trade credits and insurance cover. In March Chissano made a state visit to the United States and met President Bush. The decision was taken to embark on unconditional direct negotiations.[66] Renamo immediately announced its acceptance of such talks. The first meeting was scheduled to take place in Blantyre, Malawi, but failed to take place because of Renamo indecision and the increasingly partisan role of the Kenyans. The failure of the Blantyre talks in June 1990, despite attempts by 'Tiny' Rowland of the British corporation Lonrho and Bethwell Kiplagat physically to deliver Dhlakama to them, had put the finishing touch to the unsuccessful Kenyan/Zimbabwean phase of joint mediation. The scene then shifted to Italy and to a set of mediators judged acceptable by both sides.

The international diplomatic pressures on Renamo were also ratcheted upwards just at the time when Renamo was under military pressure internally in Zambézia from army counter-offensives and from the activities of the Naparama peasant militias.[67] To some extent Renamo's need for political status could be enhanced by a greatly extended range of international political contact.[68] Chis-

---

[65] *Notícias*, 13 March 1990.

[66] *Notícias*, 14 March 1990.

[67] Renamo bases taken by the Naparama were commonly handed over by them to the FAM, and for this reason Legrand suggests a possible successful manipulation by Mozambican military intelligence: 'Logique de guerre et dynamique de la violence en Zambézia, 1976-1991', *Politique Africaine*, 50 (June 1993), pp. 88-104.

[68] Witney W. Scheidman, 'Conflict Resolution in Mozambique' in David R. Smock

sano continued to exploit the limited opportunities open to him. In the absence of any Renamo participation, Frelimo encouraged major public debate of its new constitutional proposals. From late April onwards, brigades took the debate out from the provincial centres into the countryside (wherever security conditions allowed) and even to refugee camps in neighbouring countries. Opinion thus collected fed back, the government claimed, into an extensive further revision of the draft. During his visit to Lisbon in April 1990, Chissano invited all Mozambicans living abroad to contribute to the discussions (a move interpreted by Renamo as a strategy to coopt other opposition movements). Whatever the real significance of this public consultation, Frelimo made every effort to be seen to be taking public opinion seriously.

A central issue in the constitutional debate was whether Mozambique should adopt a multi-party system. Chissano's public position in earlier speeches (in November 1989 and January 1990) had been that the country was not yet ready for such a development,[69] since parties were likely to form along ethnic or regional lines, thus endangering national unity. Other senior figures in the regime, however, had already floated the possibility, as had the second session of the new Central Committee. The overall balance of popular opinion canvassed was also reported by the official Mozambican press to be against the idea, especially in the rural areas. Yet on 31 July 1990 Chissano announced that the Frelimo Politburo was unanimously in favour of adopting a multi-party system, on the grounds that it would be illegitimate to reject the views of those who supported pluralism by denying them the right to form new parties. The Central Committee endorsed this decision on 10 August – the eve of the second round of direct talks with Renamo in Rome. Subsequently the Frelimo leadership adopted the public position that this was the natural culmination of previous developments.[70] However, it is difficult to regard this move as anything other than a unilateral concession by the Mozambican authorities in an attempt to end the war. Indeed, Chissano quite possibly had it in mind from the beginning that there was to be a multi-party system in Mozambique, but did not include it in the published draft so as to have a further concession to make in negotiations – the fact that public opinion seemed to be against multi-partyism made the size of that projected concession appear even greater.

(ed.), *Making War and Waging Peace*, Washington, 1993.

[69] See *Mozambiquefile*, December 1989.

[70] *Boletim de Celula*, 47 (August 1990).

At the time of Frelimo's 5th Congress, Dhlakama had promised that if the Maputo government went 'all the way and accept[ed] general elections for the people freely to choose their future...the war would be over'.[71]

The Central Committee, meeting on 6-15 August 1990, also voted in favour of changing the style of the country from 'People's Republic' to 'Republic', the 'People's Assembly' was to become the 'Assembly of the Republic; and the 'People's Supreme Court' 'the Supreme Court'. Subsequently, a redraft of the Constitution went forward to the People's Assembly meeting in special session for three weeks from 5 October to discuss and approve the final version. The Assembly voted unanimously in favour of the five articles providing for a multi-party political system, and approved other changes. The new Constitution was approved by the Assembly on 2 November and came into effect on 30 November. It was considerably longer than its predecessor (containing 206 articles rather than eighty), while its preamble was completely rewritten, replacing Frelimo's exclusive claim to power and its commitment to build a socialist society with a shorter, less florid and rather different mythic place for Frelimo in the historical process, presenting the 'deeping of democracy' as the natural development of Fremlimo's achievements. Different icons, essentially those of the Western liberal tradition, were rapidly enumerated – law, rights, equality, the will of the citizens, even 'pluralism of opinion'. Frelimo's leading role was shifted into the past tense; the 'General Principles' referred back to its winning of independence for the country as 'national heritage', eliding the entire intervening period of socialist endeavour.

Opposition political parties were to be permitted for the first time, the general provisions requiring that they be national in scope. The former commitment to a planned economy vanished, market forces were explicitly recognised, and emphasis was placed on the family agricultural sector. The possibility of privatising land, which had been incorporated in the original constitutional draft of January 1990, was rejected in favour of retaining the existing land law. Under this, all land was declared state property, but titles for the use of land could be granted for up to fifty years and could be inherited. This was one of the most contentious and emotive items of the entire constitutional debate; the fear was that Mozambican owners might alienate land to foreign interests. The constitution contained new references to, and a new emphasis and tone on, the questions of religion and national

[71] *O Seculo*, 9 July 1989.

languages. The secular character of the state is maintained, but whereas Article 19 of the old Constitution stated firmly that 'There exists an absolute separation between the State and religious institutions. ...activities of religious institutions must conform with State laws', the new document affirmed that 'The State shall respect the activities of religious denominations in order to promote a climate of social understanding and tolerance, and to strengthen national unity.' In relation to language, while there was no suggestion of abandoning Portuguese, there was an altogether friendlier attitude to national languages (Article 5). This indicated a relaxation of the Frelimo élite's disdain for indigenous languages, previously seen as vehicles of tribalism, and a recognition that such languages might be not only the bearers of culture but vehicles for elementary instruction.

In relation to state institutions, there was a radical reversal of assumptions which had guided the country since independence, de-linking Frelimo from the structures of power. Representative institutions were to be chosen by elections, in which political parties compete through a direct, secret, personal and periodic vote. The President of the Republic was now to be elected by direct universal suffrage for a five-year term. Significantly, the powers of the Standing Commission of the national legislature, now called the Assembly of the Republic, were greatly reduced. Some of these powers were hived off to a new body, the National Defence and Security Council, to act as the consultative body of the President in his capacity as commander-in-chief of the defence and security forces, and with responsibility for declaring a state of siege or emergency. An independent judiciary and procuracy were enshrined in Part IV of the new Constitution. Previously the structure of people's justice, established under the terms of an Act of 2 December 1978, was closely bound to the system of people's assemblies. The apex of the structure, the Supreme People's Court (now the Supreme Court), had previously been subordinate to the People's Assembly. This subordination was now eliminated. Since the process of reform of the judiciary (and the procuracy and other aspects of the administration of justice such as *habeas corpus*) had been going on for some time, the Constitution codified a number of reforms in this area which had already taken place. A Constitutional Council was to be set up to pronounce on the constitutionality of the acts of state bodies and to supervise elections and referenda.

The national symbols, flag and insignia were to remain essentially the same, but not the national anthem (containing as it did some rather inconvenient phrasing about the struggle against the bourgeoisie); a competition was to be held to select a new one.[72] Fundamental changes to the Constitution require both the consent of the Assembly and a public debate and referendum. Lesser changes require a two-thirds majority of the Assembly. The original text stipulated that the Constitution might only be amended five years after the last constitutional revision, but this was eliminated by the final stages of the draft, presumably in the realisation that this would have closed the remaining avenue to a negotiated settlement of the conflict within the existing constitutional framework. Finally, transitional provisions laid down that pending elections the president of Frelimo remained President of the Republic, and existing deputies retained their seats in the Assembly. Until the establishment of the Constitutional Council its powers were to be exercised by the Supreme Court.

The final act

Despite the collapse of the first meeting between Frelimo and Renamo in Blantyre the two sides had been able to agree to transfer the negotiations to a Catholic lay organisation, the Sant' Egidio community in Rome. This had been made possible by fairly longstanding links between the community and Mozambique, which had already been drawn on to improve relations between the Mozambican government and the Vatican.[73] Sant' Egidio also had contacts with Renamo. The first two rounds of discussions, in early July and mid-August, involved protracted procedural disputes as both sides attempted to impose their preferred sequence on the negotiations. Delays also occurred because of Renamo's fears for its own security and the lack of trusted people able to handle negotiations at this level. For these reasons the third round of talks did not resume until November 1990, when there was a partial cease-fire along the Beira and Limpopo corridors. Renamo agreed not to attack the corridors and the government agreed not to use them as a base for offensive operations. Zimbabwean troops were

[72] Replacing symbols is an unenviable task. During discussion as to whether the dove might not form part of the symbols of the new Mozambique, Sr. Rebelo reported that he had been asked: 'Why a dove and not a turkey?' *MIO, Special Report* 2 (5 November 1990).

[73] For details on Sant' Egidio see A. Vines and K. Wilson, *Churches and the Peace Process in Mozambique*, and M. Venancio, 'Mediation by the Roman Catholic Church in Mozambique, 1988-91' in Stephen Chan and Vivienne Jabri (eds), *Mediation in Southern Africa*, London, 1993.

to be confined to specified areas. The agreement was to be monitored by a joint verification commission (JVC),

Between this agreement and the next substantive round of negotiations in May there were frequent violations of the cease-fire by Renamo and periodic threats to torpedo the whole process. The Limpopo corridor, in particular, came under attack in the first quarter of 1991, eliciting on 8 March JVC condemnation of persistent Renamo violations – the day after Renamo itself announced that the partial cease-fire agreement no longer held.[74] However, Renamo's actions were also motivated by a deep-seated suspicion of, and hostility to, the presence of the Zimbabwean military, whose troop numbers it constantly over-estimated.[75] Yet the fact that Renamo's raiding across the border into Zimbabwe virtually ceased in 1991 showed a parallel pragmatic desire to do business. There is evidence that some Zimbabwean special units remained deployed outside the corridors, and to that extent Renamo concern was justified.[76]

The much-postponed sixth round of talks finally got under way on 4 May 1991. These delays were partly attributable to Renamo having experienced technical problems in communicating with its headquarters in Mozambique, which was resolved by the Italian government installing a new communications system between Rome and the Gorongosa.[77] Other more substantive problems also emerged, however – notably over the nature of a 'caretaker' government, the date of forthcoming elections and the political agenda for the talks.[78] Renamo accused Maputo of blocking peace negotiations by refusing to discuss the dismantling of 'private armies', the secret police, the return of refugees and the release of political prisoners, but it came under intense international pressure not to jeopardise the negotiations. At the end of May both delegations in Rome signed an agenda that was more or less imposed by the mediators. The protocol agreement on a 'definitive' and 'detailed' agenda for peace negotiations leading to a cease-fire included the following as political issues to be discussed: civil liberties, press freedom, freedom of movement and political propaganda, as well as the methods by which the large refugee and *deslocados* population

---

[74] *Southscan*, 8 March 1991.

[75] See Hasu H. Patel, 'Zimbabwe's Mediation in Mozambique and Angola' in Chan and Jabri (eds), *Mediation in Southern Africa*, pp. 117-41.

[76] A. Vines, *No Democracy without Money*.

[77] Venancio, 'Mediation', p. 153.

[78] *Independent*, 25 April 1991.

were to be resettled and rehabilitated. The military questions concerned the integration of Renamo into the national armed forces (FAM), the demobilisation of some elements and the restructuring of security forces (SNASP especially). The mechanics of a cease-fire arrangement were also be be discussed.

Negotiations moved forward in fits and starts after the signing of the May protocol. However, talks were suspended during June and much of July for a 'period of reflection' proposed by the Italian mediators, and did not resume until 19 July. They were then held up further by problems with Renamo's radio link between Rome and the Renamo-held area of Canxixe, problems which may have been merely a pretext for delay but which in any case were not resolved until the end of the month. The seventh round of talks largely concerned the question of the legitimacy of the Mozambican state. The Italian mediators attempted to break the deadlock by proposing that Renamo would recognise the Mozambican state and government while in exchange the Mozambique government would grant Renamo a special kind of privileged status that would allow it to undertake certain political activities immediately after the signing of a cease-fire agreement. The government was also prepared to accept that no further laws would be promulgated which went counter to the spirit of the Rome negotiations. Renamo's rejection of, or rather lack of interest in, these proposals and its suggestion that the talks be suspended for the duration of Frelimo's 6th Congress were indicative of continuing differences within the organisation over how to proceed in the negotiation process.

The Mozambican government could not accept suggestions then put forward by Renamo that the registration of political parties should be administered by a non-Mozambican body. Even less acceptable was its proposal that there should be some kind of transitional government with direct United Nations involvement. An eighth round of talks began in September and produced an agreement (protocol no.1 on fundamental principles, signed on 18 October) not greatly removed in substance from that first proposed by the mediators in July. Essentially, on Renamo's side, while the document did not constitute formal recognition of the Mozambican government, it conceded that the existing framework of institutions would remain in place during the period between a cease-fire and the holding of elections, with the government continuing to run the country. For its part, the government agreed that any protocols agreed with Renamo would effectively 'trump' any existing laws, and that Renamo might for all practical purposes start to function as a political party.

Towards the end of 1991 negotiations again appeared deadlocked and were not resolved until a second protocol was signed on 13 November 1991, covering the registration of political parties. Although the details appear arcane, this was an important issue for Renamo, which feared that regulations might be used to hamstring its own activities as a political organisation. The ninth round of talks began in December and initially raised hopes of an early resolution of all problems, perhaps even by Christmas. In fact two of the most contentious items remained to be hammered out; namely, the organisation of elections and military issues. At the beginning of 1992 Portugal, at the request of both parties, became more heavily involved in the mediation efforts and the Italian government, the main mediator along with the Catholic Church, raised the profile of its involvement. These efforts bore fruit in a third protocol (12 March 1992), which not only cleared up outstanding differences over electoral law but effectively promised Renamo aid in completing the transition to becoming a political organisation.

The last stage of negotiations was perhaps the toughest. It concerned military issues and Renamo's persistent demands for further guarantees of the safety of its members. This stage saw the greater involvement of the local actors, Presidents Mugabe of Zimbabwe and Masire of Botswana. It also involved the first face-to-face negotiations between Chissano and Dhlakama: this meeting in August undertook to pass the agreed protocols into Mozambican law and to work for a cease-fire by the beginning of October. A second meeting between the two (in Gaborone, Botswana) was needed to resolve the issue of guarantees and the outstanding points on the creation of a new military force for the country. Finally, a cease-fire accord was signed in Rome on 4 October 1992. Strictly this was not to take formal effect until approved by the Mozambican parliament (which had already been recalled in preparation), but both sides agreed to observe it immediately. President Chissano returned to a hero's welcome in Maputo, reflecting the war-weariness of the population. The agreement, which envisaged substantial UN involvement (much greater than, for example, in Angola), laid down the structure of a new national army of 30,000 men drawn from both sides. After ratification the armed forces of both sides were required to assemble at set points. All armed groups were to be disbanded within six months and elections held by October 1993. Despite substantial delays, this process began in January 1994.

9

FROM SOCIALISM TO LIBERAL CAPITALISM?

'Long live Marxism-Leninism.'[1]

'The fundamental aim is the development of Mozambican individuals.'[2]

'....one of the fundamental problems continues to be the relationship between preserving all that is positive in African tradition while transforming society at its roots.[...] Whether the changes introduced should be called socialist or national democratic transformation, or simply nation-building or modernisation, they do amount to a significant change in the may things are done and the way people see themselves.'[3]

'And Europe is never far away from people's minds: it is still their reference point for good or ill.'[4]

By 1992 Mozambique had completed a curious circle. The glorious visions of progress and enlightenment to be achieved by collective discipline had been overwhelmed by a bitter and fratricidal conflict that was brought to an end by an elaborate peace agreement mediated – indeed, more than mediated – by the Great Powers. Outside Mozambique both the 'socialist' countries and the socialist idea had disintegrated. Of Frelimo's original principles nothing appeared to remain, other than the existence of the party itself. The country has become a recipient of vast amounts of international aid and in some ways has ceased to be a state at all as that is traditionally understood. Its extreme economic and political weakness has made it vulnerable to massive penetration by Western

---

[1] Marcelino dos Santos, SWB ME 8408 B1, 5 November 1986.

[2] Joaquim Chissano, Frelimo Second National Conference, SWB ME 0214 B1, 27 July 1988.

[3] A. Sachs and G.H. Welch, *Liberating the Law: Creating Popular Justice in Mozambique*, London, 1990, p. 24.

[4] Tom Glaser in *The Courier*, Mozambique: Country Report, 114 (March-April 1989), pp. 19-26.

agencies of all kinds, at the same time as new (though not yet clearly formulated) ideas of international order are legitimising such penetration. In brief, Mozambique has become an experimental laboratory for new forms of Western domination. To make sense of these most recent developments it is necessary to take account of changes in international politics as well as certain conceptual issues, a task which this chapter seeks at least to begin.

If constitutions may be said to be 'autobiographical', then political changes are most obviously visible in such documents.[5] A comparison of the 1975 and 1990 texts reveals how much the 'fundamental aims' of the Mozambican state have altered. In the first Constitution these aims included the elimination of the structures of colonial and traditional oppression and exploitation and the mentality underlying them; the extension and strengthening of democratic people's power; the building of an independent economy and the promotion of cultural and social progress; the defence and consolidation of independence and national unity; the building of people's democracy and the construction of the material and ideological bases of socialist society; the establishment and development of relations of friendship and cooperation with other peoples and states; and the prosecution of the struggle against colonialism and imperialism. In the new Constitution the aims of the state are defined as the defence of independence and sovereignty; the consolidation of national unity; the building of a society of social justice and the achievement of material and spiritual well-being for its citizens; the defence and promotion of human rights and the equality of citizens before the law; the strengthening of democracy, of freedom and of societal and individual stability; the development of the economy and of scientific and technological progress; the affirmation of the Mozambican personality, of its traditions and other social and cultural values; and the establishment and development of relations of friendship and cooperation with other states.

Clearly two distinctly different political languages are recognisable here, those of socialism and liberalism. At a conference in Maputo in 1990 President Chissano said, in a rather sad speech, 'We have done everything the West has asked – what more can we do?'[6] There is no question that Mozambique has been under pressure to abandon socialism and adopt a liberal language. It is

---

[5] S.E. Finer, *Five Constitutions*, London, 1979, p. 21.

[6] One of the present authors (Tom Young) was present to hear this speech. See also John Saul's observations in 'Mozambique: The failure of Socialism?', *Southern Africa Report*, 6, 2 (1990).

not sufficient, however, to suggest that these changes are simply the result of international forces – that Mozambique is a weak country and is pushed around by stronger states, adopting Marxism when it felt dependent on the Soviet bloc and liberalism as it became dependent on the West. Or, in a more generous version, that Frelimo in its early days adopted a socialist vision of social change and has been forced by the Western powers to give that up.[7] Frelimo's own accounts of these changes have tended to vacillate between claiming that they were inevitable developments (and even trying to claim credit for them) and that they were imposed. Such ambiguities suggest that these accounts are not wrong in themselves, but miss some fundamental issues. In the case of both Constitutions Mozambicans, or at least their leaders, had a considerable say in the matter and in some sense opted first for a version of socialism and latterly for a version of liberalism.

But it is also clear that these two languages are 'autobiographical' only in a rather odd sense. The 1975 text is clearly to be located in a tradition that can claim some origin in a broadly defined Marxism, but more specifically in Leninist/Stalinist constitutionalism. The 1990 Constitution, despite its affirmation of 'the traditions and values of Mozambican society' of which not one is designated, defined or reflected in that document, is in fact from beginning to end drawn from the tradition of John Locke and John Stuart Mill. What makes the autobiographical element clear is that for the constitution-framers and the political élite generally they are the only two *conceivable* political languages. The Central Committee report to Frelimo's 6th Congress, in some ways a document of extraordinary honesty, asserts that Mozambique achieved independence during 'a historical period characterised by continual rivalry between two economico/philosophical paradigms, capitalism and communism' and that it is necessary to understand that 'Frelimo's options were the solutions that offered themselves as viable to us'.[8] The effects of an ideology of the 'blank page', a term coined by Geffray to characterise Frelimo's understanding of rural Mozambique, went far beyond that understanding to encompass the country as a whole. For the new political leadership an independent Mozambique could only consist of a

---

[7] Thus Hanlon, *Mozambique: Who Calls the Shots?*, London, 1991.

[8] Frelimo 6th Congress Central Committee Report, pp. 21 and 25. The 6th Congress was 'closed'. We are extremely grateful to Polly Gaster for obtaining a copy of the Report for us. It is a fascinating document which deserves more analysis than we have been able to give it here.

blank sheet, available to replicate one or other 'economico-
philosophical paradigm'.

It might be argued that this was only to be expected from a
modernising élite, and that Frelimo's enemies would articulate a
political discourse of a different nature. Throughout its conflict
with the government Renamo did in fact argue that its struggle
was based on Mozambican traditions, which were being deliberately
attacked by Frelimo, and the evidence shows that, in some parts
of Mozambique at least, tolerance of rather than support for
Renamo was in part an effect of Frelimo's assault on traditional
values and structures.[9] But – an this is the important point – when
confronted with the need to present political positions in a recognisable language, particularly in international fora, Renamo has
presented essentially liberal ones.[10] Cynics will argue that this is
simply an effect of Renamo's Western and conservative backers.
This is true, but what is more interesting is that Renamo's
'theoreticians' have made no *attempt* to articulate the beliefs and
traditions of those they claim in some sense to represent. Indeed
if constitutional history repeats itself, first as tragedy and then as
farce, the rapidity of such cycles seems greatest in those countries
most removed from 'modernity'.[11]

These shifts recall the historic battles of socialism and liberalism.
Socialism's critique of liberalism focused on the substantive inequalities of a liberal order, while liberalism's critique of socialism
focused on the abuse of political power. Socialism demanded intervention by the state in all areas of social life to bring about
rapid emancipation for all; liberalism insisted that the state be
restrained so as not to endanger the freedom of any. But the
historic fury of this battle should not be allowed to obscure two
important points. The first concerns the nature and uses of modern
political power. Our own (Western) historical development has
ensured that we experience liberal-capitalist social orders as freedom
and identify freedom as the individual capacity to pursue projects
unhindered by others, though in practice this is true only in the
economic realm, and even within that largely in the sphere of
consumption. These historical transformations have found theoretical

---

[9] Endless cautions about the dangers of the term 'tradition', while we do not
ignore them, are a trifle irksome. The point here is that many Mozambican traditions
and practices were emphatically neither liberal nor socialist.

[10] See the Renamo Constitution of July 1991 – drawn up, it would appear, by
Bruce Fein, a lawyer acting for Renamo in the United States.

[11] The absurd mimicry of the US Constitution in the July 1991 document hardly
needs comment here.

expression in familiar liberal principles. The assumptions of neutrality between and tolerance towards all other (necessarily more limited) positions has enabled liberalism to deny that it is itself a tradition or a point of view.[12] Complementary assumptions about the universality of liberalism's own values (most notoriously in the notion of 'economic man' but also in all sorts of less rigorous notions like 'inexorable social change') have allowed it to obscure and even deny its own historical place and effects.

Yet reflection on the historical processes by which what we now experience as liberal social orders came into being leads to severe doubt on the plausibility of these assumptions. Contemporary liberalism, deploying a series of linked notions of social equilibrium and 'civil society', has largely concealed its earlier obsessions with unlimited state power, a state power which (in that wonderful phrase of Jean-Jacques Rousseau that is supposed to strike terror into the hearts of liberals but in fact exactly describes their practice) would 'force men to be free'. It has thus also concealed the degree to which it has countenanced intervention by the state to bring about the very transformations in 'human nature' that it supposedly found to be 'given'.[13] Despite an apparent reliance on arguments from 'nature', the historical agenda of this liberalism has been 'to deconstruct old customary ways of life and to produce new ones'.[14] In brief, this agenda has been about the imposition of a particular form of state and a particular form of self, and people are not conceived of as free to refuse either. The first architects of liberal thinking were well aware of this.

The contemplation of these highly authoritarian forms of intervention provides the clue to a second essential point, namely that both these languages are the bearers of political modernity; that they have as much that unites as separates them. The issue of the form and scope of political power excepted, the agendas of liberalism and socialism look much less distinct. Despite important differences in terminology, much of the agenda of 'modernisation' is common to both. There are two core elements in such thinking. The first is neatly captured in Michael Walzer's

---

[12] It is true that more recently liberal theorists have retreated from claims of neutrality. See for example J. Rawls, 'Justice as Fairness: Political not Metaphysical', *Philosophy and Public Affairs*, 14, 3 (1985) pp. 223-51: and some of the contributions to R. Bruce Douglas, G.M Mara and Henry Richardson (eds), *Liberalism and the Good*, London, 1990.

[13] I. Shapiro, *The Evolution of Rights in Liberal Theory*, Cambridge, 1986, *passim*.

[14] J. Tully,' Governing Conduct' in E. Leites (ed), *Conscience and Casuistry in Early Modern Europe*, Cambridge, 1988, p. 68.

phrase 'disconnected criticism'. As he describes it, 'The problem with disconnected criticism, and thus with criticism that derives from newly discovered or invented moral standards, is that it presses its practitioners toward manipulation and compulsion.'[15] Both the liberal and the socialist agendas have laid claim to supposedly universal political and ethical standards. But what is common to their understanding of political modernity? The second core element which provides this understanding is the creation of the 'unencumbered self', a process involving the radical destruction of the 'constitutive' attachments; that is, those attachments which are part of the self or from which, as it were, the self cannot stand back.[16] Clearly this is in part linked historically to establishing the conditions for capitalism, but it is not only about that. That this is so is shown by the second and complementary phenomenon of re-forming people. As Taylor puts it, 'radical disengagement opens the prospect of self-remaking.'[17] But this creation of unencumbered selves, the products of 'freedom', makes possible entirely new forms of social and political power. Such emancipated individuals are much easier to weld into new collectivities and to subject to various kinds of social discipline. As students of war have often noted, 'by revolutionising society, the state was able as never before to exploit the energies of society for war.'[18] Clearly what lies at the heart of political 'modernity', in its socialist or liberal versions, is political mobilisation.

It was these features of political modernity which were appropriated by the post-colonial élites where they were not entirely venal. The new African states were run by leaders who looked to essentially Western visions of modernity and progress – as has been shown, Frelimo was no exception to this rule. An essential part of that vision was the centrality of the state in bringing about rapid progress. But, 'alien in origin, these [states] possessed neither symbolic depth, nor a common language of deep accountability, nor any indigenous conventions of high-political restraint.'[19] Two processes clearly constrained the implementation of these visions. First, such states had to operate within specific social settings. 'A

---

[15] M. Walzer, *Interpretation and Social Criticism*, Cambridge, MA, 1987, p. 64

[16] For this usage see M. Sandel, 'The Procedural Republic and the Unencumbered Self', *Political Theory*, 12 (1984), pp. 81-96.

[17] C. Taylor, *Sources of the Self*, Cambridge, 1989, p. 171.

[18] P. Paret, *Clausewitz and the State*, Oxford, 1976, p. 32.

[19] J. Lonsdale, 'Political Accountability in African History' in P. Chabal (ed.), *Political Domination in Africa*, Cambridge, 1986, p. 144.

massive obstacle to the rampant doctrinaire state is the great pluralism of African societies.'[20] The state, to be effective, found itself having to deal with social forces which were not congruent with Western state models and thus to develop various forms of clientelism, patronage and ethnic coalition-building. Secondly, of course, society as it were seeps into the state, the lower level functionaries upon whom the leadership rely to implement the visions of progress having often very imperfectly internalised such visions and their accompanying conceptual and political practices. Thus the ubiquitous phenomena in Africa, at the very heart of the state in the Western sense, of armies that split along ethnic lines, bureaucracies that do not administer and so on.[21]

Despite the fact that political modernity has proved much more difficult to attain in Africa than had been anticipated, the connection between 'unencumbered'/remade selves and 'disconnected criticism' grounds a very powerful dynamic in Western culture that sanctions doing good to people by remaking them according to a universalising logic.[22] Western liberal discourse of course has its cynical and duplications side in the context of Cold War and/or Great Power politics (though this is often exaggerated), but the World Bank, Amnesty International and the various other authors of this discourse have a great deal in common and genuinely think they stand for a better world. *Because* liberalism is a massive historical forgetting and because it is caught up in its own notions and language of equality (of individuals and states), the liberal social order being offered to Mozambique and other Third World countries has to be the current model in which the state must be restrained, with the economy allowed to operate 'freely' and citizens permitted to related to each other through contract and rights. That is the only form of liberal state and civil society that we (now) know. Thus the dilemma facing such interests and positions is clear: historical amnesia, 'universalist' dogmas and assumptions of equality (about both individuals and states) preclude the overt recommendation to Third World countries of a Hobbesian Leviathan

---

[20] L. Sanneh, 'Religion and Politics in Africa: A Thematic Approach' in D. Rimmer (ed.), *Africa Thirty Years On*, London, 1991, p. 111.

[21] See C. Clapham, 'The African State' in Rimmer (ed.), *Africa Thirty Years On*. See also the important contribution by S. Kaviraj, 'On State, Society and Discourse in India' in J. Manor (ed.), *Rethinking Third World Politics*, Harlow, 1991.

[22] This, of course, is not to say that there are not other tendencies (relativist ones, for example), but they have had much less effect. There has not ever been and is not now any respect in the West for non-Western cultures where these deviate significantly from 'universal' norms.

that will do the grim business of 'deconstructing' old ways of life and creating the social preconditions for a liberal state.[23] Thus, the only alternative is to find functional equivalents of Leviathan which can bring about those social transformations.

It is within this space that 'governance' and 'civil society' have come to be central operational concepts in Western policy. There are, it is true, diplomatic advantages in governance while considerations of sovereignty, however threadbare they may seem to liberal scholars,[24] regulate at least rhetorical relations between states and make it impossible to demand that sovereign states adopt specific forms of government. Thus Britain's Mrs Lynda Chalker (then Minister of Overseas Development): 'It's not for me to say how any other country except my own should be run.[...] But there is one thing I *will say*: whatever your system of government, only those countries which apply the principles of good government will be successful in the long run.'[25] Behind such homilies is a growing tendency to link policy 'correctness' (that is, some form of market economy) and policy implementation to other features of the wider society. In other words, the unspoken assumption is that mere pressure on states to change policies will not work because these states are not able to implement such policies.

Such considerations are clearly at work in a variety of initiatives, from the World Bank's capacity enhancement programme to the funding of political parties.[26] World Bank analysts have long moved beyond a crude 'markets-solve-everything' view. They suggest that 'private enterprise needs an enabling environment and only government can provide this. So the problems of governance must be faced; they cannot simply be willed away by privatisation, economic liberalisation and reliance on market processes.'[27] But there is also an emphasis that goes beyond the restructuring of governance to the restructuring of civil society – an implicit recognition

---

[23] For an argument of implacable intellectual honesty within a liberal framework that comes close to such a position, see R.D. Jeffries, 'The State, Structural Adjustment and Good Government in Africa', *Journal of Commonwealth and Comparative Politics*, 31, 1 (1993), pp. 22-35.

[24] Cf.C.Beitz, 'Sovereignty and Morality in International Affairs' in D. Held (ed.), *Political Theory Today*, Cambridge, 1991.

[25] Opening speech at Wilton Park Special Conference on Promoting Good Government in Africa, 27-31 January 1992.

[26] World Bank, *A Framework for Capacity Building in Policy Analysis and Economic Management in sub-Saharan Africa*, 1989.

[27] P. Landell-Mills, 'Creating Transparency, Predictability and an Enabling Environment for Private Enterprise', Wilton Park special conference, 1992, p. 7.

that there will be no liberal state until there are liberal persons. Comparing the management of public enterprises in Eastern Europe with those in Africa, Landell-Mills, a senior policy adviser at the World Bank, regrets that 'African managers cannot easily set aside their loyalties to their community.[... They] cannot easily escape the heavy social obligations that take up a large proportion of their time.'[28] For such analyses the idea that Africans might have general and non-contractual obligations to their communities is an obstacle to efficiency – an obstacle that outside agencies whose concern is to promote economic development must somehow remove.

Not surprisingly, 'civil society' has been colonised by so-called NGOs. Despite a surface hostility towards the World Bank and the network of Western interests and agencies of which it is part, there are considerable common elements in their different agendas. The radical noises made by NGOs about Western 'interests' should not obscure their common vision of what development means – a vision arising from Western notions of the state and the self. The most radical part of NGO discourse is the emphasis on 'grassroots' participation and the strong demand that this become part of the development process. But this terminology is always to be understood entirely within Western preconceptions. 'Social justice also demands the eradication of all forms of discrimination, whether on grounds of race, creed, tribe or sex.'[29] Although NGO literature is replete with contradictions (demanding the protection of cultures in one breath and the elimination of 'cultural bias' in the next), the agenda is known in advance – 'progressive', 'grassroots' organisations are simply to be 'mobilised' around it.[30] For its part the Bank, though no doubt controlled by Western states, has a vision of economic order rooted in standard liberal conceptions and not simply the plaything of particular Western interests. The radical vision of NGOs is not basically different – it shares the Bank's doubts about the capacities of Third World governments, increasingly shares its stress on 'civil society' and entirely shares its lack of interest in and contempt for cultural traditions that do not square with Western notions of 'rights' and 'justice'.

Much of the recently induced change in Mozambique, though of course shaped by much more particular factors and various contingencies, has followed these contours. That in fact Mozam-

---

[28] Landell-Mills, p. 6.

[29] J. Clark, *Democratising Development*, London, 1991, p. 30.

[30] For an interesting analysis of this literature see D. Williams, 'Liberalism and the Development Discourse', *Africa*, 63, 3 (1993), pp. 419-29.

bique was pressured to adopt liberal democracy, despite Frelimo's official propaganda that it was a 'natural' development, has been said in almost as many words by Chissano himself.[31] To change constitutions and at least the form of institutional structures is relatively easy, and the pressures to do so have become more and more overt. The logic of liberalism goes well beyond a demand for changes in particular policies (the routine stuff of relations between states) and calls for the restructuring of the state and related matters such as property relationships, as the constitutional changes show. Below the formal constitutional level, in a variety of new statutes and regulations, Mozambique has been required to restructure the state in ways which give certain rights to citizens against the state, withdraw the state from many activities, and create new forms of representation within the state. There are of course possibilities for certain kinds of resistance of the 'foot-dragging' type to these pressures, but what is important is that pressure to design new (Western) institutional structures is intense and un-relenting. Such new structures naturally require new kinds of people to man them – especially those able at least to reproduce liberal dogma, primarily though not exclusively in economic matters.[32] In practice, despite Mozambique's equipping itself with all the trappings of a democratic state, the sheer leverage of outside powers and in particular the coordinating role of the IMF/World Bank, with the full support of the Great Powers, has subjected the country to an extraordinary degree of foreign tutelage.

On its own account, 'partly by design, partly by default, the Bank today has a near monopoly on development strategy dialogue with the [Mozambican] Government.'[33] Others have suggested more bluntly that the Bank has 'in effect [taken] over the economic policy implementation functions of the Mozambican govern-ment'.[34] The economic changes forced on the country have been centrally concerned with reforming the role of the state and with the creation of markets/private economic forces, both of which processes are to be carried out in line with 'international standards'. The first has involved increasingly calibrated interference in the detail of economic policy-making as well as the deployment of

[31] See e.g. interview in *Africa Hoje*, October 1993.

[32] David N. Plank, 'Aid, Debt and the End of Sovereignty: Mozambique and its Donors', *Journal of Modern African Studies*, 31, 3 (1993), pp. 407-30, has some useful comments on this.

[33] This quote is from an internal Bank working document dated 25 January 1993.

[34] P. Gibbon *et al.* (eds), *A Blighted Harvest: The World Bank and African Agriculture in the 1980s*, London, 1993, p. 42.

senior personnel. The second has involved such policies as privatisation of state assets and the removal of price controls. Thus by 1994, although the Great Powers continued to be generous with aid, the details of their shaping of economic policy included insistence on the introduction of value added tax, the lifting of all price controls, direct constraints on subsidies to public enterprises, the complete restructuring of the banking system including precise instructions on staff reductions, and the compulsory sale of state companies according to a strict timetable.[35] Behind the scenes, and not easily documented, there has been massive interference at a detailed level, up to and including the forced redeployment of named officials.

Despite the Bank's emphasis on the 'technical' nature of many of these economic reforms, there are strong parallels between these changes and those in the political realm, in particular the relationship between the state and the 'market' on the one hand and the state and 'civil society' on the other. Western powers and interests are involved in this, some channeling their aid through NGOs in order to avoid working through the Mozambican government, an orientation that dovetails with the ideological proclivities of many NGOs themselves. Many Western NGOs, often encouraged by their home governments, are setting up Mozambican equivalents with which they can deal directly (a sort of 'civil society' strategy, but one which parallels the interlocutor strategy at the state level).[36] Aid is being deliberately directed to assist in the construction of new social groups committed to the market economy. The Commonwealth Secretariat talks of the need 'to break the logic and patterns of thought associated with a command economy and explain how markets work'[37] (one wonders how much market failure is part of this 'teaching').

Whatever the eventual outcome (we return to this below), the transitional costs of these policy shifts have been immense. The success of the economic policies remains unclear even in the donors' own terms, since the rapid growth of the first two years of structural adjustment had slowed down by 1990 (see Table 9.1). Privately, even some Bank analysts suggest that in the earlier period (1987-90) the country experienced a 'boomlet', including

---

[35] *Indian Ocean Newsletter*, 25 June 1994.

[36] Donor pledges to Mozambican NGOs greatly exceed the funds requested! See *Mozambiquefile*, August 1994.

[37] Commonwealth Secretariat, *Capacity-Building in Mozambique: The Commonwealth Contribution*, London, 1991. This document usefully illustrates the sheer range of foreign involvement in the construction of the new Mozambique.

'once-off efficiency gains', and that 'some of the increase in [agricultural] production...is partly a statistical phenomenon of registration'.[38]

Table 9.1. REAL ANNUAL GROWTH RATES, 1987-90 (%)[39]

	1987	1988	1989	1990
GDP	5	6	5	2
Agricultural production	7	7	3	1
Industrial production	9	8	7	-10

Even if growth resumed an upward curve from 1993 onwards, it remains difficult to disentangle the effects of the reforms from the enormous influx of aid that has occurred since the late 1980s.[40] The period of growth also coincided with a steep rise in the country's external debt, continuing high foreign trade deficits and something close to a collapse of its industrial sector.

Despite the ostensible objectives of the PRE proclaimed by both the World Bank and the Mozambican government, including a shift in resources back to the rural areas and peasant producers in particular, it is not clear that this has occurred. Marketed production did not sustain large increases over the period 1987-92 as peasants complained of high prices for tools and consumer goods, itself partly an effect of sharp devaluations. It has been argued that the Mozambican peasantry have experienced few improvements in terms of trade and still suffer from weak marketing networks and poor agricultural support services. Agriculture's share of the government budget has continued to fall, and the bulk of that still goes into 'big projects'.

While the gains are unclear, the losses have been palpable. The loss of overall macro-economic control undoubtedly caused the Frelimo government and Mozambican society severe difficulties. There is no disagreement on the general fact that real wages declined during this period, possibly by as much as 24% in 1987-92.[41] Attempts to compensate the working population by minimum wage legislation have constantly fallen behind price rises.[42] For urban people the abolition or reduction of food subsidies has

---

[38] See footnote 36.

[39] Gibbon *et al.*, *Blighted Harvest*, p. 46.

[40] See *Mozambiquefile*, January 1994. For growth figures see IMF, *Request for Additional Funding under the Enhanced Structural Adjustment Funding*, 13 May 1994.

[41] See *Mozambiquefile*, October 1993, and IMF, *Mozambique: Recent Economic Developments*, 22 July 1993, p. 14.

[42] For detailed figures see *Mozambiquefile*, August 1992.

caused severe hardship. During 1988 the prices of rice, maize and sugar increased by between 300 and 500%.[43] The impact of devaluation and the abandonment or erosion of rationing systems for basic foods was exacerbated by sharp reductions in expenditure on health and education, from some 24% of the budget in 1986 to 3.2% in 1990.[44] Increased charges for medical services, combined with ill-understood systems of means-testing, meant that many people lost access to even rudimentary health care. Infant mortality remains stubbornly high.

These economic changes were bound to have social effects. Strikes occurred throughout the economy in 1990 and were reflected in open demonstrations of protest at the May Day rally, both that year and the following year.[45] While the official trade union movement, the OTM (Organização de Trabalhadores Moçambicanos), which became delinked from Frelimo as a result of the constitutional changes, has struggled to constrain protest within official structures, violent economic protest has flared outside those structures, as in the riots against 100% bus fare increases in Maputo in November 1993 which left two dead, many injured and looting all along the Avenida Eduardo Mondlane.[46] Increasingly desperate people have resorted to individual solutions, including moonlighting and crime. Generally there has been a coarsening of urban life, reflected in soaring crime rates (including much higher levels of violence and entirely novel sorts of crime such as the murder of judges and senior police officers), rioting, 'necklacing' of criminals by angry crowds, and rural vigilantism.[47] Related phenomena are mutinies, thefts and outright looting by soldiers.[48] Thus it is not far-fetched to suppose that 'the broader social fabric has deteriorated to one of individual survival at all costs'.[49]

Nor have the effects of structural adjustment been limited to the 'masses' although the effects have of course been harshest for them. Whatever the surface plausibility of the model of market

[43] J. Marshall, 'Structural Adjustment and Social policy in Mozambique', *Review of African Political Economy*, July 1990, pp.28-43, esp. p. 32.

[44] See M. Bowen, 'Beyond Reform: Adjustment and Political Power in Contemporary Mozambique', *Journal of Modern African Studies*, 30, 2 (1992), pp. 255-79.

[45] For details see MIO, *News Review*, 172.

[46] *Mozambiquefile*, December 1993.

[47] See *Mozambiquefile*, September 1991, on an outburst of lynchings and beatings in August of that year.

[48] On events in Zambézia province, see for example *Mozambiquefile*, September 1992 and March 1993.

[49] J. Marshall, 'Structural Adjustment and Social Policy in Mozambique', p. 29.

capitalism in a country like Mozambique, the form of transition has created many possibilities for personal enrichment for the political élite and the well-connected. The conjunction of difficult economic circumstances with the legitimation of private gain has exposed officials to temptations, while privatisation in its various guises has offered great rewards. Corruption on a small scale had doubtless always existed, but had been kept in check by the Frelimo leadership's moral integrity and socialist ideology. From the late 1980s, however, corruption became rife within the state sector of the economy and notoriously within the armed forces. As one government minister put it, 'There was a moral constraint that was lifted with PRE. Now to be honest means to be stupid.'[50] The main beneficiaries of the disposal of state farms, for example, have been either foreigners or government and army officials.[51] The latter have rapidly acquired the trappings of individual wealth.[52] In particularly flagrant cases relatively low-level officials have been prosecuted, but senior figures have remained untouched. A 1990 law required ministers and senior officials to declare their incomes and assets within sixty days of surrendering their office. Four years later none had done so.[53]

But corruption of the crude kind is merely one of the most obvious effects of a transition to a market economy in circumstances of acute deprivation. The huge presence of foreign organisations of all kinds has had a severe impact on the state's capacity to deploy its own personnel, as large numbers of the more highly qualified have taken up employment with non-state organisations, often foreign NGOs. Much the same applies to the public sector more generally.[54] Beyond the fairly obvious difficulty of holding on to qualified personnel in the state sector, much of the effects of this foreign presence are of course unconscious. Standards of living, notions of status, the trappings and assumptions of Western lifestyles are communicated by example as NGOs take on more local staff. Western norms ('international standards') become those to which people, especially those with any training, aspire.

The common feature of all these aspects of a transition to liberal

[50] Quoted in Hanlon, *Mozambique: Who calls the shots?*, p. 235.

[51] Gibbon *et al.*, *Blighted Harvest*, p. 50. The distinction between 'legal' and 'illegal' acquisition is often rather academic, e.g. see *Mozambiquefile*, April 1994.

[52] For some details see *Africa Analysis*, 3 September 1993, and discussion in the Mozambican Assembly reported in *Mozambiquefile*, April 1992.

[53] *Mozambiquefile*, December 1994.

[54] For details of such developments in the University and Radio Mozambique see *Mozambiquefile* April 1994.

capitalism has been an increasing dependence on foreign aid of all kinds. Relative to its size Mozambique is now the most heavily indebted country in the world, with foreign debt in 1992 totalling some $5 billion (about five times the country's GDP).[55] The interest on it has had to be constantly rescheduled in order for the fiction of repayment to be maintained at all. The country's exports are negligible (the two largest items are prawns and cashew nuts), and until 1992 'foreign grants continued to cover half of all Mozambique's merchandise imports'.[56] Most development projects are carried out with foreign aid, and even the current budget relies on donor contributions. A whole culture has grown up of appealing for foreign aid for any and every expenditure or 'project'. None of this is likely to change in the forseeable future. But this extreme material dependence must induce dependence of other kinds, a debilitating loss of self-esteem and sense of self-capacity. This has inevitably had its most profound effects at the political level. There has been a general political fragmentation and loss of political authority at every level which goes well beyond issues of corruption and dependence. It includes the abandonment of an ideological cohesion that, whatever its difficulties, gave the ruling group a certain coherence. And the vacuum has not been replaced by any public discussion but by the unquestioning acceptance that IMF/World Bank strategies are the only possibilities there are. Thus the strategies of the Mozambican state have been reduced to little more than mediating the demands of donors and its domestic constituencies.[57]

All of these features of the contemporary Mozambican situation were sharply highlighted by the operations of ONUMOZ (the UN peacekeeping force) in the country during the two-year period between the conclusion of the General Peace Agreement and the elections which took place in 1994.[58] The status of forces agreement granted ONUMOZ personnel diplomatic immunity, unlimited freedom of movement and exemption from all taxes and duties.

---

[55] IMF, *Mozambique Recent Economic Developments,* 22 July 1993, p. 1.

[56] Ibid. p. 30.

[57] David N. Plank, 'Aid, Debt, and the End of Sovereignty'.

[58] Much of the commentary on the elections in the following section draws on the experience and observation of Tom Young as an official UN election observer, the opportunity to observe the UN being at least as valuable as the opportunity to observe the elections. During this period various individuals provided information and assessments on a non-attributable basis, for which we are grateful. Much of the factual information is taken from the invaluable *Mozambique Peace Process Bulletin* edited by Joe Hanlon.

Beyond these extensive formal powers and rights, the UN operation in Mozambique was run by its special representative Aldo Ajello in a very 'political' way. Clearly in part under pressure to secure a UN success in Africa after the débâcles in Somalia and Angola, Ajello, a forceful speaker and (by all accounts) negotiator, became an important part of the Mozambican political process – pressuring, encouraging and cajoling the various actors involved.

The elections formed a central part of the peace process and were largely engineered, paid for and monitored from outside. The creation of 'democratic politics' before the elections was also largely orchestrated by outside interests. Renamo itself received a huge amount of money legitimately, in the form of a UN-administered trust fund (the bulk of the funds were provided by Italy), to transform itself into a political party. It almost certainly received more behind the scenes. Constant demands by Renamo for money, backed by threats to boycott the whole process, formed an almost permanent feature of the two-year period, threats which just before the electoral campaign netted another $5 million. Some twenty other 'unarmed' parties came into existence, although not all met the criteria for registration. A second UN trust fund was intended for these parties, none of which secured any significant public support or even awareness, but all were entitled to money from the fund. It was to be released in tranches of $50,000, with the next tranche only being released after the first had been accounted for. After the election none of these minor parties showed much enthusiasm to account for their use of the money as the electoral law required.

The elections were 'run' by the Mozambican National Electoral Commission (CNE), but its technical arm, the STAE, was largely trained and funded by the UNDP (UN Development Programme). The CNE's transport capacity was largely funded from outside, including the helicopters leased (still in camouflage paint) from the South African air-force and flown by South African pilots.[59] The operation of election observation itself at every stage exhibited the painful efforts to maintain Mozambican 'sovereignty' while confirming the fact of ONUMOZ – essentially outside rule. Although observers had to enter the country through Maputo or Beira, their passports were collected and sorted by UN officials while Mozambicans stamped them. Election observers were told by UN officials in Johannesburg not to inform the Mozambicans that they were bringing in meticais. This mentality was adopted by many observers

---

[59] Who told Tom Young that in Nampula, at least, ONUMOZ always overrode the CNE in the allocation of aviation fuel!

who, despite the instructions merely to observe, instructed local people what to do. The UN operation at its middle and lower levels was run by young Westerners who were doubtless up with all the current ideological fads but knew little about Mozambique. To be a 'new missionary' in the late twentieth century requires no learning – merely a walkie-talkie and a four-wheel-drive.

As for the significance of the elections themselves, much remains unclear. In a country as profoundly exposed to Western influence as Mozambique it would be strange if liberal democracy did not represent the aspirations of some, or at least constitute their notion of progress. In urban areas especially, political activists seemed very young and to be quite genuine in their desire and commitment to elections. Among such activists there was undoubtedly a resentment at any suggestion that the elections were not theirs.[60] But the significance of other features of the situation remain less obvious. It needs to be borne in mind that virtually all those involved in the elections were being paid, and by Mozambican standards paid quite well. This did not prevent strikes and riots by polling staff, extending in some cases to hostage-taking.[61] That many of the electors had little understanding of the electoral process was evidenced by empirical observation, the large number of spoilt papers and some accidental effects of the layout of the ballot papers themselves.[62] Voter apathy was widely observed by commentators of all persuasions – 'most people say they are registering because they have been told they must.'[63] The election campaigns were lacklustre. Few parties exploited the radio and television time they had been given, despite the funds allocated for such purposes. Campaigning in the form of rallies and open-air meetings was lifeless and rather formalistic. One observer called them the 'elections of silence'.[64]

Liberal democracy works best as a form of political decision-

---

[60] Often this was exacerbated by the great disparity in the technological capabilities of the ONUMOZ, the Mozambican government and the CNE. In Nampula the humblest UN election observer knew there was to be a third day of voting before any of the Mozambican election officials or even the provincial headquarters of the CNE knew this.

[61] For details see *Mozambiquefile*, December 1994

[62] The União Democratica, which happened to be the last party on the Assembly elections ballot papers, clearly benefited from Chissano being the last candidate on the presidential election ballot forms. Some electors voted for the last name on both forms.

[63] *Mozambique Peace Process Bulletin*, 12 (September 1994).

[64] *Expresso*, 12 November 1994.

making and political legitimation in societies whose members think of themselves as individuals, characterised by material interests among which there can be trade-offs. It fits with notions of markets and civil society which see these as simply spheres of interaction for such individuals. Yet far from 'the market' and civil society being 'spontaneous' social developments, as liberal myth requires, to be effective they must be penetrated and shaped by a modernising state and moreover one which is driven by a ruling élite armed with new forms of expertise and motivated by more than just a desire for self-aggrandisement and self-enrichment – it also needs a vision of how 'to deconstruct old customary ways of life and to produce new ones'.[65]

To say the least, it is possible to doubt whether these conditions exist in Mozambique. The UN, the Western great powers and the growing group of international bureaucrats who stand for the 'new world order' desperately needed a success in Africa and can be forgiven for their triumphalism: Ajello in his last major speech before terminating the mission to Mozambique suggested that the elections constituted 'proof of the highest order of democratic maturity'.[66] It would be as foolish to suggest that a liberal-capitalist transformation is impossible in Mozambique as to say that the previously attempted socialist one was always doomed to failure. We can take refuge in the cliché that it is too early to say. Yet our earlier analysis showed that much of Frelimo's Marxism was of a mimetic kind that bore little relation to the society on which it was being imposed. It is not yet clear that Frelimo's recently adopted liberalism will be so different. As a seasoned participant in the old Mozambican politics commented, 'now that the elections are over, people expect democracy to bring prosperity, just as they believed Marxism would bring development after independence. It may be just another unrealistic dream.'[67] Or could it be that a different reality lies beyond both these dreams?

---

[65] See footnote 14.

[66] Supervising and Monitoring Commission, 6 December 1994. The total cost of the election was estimated at $63 million, of which Mozambique contributed $4.5 million.

[67] Jose Cabaco, quoted in the *Financial Times*, 9 December 1994.

BIBLIOGRAPHY

Published books and articles on Mozambique and Southern Africa

P. Abbott and Manuel Rodrigues, *Modern African Wars: Angola and Mozambique, 1961-1974,* London: Osprey, 1988.

D.M Abshire and M.A Samuels (eds), *Portuguese Africa: A handbook,* London: Pall Mall Press, 1969.

E. Adam, 'Mozambik. Im 12 Jahr am Ende?', *Afrika-Spectrum,* March 1986, pp. 337-62.

Edward A. Alpers, 'Ethnicity, Politics and History in Mozambique', *Africa Today,* 21,4 (fall 1974), pp. 39-52.

——, 'The Struggle for Socialism in Mozambique, 1960-1972' in Carl G. Rosberg and Thomas M. Callaghy (eds), *Socialism in Sub-Sabaran Africa,* Berkeley: University of California Press, 1979. pp. 267-95.

G. Arnold, 'The Mozambique Road', *Africa Report,* July-August 1979, pp. 20-2.

Kaúlza de Arriaga, *A Luta em Moçambique 1970/1973,* Braga: Intervenção, 1977.

——, *Coragem, Tenacidade e Fé,* Lourenço Marques: Empresa Moderna, 1973.

Steve Askin, 'Mission to RENAMO: The militarization of the religious right', *Issue,* 18, 2, (1990), pp. 29-38.

M. Azevedo, '"A Sober Commitment to Liberation?" Mozambique and South Africa, 1974-1979', *African Affairs,* 79, 317 (1980), pp. 567-84.

Norman A. Bailey, 'Government and Administration' in Abshire and Samuels (eds), *Portuguese Africa: A handbook,* London: Pall Mall Press, pp. 133-45

A. Bady, 'Les villages communitaires. Bases du pouvoir populaire mozambicain', *Le Mois en Afrique,* 215-216 (December/January 1984), pp. 18-31.

P. Balmes, 'Le Mozambique', *Afrique Contemporaine,* 106 (November/December 1979), pp. 8-15.

C. Barker, 'Bringing health care to the People' in John Saul (ed.), *A Difficult Road: The Transition to Socialism in Mozambique,* New York: Monthly Review Press, 1985, pp. 316-46.

J. Barker, 'Gaps in the Debate About Agriculture: Senegal, Tanzania and Mozambique', *World Development,* 13(1985), pp. 59-76.

N. Baron, 'The Struggle Continues: Diary of a Kidnapping in Mozambique by Robert Rosskamp: an analysis' in A. Vines and K.B. Wilson (eds), *War in Mozambique: Local Perspectives* (in press).

Simon Baynham, 'British Military Training Assistance in Southern Africa: Lessons for South Africa?', *Africa Insight,* 22,3 (1992), pp. 218-24.

I. Beckett, 'The Portuguese Army: The Campaign in Mozambique, 1964-1974' in I. Beckett and J. Pimlott (eds), *Armed Forces and Modern Counterinsurgency*, London: Croom Helm, 1977, pp. 136-62

G.J. Bender, *Angola under the Portuguese*, London: Heinemann, 1978.

Gregor H. Binkert, 'Agricultural Production and Economic Incentives: Food Policy in Mozambique' (Harvard Institute for International Development, discussion paper 154 September 1983).

David Birmingham, *Frontline Nationalism in Angola and Mozambique*, London: James Currey, 1992.

J.P. Borges Coelho, *O Início da Luta Armada em Tete, 1968-1969*, Estudos 7, Maputo: Arquivo Histórico de Moçambique, 1989.

P. Botha, 'Mozambique; The Democratic People's Revolution Fails', *Africa Insight*, 13 (1983), pp. 130-4.

M. Bowen, 'Beyond Reform: Adjustment and Political Power in Contemporary Mozambique', *Journal of Modern African Studies*, 30,2 (1992), pp. 255-79.

——, 'Economic Crisis in Mozambique', *Current History*, May 1990, pp. 217-28.

A. de Bragança, 'Independência sem descolonização', *Estudos Africanos* 5-6, (1986), pp. 7-28.

—— and J. Depelchin, 'From the Idealization of Frelimo to the Understanding of Mozambique's Recent History', *Review*, 9, 1 (winter 1988), pp. 95-117.

Luis de Brito, 'Une relecture nécessaire. La genèse du parti-État FRELIMO', *Politique Africaine*, 29 (1988), pp. 15-27.

Grete Brochmann and Arve Ofstad, *Mozambique: Norwegian Assistance in a Context of Crisis*, Bergen: Chr. Michelsen Institute, 1990.

M. Cahen, 'Corporatisme et colonialisme. Approche du cas mozambicaine, 1933-1979: I. Une genèse difficile, une mouvement squelettique', *Cahiers d'Études Africaines*, 92, XXIII-4, 1983, pp. 383-417.

——, 'Corporatisme et colonialisme. Approche du cas mozambicaine, 1933-1979: II.Crise et survivance du corporatisme colonial, 1960-1979', *Cahiers d'Études Africaines*, 93, XXIV-1, 1983, pp. 5-24.

——, 'Africanisme portugais. Une tradition en danger?', *Politique Africaine*, 41(1991), pp. 149-53.

——, 'État et pouvoir populaire dans le Mozambique indépendant', *Politique Africaine*, 19(1985), pp. 36-60.

——, *La Révolution Implosée*, Paris: L'Harmattan, 1987.

——, 'Le Portugal et l'Afrique. Le cas de relations luso-mozambicaines 1965-1985', *Afrique Contemporaine*, January-March 1986, pp. 3-55.

——, *Mozambique. Analyse politique de conjoncture*, Paris: Indigo Publications, 1990.

——, 'Check on Socialism in Mozambique', *Review of African Political Economy*, 57 (1993), pp. 46-59

E. Cain, 'Mozambique's Hidden War' in C. Moser (ed.), *Combat on Communist Territory*, Washington, DC: Free Congress Foundation, 1985, pp. 38-71.

H. Campbell, 'War, Reconstruction and Dependence in Mozambique', *Third World Quarterly*, vol.6, 1984, pp. 839-67.

B. Caplan, 'Mozambique beckons the West', *The Banker*, 130, 658 (December 1980), pp. 33-9.

F. Cardoso, 'Some experiences in economic development particularly in industry after the fall of colonialism in Mozambique', *Wissenschaftliche Beiträge*, supplementary issue 1977, pp. 111-18.

A.Y. Casal, 'A Crise da Produéção Familiar e as Aldeias Comunais em Moçambique', *Revista Internacional de Estudos Africanos*, no. 8-9, Jan.-Dec. 1988, pp. 157-91.

Centro de Estudos Africanos, *A Situação nas Antigas Zonas Libertadas de Cabo Delgado*, Maputo, 1983.

Poder popular e desagregação nas aldeias comunais do planalto de Mueda, Centro de Estudos Africanos, Maputo, 1986.

Nã Vamos Esquecer!, year 2, 4 July 1987. Bulletin of the History Workshop, Universidade Eduardo Mondlane. Special issue on the liberated zones.

P. Chabal, 'People's War, State Formation and Revolution in Africa: a comparative analysis of Mozambique, Guinea-Bissau and Angola', *Journal of Commonwealth and Comparative Politics*, 21 (1983), pp. 104-25.

—— (ed.), *The Postcolonial Literature of Lusophone Africa*, London, 1996.

Michael Charlton, *The Last Colony in Africa: Diplomacy and the Independence of Rhodesia*, Oxford: Basil Blackwell, 1990.

R. Chilcote, 'Conflicting Nationalist Ideologies in Portuguese Africa: The Emergence of Political and Social Movements, 1945-1965, African Studies Association Conference, October 1966.

I. Christie, *Machel of Mozambique*, Harare: Zimbabwe Publishing House, 1988.

J. Christman and W. Kuhne, 'Mozambique: Adrift Between the Superpowers', *Journal of Defense and Diplomacy*, November 1986, pp. 14-18.

Gervase Clarence-Smith, *The third Portuguese empire, 1825-1975: A study in economic imperialism* Manchester University Press, 1985.

'The Roots of the Mozambican counter-revolution', *Southern African Review of Books*, April/May 1989, pp. 7-100.

M. Clough, 'American Foreign Policy Options', *Africa Report*, November-December 1982, pp. 14-17.

Barbara Cole, *The Elite: The story of the Rhodesian Special Air Service*, Transkei: Three Knights Publishing, 1984

Jean-Pierre Colin, 'Le Mozambique un an apres l'indépendance', *Politique Étrangère*, 5 (1976), pp. 433-58.

C. Collins, 'Mozambique: Dynamising the People', *Issue*, 8, 1 (spring 1978), pp. 12-16.

F.J Couto et al., *Eigenständige Entwicklungen in Mosambik*, Frankfurt: Otto Lembeck, 1982.

C. Crocker, *High Noon in Southern Africa: Making Peace in a Rough Neighbourhood*, New York: W.W. Norton, 1992.

J. Crush, Alan Jeeves and David Yudelman, *South Africa's Labor Empire*, Boulder, CO: Westview Press, 1991.

Teresa Cruz e Silva, 'A IV Região" da Frelimo no sul de Moçambique: Lourenço Marques, 1964-65', *Estudos Africanos*, 8 (1990), pp. 127-41.

C. Darch, 'Are There Warlords in Provincial Mozambique? Question of the Social Base of MNR Banditry', *Review of African Political Economy*, 46/47, (1990), pp. 34-49.

B. Davidson, 'The Revolution of People's Power: Notes on Mozambique 1979', *Race and Class*, 21 (1979), pp. 127-40.

Robert Davies, *South African Strategy towards Mozambique in the post-Nkomati Period*, Uppsala: Scandinavian Institute of African Studies, Research report no.73, 1985.

——, 'South African Strategy towards Mozambique since Nkomati', *Transformation* no.3, 1987, pp. 4-30

——, 'Implications for Southern Africa of the current impasse in the peace process in Mozambique', Bellville: University of the Western Cape Centre for Southern African Studies, working paper, no.9, 1991.

Stephen M. Davis, *Apartheid's Rebels: Inside South Africa's Hidden War*, New Haven, CT: Yale University Press, 1987.

J. Depelchin, 'African Anthropology and History in the light of the History of Frelimo', *Contemporary Marxism*, 7 (1983), pp. 69-88.

Georgi Derlugyan, 'Mozambique: A tight knot of problems', *International Affairs*, 3, March 1990, pp. 103-11.

——, 'Social Decomposition and Armed Violence in Postcolonial Mozambique', *Review* (Fernand Braudel Center), 13, 4 (1990), pp. 439-62.

A Descolonização Portuguesa, vol.2. Lisbon: Instituto Amaro da Costa, 1982.

Cole P. Dodge and Magne Raundalen, *Reaching Children in War: Sudan, Uganda and Mozambique*, Bergen: Sigma Forlag, 1991.

Helen Dolny, 'The Challenge of Agriculture' in John Saul (ed.). *A Difficult Road: The Transition to Socialism in Mozambique*, New York: Monthly Review Press, 1985, pp. 211-52.

James Duffy, *Portuguese Africa*, Cambridge, MA: Harvard University Press, 1959.

A.E. Duarte Silva, 'O Vietname português', *Expresso Revista*, 2 October 1993, pp. 44-6.

B. Egero, *Mozambique, a Dream Undone: The Political Economy of Democracy, 1975-1984*, Uppsala: Scandinavian Institute of African Studies, 1987.

——, 'Mozambique before the Second Phase of Socialist Development', *Review of African Political Economy*, 25 (1982), pp. 83-91.

H. Ellert, *The Rhodesian Front War: Counter-Insurgency and guerrilla warfare, 1962-1980*, Gweru: Mambo Press, 1989.

S. Ellis and Tsepo Sechaba, *Comrades against Apartheid: The ANC and the South African Communist Party in Exile*, London: James Currey, 1992.

Paul Fauvet, 'Roots of Counter-Revolution: the Mozambican National Resistance', *Review of African Political Economy*, 29 (1984), pp. 108-21.

P. Fauvet and A. Gomes, 'The Mozambique National Resistance', supplement to *AIM Information Bulletin* 69 (March 1982).

A. de Figueiredo, 'Portugal's New Role', *Africa Report*, May-June 1975, pp. 6-9.

——, 'Portugal's Year in Africa: The Continuing Record of Lost Opportunities', photocopied MS 1983/4

W. Finnegan, *A Complicated War: The Harrowing of Mozambique*, Berkeley: University of California Press, 1993.

J. Fitzpatrick, 'The Economy of Mozambique: Problems and Prospects', *Third World Quarterly*, 3, 1 (January 1981), pp. 77-87.

Ruth First, 'The Gold of Migrant Labour', *Review of African Political Economy*, (Tribute edition to Ruth First), 25 (Sept.-Dec. 1982).

——, *The Mozambican Miner: a study in the export of labour*, Maputo: Centro de Estudos Africanos, 1987.

K. Flower, *Serving Secretly*, London: John Murray, 1987.

C. Gaspar, 'Portugal's Policies toward Angola and Mozambique since Independence' in R.J. Bloomfield (ed.), *Regional Conflict and US Policy*, Boston, MA: World Peace Foundation, 1988, pp. 40-74.

Christian Geffray, *La cause des armes au Mozambique. Antropologie d'une guerre civile*, Paris: Karthala, 1990.

C. Geffray, 'Fragments d'un discours du pouvoir (1975-1985). Du bon usage d'une méconnaissance scientifique', *Politique Africaine*, 29 (1988), pp. 71-85.

—— and M. Pedersen, 'Nampula en guerre', *Politique Africaine*, 29 (1988), pp. 18-40.

D. Geldenhuys, 'South Africa's Regional Policy' in M. Clough (ed.), *Changing Realities in Southern Africa*. Berkeley, CA: Institute of International Studies, 1982.

Anna Maria Gentili, 'Da Lourenço Marques a Maputo', *Africa* (Rome), 2 (1985), pp. 183-220.

——, 'Les origines rurales du nationalisme Mozambicain. Les coopératives Liquilanilu du Plateau du Mueda, 1957-63' in *Histoire Sociale de l'Afrique de l'Est*, Actes du Colloque de Bujumbura, 17-24 Oct. 1989, Département d'Université de Burundi, Paris, 1991.

T. Gifford, 'Struggle in Mozambique', *Third World*, 1,3 (November 1972).

I.L.L. Griffiths, 'The Quest for Independent Access to the Sea in Southern Africa', *Geographical Journal*, 155, 3 (November 1989), pp. 378-91.

João Paulo Guerra, *Os 'flechas' atacam de novo*, Lisbon, 1988.

A. Gundersen, 'Popular Justice in Mozambique: Between State Law and Folk Law', *Social and Legal Studies*, 1, 2 (1992), pp. 257-82.

G.Gunn, *Cuba and Mozambique*, CSIS Africa Notes, 80 (1987).

——, 'Learning from Adversity: The Mozambican Experience' in R.J. Bloomfield (ed.), *Regional Conflict and US Policy*, Algance, MI: World Peace Foundation, Reference Publications Inc, 1988, pp. 134-85.

Lord Hailey, *An African Survey*, Oxford University Press, 1957.

M. Hall, 'The Mozambican National Resistance Movement', *Africa*, 60, 1 (1990), pp. 39-68.

R.G. Hamilton, *Voices from an Empire*, Minneapolis: University of Minnesota Press, 1975.

J. Hanlon, *Mozambique: The Revolution under Fire*, London: Zed Press, 1984.

——, *Mozambique: Who Calls the Shots?*, London: James Currey, 1991

Adrian Hastings, *Wiriyamu*, London Search Press, 1974.

L. Harris, 'Agricultural Cooperatives and Development Policy in Mozambique', *Journal of Peasant Studies*, 7 (1980), pp. 338-52.

D. Hedges, 'Apontamento sobre as relações entre Malawi e Moçambique, 1961-1987', *Cadernos de Historia*, 6 (1987) pp. 5-28.

R. d'A. Henderson, 'Principles and Practice in Mozambique's Foreign Policy', *The World Today*, 34, 7 (1978), pp. 276-86.

Thomas H. Henriksen, 'Marxism and Mozambique', *African Affairs*, 77 (1978), pp. 441-62.

——, *Revolution and Counterrevolution: Mozambique's War of Independence, 1964-1974* Westport, CT: Greenwood Press, 1983.

——, *Mozambique: A History*, London: Rex Collings, 1978.

K. Hermele, *Country Report Mozambique*, Stockholm: SIDA Planning Secretariat, 1988.

——, *Land Struggles and Social Differentiation in Southern Mozambique: A Case Study of Chokwe Mozambique*, Uppsala: Scandinavian Institute of African Affairs, research report no. 82, 1988.

Herb Howe, 'Mozambique at a Standstill', *Defence Africa and the Middle East*, 11, 2 (March 1985), pp. 14-15.

A.F. Isaacman, *The Tradition of Resistance in Mozambique: anti-colonial activity in the Zambesi Valley, 1850-1921*, London: Heinemann, 1976.

——, 'A Luta Continua: Creating a New Society in Mozambique', Southern Africa Pamphlets 1, State University of New York/Centro de Estudos Africanos, 1978.

——, 'Coercion, Paternalism and the Labour Process: The Mozambican Cotton Regime, 1938-1961', *Journal of Southern African Studies*, 18, 3, (1992), pp. 487-526.

——, 'Transforming Mozambique's Rural Economy', *Issue*, 8,1 (spring 1978), pp. 17-24.

——, 'Chissano's Friends and Enemies', *Africa Report* (Sept.-Oct. 1987), pp. 48-51.

——, and B. Isaacman, *Mozambique: From Colonialism to Revolution, 1900-1982*, Boulder, CO: Westview Press/Aldershot: Gower, 1983.

——, 'On the Road to Economic Recovery', *Africa Report*, (May-June 1980), pp. 4-7.

——, 'South Africa's Hidden War', *Africa Report* (Nov.-Dec. 1982), pp. 4-8.

——, 'In Pursuit of Nonalignment', *Africa Report*, (May-June 1983), pp. 47-54.

W. James, *Our Precious Metal: African Labour in South Africa's Gold Industry, 1970-1990*, London: James Currey, 1992.

Jorge Jardim, *Moçambique: Terra Queimada*, Lisbon: Editorial Intervenção, 1976.

R. Jaster, 'The Security Outlook in Mozambique', *Survival*, Nov./Dec. 1985, pp. 258-64.

——, *South Africa and its Neighbours: The dynamics of regional conflict* London: International Institute of Strategic Studies, Adelphi Paper 209 (1986).

P. Jenkins, 'Mozambique' in K. Mathey (ed.), *Housing Policies in the Socialist Third World*, London: Mansell, 1990, pp. 147-79.

Anton Johnston, 'Study, Produce, and Combat! Education and the Mozambican State 1962-1984', *Studies in Comparative and International Education* 14, Institute of International Education, University of Stockholm, 1989.

Brendan F. Jundanian, 'Resettlement Programs: Counterinsurgency in Mozambique', *Comparative Politics*, 6 (1974), pp. 519-40.

I.M. Kaplan (ed.), *An Area Handbook for Mozambique*, Washington, DC: US Government Printing Office, 1977.

R. Kasrils, *Armed and Dangerous: my undercover struggle against Apartheid.* Oxford: Heinemann, 1993.

H. Kitchen (ed.), *Angola, Mozambique and the West*, Washington, DC: Praeger, 1987.

S. Kruks, 'From Nationalism to Marxism: The Ideological History of Frelimo, 1962-77' in I.L. Markowitz (ed.), *Studies in Power and Class in Africa*, Oxford University Press, 1987, pp. 237-56.

W. Kuhne, 'What does the case of Mozambique tell us about a Soviet ambivalence towards Africa?' in Kitchen (ed.), *Angola, Mozambique and the West* pp. 105-116.

C.S. Lancaster, 'Ethnic Identity, History, and "Tribe" in the Middle Zambezi Valley', *American Ethnologist*, 1 (1974), pp. 707-30.

J. Legrand, 'Logique de guerre et dynamique de la violence en Zambézia, 1976-1991', *Politique Africaine*, 50 (June 1993), pp. 88-104.

R. Lefort, 'Un nouveau départ', *L'Année Politique Africaine*, 1977, pp. 33-6.

——, Colin Legum, 'The MNR', *CSIS Africa Notes*, 16, 15 (July 1983).

——, 'The Counter-Revolutionaries in Southern Africa', *Third World Reports*, 1, (18 March 1983).

S. Levy, 'Broken Promises', *Africa Report* (Jan-Feb. 1986), pp. 77-80.

M. Mackintosh, 'Economic Policy Context and Adjustment Options in Mozambique', *Development and Change*, 17 (1986), pp. 557-81.

—— and M. Wuyts, 'Accumulation, Social Services and Socialist Transition in the Third World: Reflections on Decentralised Planning based on the Mozambican Experience', *Journal of Development Studies*, 24, 4 (1988), pp. 136-79.

N. Macqueen, 'Mozambique's Widening Foreign Policy', *The World Today*, 40, 1 (January 1984), pp. 22-8.

Lina Magaia, *Dumba Nengue: Run for Your Life (Peasant Tales of Tragedy in Mozambique)*, Trenton, NJ: Africa World Press, 1988.

O. Marleyn, D. Wield and R. Williams, 'Notes on the Political and Organisational Offensive in Mozambique and its Relationship to Agricultural Policy', *Review of African Political Economy*, 24 (1982), pp. 114-20.

J. Marshall, 'Making Education Revolutionary' in John Saul (ed.), *A Difficult Road: The Transition to Socialism in Mozambique*, New York: Monthly Review Press, 1985, pp. 156-210.

——, 'Structural adjustment and Social Policy in Mozambique', *Review of African Political Economy*, 47 (1990), pp. 28-43.

——, *Education in a Mozambican Factory*, Bellville: University of the Western Cape Centre for Adult and Continuing Education, 1990.

Judith Marshall, *Literacy, State Formation and People's Power*, Cape Town, 1990.

D. Martin and P. Johnson, *The Struggle for Zimbabwe*, London: Faber and Faber, 1981.

D. Martin and P. Johnson, 'Moçambique to Nkomati and Beyond' in P. Johnson and O. Martin (eds), *Destructive Engagement: Southern Africa at War*, Harare: Zimbabwe Publishing House, 1986, pp. 1-43.

D. Martins da Silva, 'Como se organiza o Estado Mocambicano', *Justica Popular* 10 (June 1985), pp. 21-5.

Kenneth Maxwell, 'Portugal and Africa: the Last Empire' in Prosser Gifford and W.M. Roger Louis (eds), *The Transfer of Power in Africa: Decolonization, 1940-1960*, New Haven, CT: Yale University Press, 1982, pp. 337-85.

C. Meillassoux and C. Verschuur, 'Les paysans ignorés du Mozambique', *Le Monde Diplomatique*, October 1985.

Clotilde Mesquitéla, *Moçambique 7 de Setembro: Memórias da Revolução*, Lisbon: Edições a Rua, 1978.

Steven Metz, 'The Mozambique National Resistance and South African Foreign Policy', *African Affairs*, 85 (1986), pp. 491-507.

P. Meyns, 'Liberation Ideology and National Development Strategy In Mozambique', *Review of African Political Economy*, 22 (1981), pp. 42-64.

Keith Middlemass, 'Mozambique: Two Years of independence', Proceedings of a Seminar on Mozambique held in the Centre of African Studies, University of Edinburgh, 1 & 2 December 1978.

——, 'Independent Mozambique and Its Regional Policy' in J. Seiler (ed.), *Southern Africa since the Portuguese*, Boulder, CO: Westview Press, 1980.

——, *Cabora Bassa: Politics and Engineering in Southern Africa*, London: Weidenfeld and Nicolson, 1975.

——, 'Twentieth Century White Society in Mozambique', *Tarikh*, 6,2 (special edn on 'White Society in Africa'), published for Historical Society of Nigeria.

William Minter, *Portuguese Africa and the West*, Harmondsworth: Penguin, 1972.

——, 'Major Themes in Mozambican Foreign Relations, 1975-77', *Issue*, (spring 1978), pp. 43-9.

J. H. Mittelman, 'State power in Mozambique', *Issue*, Vol. VIII, 1, (spring, 1978), pp. 4-11.

——, 'Mozambique: The Political Economy of Underdevelopment', *Journal of Southern African Affairs*, 3, 1 (1978), pp. 35-54.

——, *Underdevelopment and the Transition to Socialism in Mozambique and Tanzania*, New York: Academic Press, 1981.

Paul Moorcraft, *African Nemesis: War and Revolution in Southern Africa, 1945-2010*, London, Brassey's, 1990.

——, 'Mozambique's Long Civil War: RENAMO, puppets or patriots?', *International Defense Review*, 10 (1987), pp. 1313-16.

Glenda Morgan, 'Violence in Mozambique: Towards an Understanding of Renamo', *Journal of Modern African Studies*, 28, 4 (1990), pp. 603-19.

J. Stephen Morrison, ' The Battle for Mozambique', *Africa Report*, (Sept.-Oct. 1987), pp. 44-7.

Barry Munslow, *Mozambique: the Revolution and its Origins*, Harlow: Longman, 1983.

——, (ed.), *Samora Machel: An African Revolutionary*, London: Zed Press, 1985

——, 'State Intervention in Agriculture: The Mozambican experience', *Journal of Modern African Studies*, 22 (1984), pp. 220-1.

—— and P. O'Keefe, 'Rethinking the Revolution in Mozambique', *Race and Class*, 26 (1984), pp. 15-31.

Y.T. Museveni, 'Fanon's Theory on Violence: its Verification in Liberated Mozambique' in N.M. Shamuyarira (ed.), *Essays on the Liberation of Southern Africa*, University of Dar es Salaam Studies in Political Science 3 (1972)

P. Nesbitt, 'Terminators, Crusaders and Gladiators: Western (private and public) support for Renamo and Unita', *Review of African Political Economy*, 43 (1988), pp. 111-24.

Malyn Newitt, *Portuguese Settlement on the Zambesi*, London: Longman, 1973.

——, 'Towards a history of modern Moçambique', *Rhodesian History*, 7, 5 (1974), pp. 33-47.

——, *Portugal in Africa*, London: Hurst, 1981.

——, *A History of Mozambique*, London: Hurst, 1995.

Anders Nilsson, 'South African Aggression on Mozambique through MNR', paper presented to ECASAAMA Conference, Bonn, 8-18 December, 1988.

——, *Unmasking the bandits: The true face of the MNR*, London, 1990

——, 'From Pseudo-Terrorists to Pseudo-Guerrillas: The MNR in Mozambique', *Review of African Political Economy*, 58 (1993), pp. 35-42.

Bridget O'Laughlin, 'Interpretations Matter: Evaluating the War in Mozambique', *Southern Africa Report*, January 1992, pp. 23-33.

Bernardino G. Oliveira, *Aqui Portugal Moçambique*, privately published, 1978.

J.D. Omer-Cooper, *The Zulu Aftermath*, Harlow: Longman, 1966.

W.C. Opello, 'Revolutionary Change in Mozambique: Implications for the Emerging Postindependence Society' in J.R. Scarritt (ed.), *Analysing Political Change in Africa: Applications of a New Multi Dimensional Framework*, Boulder, CO: Westview Press, 1980, pp. 256-300.

——, 'Guerilla War in Portuguese Africa: An assessment of the balance of forces in Mozambique', *Issue*, 4,2 (Summer 1974), pp. 29-37.

M. Ottaway, 'Soviet Marxism and African Socialism', *Journal of Modern African Studies*, 16, 3 (1978), pp. 477-85

——, 'Mozambique; From Symbolic Socialism to Symbolic Reform', *Journal of Modern African Studies*, 262 (1988), pp. 211-26.

——, 'Economic Reform and War in Mozambique', *Current History*, May 1988, pp. 201-23.

E.F Pachter, 'Contra-Coup: Civilian Control of the Military in Guinea, Tanzania and Mozambique', *Journal of Modern African Studies*, 20, 4 (1982), pp. 595-612.

P. Pandya, 'Foreign Support to ZANU and Zanla during the Rhodesian War', *ISSUP Strategic Review*, November 1987, pp. 1-31.

Hasu H. Patel, 'Zimbabwe's Mediation in Mozambique and Angola' in Stephen Chan and Vivienne Jabri (eds), *Mediation in Southern Africa*, Basingstoke: Macmillan, 1993, pp. 117-41.

John Paul, *Mozambique; Memoirs of a Revolution*, Harmondsworth: Penguin, 1975.

Rene Pélissier, 'Angola, Mozambique. Des guerres interminables et leurs facteurs internes', *Hérodote*, 46 (1987), pp. 83-107.

——, *Le Naufrage des Caravelles. Études sur la fin de l'Empire portugais (1961-1975)*, Orgeval, 1979.

Jeanne Penvenne, 'The unmaking of an African Petite Bourgeoisie: Lourenço Marques, Mozambique', Mozambique Working Paper 57, African Studies Center, Boston University, 1982.

——, 'A Luta Continua! Recent Literature on Mozambique', *International Journal of African Historical Studies*, 18, (1985), pp. 109-38.

Rui Pereira, 'Antropologia aplicada na política colonial portuguesa do Estado Novo', *Revista Internacional de Estudos Africanos*, 4/5 (1985), pp. 191-234

M. Anne Pitcher, *Politics in the Portuguese Empire: The State, Industry and Cotton, 1926-1974*, Oxford: Clarendon Press, 1993.

David N. Plank, 'Aid, Debt, and the End of Sovereignty: Mozambique and its Donors', *Journal of Modern African Studies*, 31,3 (1993), pp. 407-30.

M.S Radu, 'Mozambique: Nonalignment or New Dependence', *Current History*, 83, 491 (March 1984), pp. 101-35.

P. Rich (ed.), *The Dynamics of Change in Southern Africa*, Basingstoke: Macmillan, 1994

A. Rita-Ferreira, 'Moçambique pos-25 de abril. Causas do êxodo da população de origem europeia e asiática', *Moçambique. Cultura e história de um país*, papers of the 5th seminar of African culture, Centre of African Studies, Institute of Anthropology, Coimbra University, 1988.

Otto Roesch, 'Rural Mozambique since the Frelimo Party Fourth Congress: The Situation in the Baixo Limpopo', *Review of African Political Economy*, 4 (1988), pp. 73-91.

——, 'Renamo and the Peasantry in Southern Mozambique: A View from Gaza Province', *Canadian Journal of African Studies*, 26 (March 1992), pp. 462-84.

A. Sachs and G.H. Welch, *Liberating the Law: Creating Popular Justice in Mozambique*, London: Zed Books, 1990

Marcelino dos Santos, 'The revolutionary perspective in Mozambique', *World Marxist Review*, 11 (1968), pp. 43-5.

John Saul, 'The Content: a transition to socialism?' in Saul (ed.), *A Difficult Road*, pp. 75-151.

—— (ed.), *A Difficult Road: The Transition to Socialism in Mozambique*, New York: Monthly Review Press, 1985.

——, 'Mozambique: The Failure of Socialism?', *Southern Africa Report*, 6, 2 (1990).

Witley W. Scheidman, 'Conflict Resolution in Mozambique: A Status Report', *CSIS Africa Notes*, 121 (Feb. 1991).

——, 'Conflict Resolution in Mozambique' in David R. Smock (ed.), *Making War and Waging Peace*, Washington, DC: US Institute of Peace Press, 1993.

W. Schoeller, 'Mosambik. Struktur und Krise einer Dienstleistung-Ökonomie in Südlichen Afrika', *Afrika Spectrum*, 81, 3(1981), pp. 345-68.

H. Schröer, 'Der Kampf an der Produktionsfront. Die materiellen, sozialen and politischen Bedingungen der Industrialisierung Mozambiks' in F.J. Couto *et al.*, *Eigenständige Entwicklung in Mosambik*, Frankfurt: Otto Lembeck, 1982.

——, *Frelimo und Industriearbeiter in postkolonialen Konflikten*, Saarbrücken: Breitenbach 1983.

C.V. Scott, 'Socialism and the "Soft State" in Africa: An Analysis of Angola and Mozambique', *Journal of Modern African Studies*, 26, 1 (1988), pp. 23-36.

Annette Seegers, 'Revolutionary Armies of Africa: Mozambique and Zimbabwe' in Simon Baynham (ed.), *Military Power: Politics in Black Africa*, London: Croom Helm 1986, pp. 129-63.

——, 'From Liberation to Modernization: Transforming Revolutionary Paramilitary Forces into Standing Professional Armies' in B.D. Arlinghaus and P.H. Baker (eds), *African Armies: Evolution and Capabilities*, Boulder, CO: Westview Press, 1986, pp. 52-83.

J. Seiler (ed.), *Southern Africa the Portuguese*, Boulder, CO: Westview, 1980.

U. Semin-Panzer, 'Transformation der Landwirtschaft und Überwindung von Unterentwicklung in Moçambique', *Afrika Spectrum*, 13, 3 (1977), pp. 287-307.

J. Sidaway, 'Contested Terrain: Transformation and Continuity of the Traditional organisation in post-Independence Mozambique', *Tijdschrift voor economische en sociale geografie*, 82 (1991), pp. 367-76.

——, 'Urban and regional planning in post-Independence Mozambique', *International Journal of Urban and Regional Research*, 17 (1993), pp. 241-59.

P. Sketchley, 'Problems of the Transformation of Social Relations of Production in post-independence Mozambique', *People's Power*, 15 (winter 1979), pp. 28-40.

J. Slovo, 'Lessons of the Mozambican Revolution', *African Communist*, 73 (3rd quarter, 1978), pp. 20-39.

A.K. Smith, 'The Peoples of Southern Mozambique: An Historical Survey', *Journal of African History*, XIV (1973), pp. 565-80.

P. Spacek, 'Nation building in Mozambique', *Sechaba* 4 (1970), pp. 12-15.

C.F. Spence, *Moçambique: East African Province of Portugal*, Cape Town: Howard Timmins, 1963.

E. Stephan, *Moçambique. Vitima do Colonialismo*, Lisbon: Preto, 1975.

G. Taju, 'Renamo: Os Factos que Conhecemos', *Cadernos de Historia*, 7 (1988), pp. 5-44.

F. Tarp, 'Prices in Mozambican Agriculture', *Journal of International Development*, 2, 2 (1990), pp. 172-208.

Andre E.A.M. Thomashausen, 'The Mozambique National Resistance' in C.J. Maritz (ed.), *Weerstandsbewegings in Suider-Afrika*, Potchefstroom University, South Africa, 1987.

V. Tickner, 'Structural Adjustment and Agricultural Pricing In Mozambique', *Review of African Political Economy*, 53 (1992), pp. 25-42.

J.E. Torp, 'Industrial Planning and Development in Mozambique: Some preliminary considerations', Uppsala: Scandinavian Institute for African Studies (research report 50), 1979.

——, *Mozambique: Politics, Economics and Society*, London: Pinter, 1990.

Tortura na Colonia de Moçambique 1963-1974. Depoimentos de presos politicos, Oporto: Edições Afrontamento, 1977.

Anthony R. Tucker, 'South Africa's War in Mozambique', *Armed Forces*, June 1989.

Leroy Vail and Landeg White, *Capitalism and Colonialism in Mozambique: A Study of Quelimane District*, London: Heinemann, 1980.

Irene S. van Dongen, 'Agriculture and other Primary Production' in D.M. Abshire and M.A. Samuels (eds), *Portuguese Africa: A handbook*, London: Pall Mall Press, 1969, pp. 253-93.

W.S. van der Waals, *Portugal's War in Angola, 1961-1974*, Rivonia: Ashanti Press, 1993.

P. Vanneman, 'Mozambique: A New Soviet Opportunity', *Strategic Review*, 3, 4 (fall 1975), pp. 45-53.

Moises Venancio, 'Mediation by the Roman Catholic Church in Mozambique, 1988-91' in Chan and Jabri (eds), *Mediation in Southern Africa*, Basingstoke: Macmillan, 1993, pp. 142-58.

A.I.J. Venter, 'Why Portugal lost its African Wars' in Venter (ed.), *Challenge: Southern Africa within the African revolutionary context: An Overview*, Gibraltar: Ashanti Publishing, 1989, pp. 224-72.

C. Verschuur *et al.*, *Mozambique. Dix Ans de Solitude*, Paris: L'Harmattan, 1986.

S. Vieira, W.G. Martin, I. Wallerstein (eds), *How Fast the Wind? Southern Africa, 1975-2000*, Trenton, NJ: Africa World Press Inc, 1992.

Joaquim Vieira, 'Moçambique: a 'guerra global' in João de Melo (ed.), *Os anos de guerra: 1961-1975. Os Portugueses em Africa. Crónica, ficção e história*, Lisbon: Publicações Don Quixote, 1988, pp. 7-26.

Alex Vines, *Renamo: From Terrorism to Democracy in Mozambique?*, 2nd rev. edn, London: James Currey, 1996.

——, 'Diary', *Southern African Review of Books*, 4, Issue 20/21 (July/Oct. 1991).

——, '"No Democracy without Money": The road to peace in Mozambique (1982-1992)', London: CIIR, briefing paper 1994.

—— and K. Wilson, 'Churches and the peace process in Mozambique' in P. Gifford (ed.), *The Christian Churches and the Democratisation of Africa*, Leiden: E.J. Brill, 1995, pp. 130-47.

G. Walt and A. Melamed (eds), *Mozambique: Towards a People's Health Service*, London: Zed Books, 1983.

A. Wardman, 'The Cooperative Movement in Chokwe, Mozambique', *Journal of Southern African Studies*, 11, 2 (1985), pp. 295-304.

D. Webster, 'Migrant Labour, Social Formation and the Proletarianisation of the Chopi of Southern Mozambique', *African Perspective*, 1, (1978), pp. 157-74.

J. Wheeler, 'From Rovuma to Maputo: Mozambique's guerrilla war', *Reason*, Dec. 1985.

L. White, 'Review Article: The Revolutions Ten Years On', *Journal of Southern African Studies*, 11, 2 (1985), pp. 320-32.

D. Wield, 'Mozambique: Late colonialism and early problems of transition' in G. White *et al* (eds), *Revolutionary Socialist Development in the Third World*, Brighton: Wheatsheaf, 1983, pp. 75-113.

K.B. Wilson, 'War, Displacement, Social Change and the Re-Creation of Community: An exploratory study in Zambezia, Mozambique', preliminary report of a field study in Milange District, March-April 1991. Refugee Studies Programme, May 1991.

——, 'The Socio-Economic Impact of War and Flight in Posto Derre, Morrumbala District, Zambezia', January 1992 (forthcoming in the Archivo histórico de Moçambique).

——, 'Cults of Violence and Counter-Violence in Mozambique', *Journal of Southern African Studies*, 18, 3 (Sept. 1992), pp. 527-82.

G. Winrow, *The Foreign Policy of the GDR in Africa*, Cambridge University Press, 1990.

M. Wuyts, 'The Mechanization of Present-Day Mozambican Agriculture', *Development and Change*, 12 (1981) pp. 1-27.

——, *Money and Planning for Socialist Transition: The Mozambican Experience*, Aldershot: Gower, 1984.

——, 'Money, Planning and Rural Transformation in Mozambique', *Journal of Development Studies*, 22 (1985), pp. 180-207.

——, 'Mozambique: Economic Management and Adjustment Policies' in D. Ghai (ed.), *The IMF and the South*, London: Zed Books, 1991, pp. 215-35.

N. Zafaris, 'The People's Republic of Mozambique; Pragmatic Socialism', in P. Wiles (ed.), *The New Communist Third World*, London: Croom Helm, 1982, pp. 114-64.

Reports

Amnesty International, 'The Use of Flogging in the People's Republic of Mozambique', February 1984.

——, 'The Use of the Death Penalty in the People's Republic of Mozambique', July 1983.

Commonwealth Secretariat, *Capacity-Building in Mozambique: The Commonwealth Contribution*, London, 1991.

The Courier, Mozambique: Country Report, 114 (March-April 1989), pp. 19-26.

Environmental Investigation Agency, 'Under Fire: Elephants in the Front Line', London, 1992.

Robert Gersony, *Summary of Mozambican Refugee Accounts of Principally Conflict-related Experience in Mozambique*, Washington, DC: Department of State, Bureau for Refugee Programs, 1988.

IMF, *Request for Additional Funding under the Enhanced Structural Adjustment Funding*, 13 May 1994,
——, *Mozambique: Recent Economic Development*, 22 July 1993.
P. Johnson and D. Martin, *Apartheid terrorism: The destabilization report*, prepared for the Commonwealth Committee of Foreign Ministers on Southern Africa, London, and Bloomington, IN: University of Indiana Press, 1989.
P. Landell-Mills, 'Creating Transparency, Predictability and an Enabling Environment for Private Enterprise', paper given at Wilton Park special conference, 1992.
UNDP/World Bank, *Mozambique Issues and options in the Energy Sector*, 1987.
A. Vines, *Conspicuous Destruction: War, Famine and the Reform Process in Mozambique*, Human Rights Watch, New York, 1992.
World Bank, *Mozambique Economic Report: An Introductory Economic Survey*, 1985.
——, *Mozambique Public Expenditure Review*, report 7615 (1989), vols 1 and 2.
——, *Economic Policy Framework*, 1987-9.
——, *A Framework for Capacity Building in Policy Analysis and Economic Management in Sub-Saharan Africa*, 1989.
US Department of State, *Mozambique: A Country in Transition*, Intelligence Research Report 175, June 1988.
Summary of World Broadcasts.

Dissertations and other unpublished works

Anthony Callan, 'Patrons and Patriots: An Investigation into the Dynamics of the external support network of Renamo and its domestic implications', MA, School of Oriental and African Studies, University of London, 1989.
J.A. Bleakley, 'The Use of Military Power in the Former British & Portuguese Colonies of Central and Southern Africa', M. Phil., Pembroke College, Cambridge, 1989.
M.L. Bowen, 'Let's Build Agricultural Producer Cooperatives': Socialist Agricultural Development Strategy in Mozambique 1975-1983', Ph. D., University of Toronto, 1986.
Luis de Brito, 'Le Frelimo et la Construction de l'Etat National au Mozambique', Ph.D., Université de Paris VIII, 1991.
S. Jackson, 'China's Third World Foreign Policy: The case of Lusophone Africa, 1961-1984', 1994.
W. Minter, 'The Mozambican National Resistance (RENAMO) as described by ex-participants', Washington, DC, 1989.
Jovito Nunes, 'Peasants and Survival: The Social Consequences of Displacement – Mocuba, Zambézia', April 1992.
P. Raikes, 'Food Policy and Production in Mozambique Since Independence', paper given to Workshop on Food Systems in Central and

Southern Africa, Centre for African Studies, School of Oriental and African Studies, University of London, 1-2 July 1983.

T.O. Ranger, 'The meaning of violence in Zimbabwe', paper given at a conference on violence and decolonisation in Africa, Cambridge, April 1991.

Lars Rudebeck, 'Conditions of People's Development in Postcolonial Africa', 1988/9.

J. Sidaway, 'Urbanity, Image and the State in post-colonial Mozambique' (n.d.).

Malcolm G. Spaven, 'Rural Resettlement and Socialist Construction: Communal Villages in Mozambique', M.Sc., University of Aberdeen, 1981.

C.F. Spence's diary of events in Mozambique, 25 April 1974/22 March 1976.

R.J. Tibana, 'The Politics of Mozambique's Famine: Gaps in Socialist Policies and the South African Total War', paper given at the Political Studies Association Annual Conference, Plymouth Polytechnic, 10-12 April 1988.

A. Thomashausen, 'People's Courts in Mozambique', paper given at the workshop on New Approaches in Respect of the Administration of Justice, Institute of Foreign and Comparative Law, University of South Africa, 10 July 1987.

S. Vieira, 'Vectors of Foreign Policy of the Mozambique Liberation Front (1982-1975)', Universidade Eduardo Mondlane, seminar paper, 1988.

A. Vine, 'Change and the Military in Mozambique', paper given at a US Defense Intelligence College Conference on Change and the Military in Africa, Alconbury, England, 6-7 May 1993.

——, '"Hunger that Kills": Food Security and the Mozambican Peace Processes', paper given to Centre for Southern African Studies, University of York, research seminar series, 1992.

Frelimo and Mozambique government documents (published in Maputo unless otherwise stated)

25 de Setembro. Dia da revolução moçambicana.

Comissão Nacional do Plano, *Informação Estatistica. Alguns Indicadores Economicos e Sociais*, May 1980.

——, *Informação Estatistica, 1975-84.*

National Planning Commission, *Economic Report, 1984* (English text), Jan. 1984.

Commissão de Implementação dos Conselhos de Produção, *Resoluções de IV Plenario dos Conselhos de Produção sobre Restruturação dos Sectores e Estruturas.*

'Documentos: II Conferencia Nacional do Trabalho Ideológico', Beira, 5-10 June 1978.

Vencer a batalha de classe, report of the 4th National Conference of the Frelimo Defence Department, 25 July-2 August 1975.

'Literacy and Adult Education in the People's Republic of Mozambique', anonymous paper delivered at a Conference on Adult Education and Development, Dar es Salaam, 21-26 June 1976.

O Processo Revolucionário da Guerra Popular de Libertação. Artigos coligidos do orgão de informação da Frelimo 'A Voz da Revolução' desde 1963 até 1974', Colecção textos e documentos da Frelimo (undated).

Report by Prime Minister Machungo's Consultative Group for Mozambique, 9-10 July 1987.

Mozambique Briefing Economic Recovery Programme (Information Department of the Frelimo Central Committee, 1987).

Vamos Construir um Estado do Povo ao Serviço do Povo.

Noções sobre o Estado, Instituto Nacional do Livro e do Disco, 1980.

Normas de Trabalho e Disciplina no Aparelho de Estado, Centro Nacional de Documentação e Informação, Série A, Doc. Inf. no. 2, 1979.

Frelimo, *Relatorio sobre a Preparacao do 4 Congresso.*

Relatório sobre a Preparação do 4 Congresso, Frelimo, Colecção 4 Congreso, 1983.

Anteprojecto de Revisão da Constituição. Texto do anteprojecto; Texto explicativo; Grandes temas, Colecção Textos e Documentos da Frelimo, 1990.

Central Committee Report to the Third Congress of Frelimo, Mozambique Angola Guiné Information Centre, 1977.

Government of the People's Republic of Mozambique, *Mid-term Evaluation of the 1988-89 Emergency Appeal, 30 April – 31 October 1988,* produced in association with the United Nations, November 1988.

Government of Mozambique, Country Presentation to the United Nations Conference on the Least Developed Countries, Paris, 3-14 September 1990.

Principles of Revolutionary Justice: The Constitution; Documents on Law and State in the People's Republic of Mozambique, State Papers and Party Proceedings Series 2 (1979), no. 2, Mozambique Angola Guine Information Centre, 1977.

Samora Machel's speeches and writings (all published in Maputo)

Sowing the Seeds of Revolution, Harare: Zimbabwe Publishing House, 1981.

'Fazer da escóla uma base para o povo tomar o poder' (July 1974), *Colecção Estudos e Orientações* no. 6.

A nossa luta é uma Revolução, Lisbon: CIDAC, 1976.

'Produzir é um acto de militância' (October 1976), *Colecção Estudos e Orientações* no. 9; B. Munslow, *Samora Machel: African Revolutionary,* ch. 7.

'Consolidating People's Power in Mozambique' (31 August 1977), *Notícias,* 1 September 1977.

'Knowledge and science should be for the total liberation of man' (December 1977), *Race and Class,* XIX, 4 (1978).

'A luta contra subdesenvolvimento é uma batalha cultural' (3 July 1976), *Colecçao Textos e Documentos* no. 4.

'Fazer viver a línha do Partido em cada trabalhador' (1 May 1979), *Colecçao Palavras de Ordem* no. 9.

'Organizemos os nossos recursos para resolver os problemas do povo' (6 July 1979), *Colecçao Palavras de Ordem* no. 10; *Samora Machel: African Revolutionary*, ch. 8.

'Colher no 25 de Setembro força renovada para o combate' (25 September 1979), *Colecçao Palavras de Ordem* no. 131.

'Transformar o aparelho de estado no instrumento da vitória' (7 February 1980), *Colecçao Palavras de Ordem* no. 18; *Samora Machel: African Revolutionary*, ch. 4.

'Desalojemos o inímigo interno do nosso aparelho de estado' (18 March 1980), *Colecçao Palavras de Ordem* no. 19; *Samora Machel: African Revolutionary*, ch. 5.

'Organizar a sociadade para vencer o subdesenvolvimento' (February 1982), *Colecçao Estudos e Orientações* no. 14; *Samora Machel: African Revolutionary* ch. 9.

'Rompamos definitivamente com a burguesia para consolidar o poder popular' (22 June 1982), *Colecçao Palavras de Ordem* no. 23.

'O apartheid é o Nazismo da nossa época' (3 March 1983), *Colecçao Palavras de Ordem* no. 24.

'Cada revolucão é uma contribuição para o Marxismo' (11 April 1983), *Notícias*, 14 April 1983; *Samora Machel: African Revolutionary,* ch. 6.

'Nossas estruturas não devem ser refúgio para incompetentes' (24-25 May 1984), *Tempo*, 10 June 1984.

Bibliographies

M. Cahen, 'Publications du Centro de Estudos Africanos de l'Université Eduardo Mondlane', *Politique Africaine*, 5 (1982), pp. 113-15.

M.E. Chonchol, *Guide Bibliographique de Mozambique*, Paris: L'Harmattan, 1979.

C. Darch, *Mozambique* (World Bibliographical Series, vol. 78), Oxford: Clio Press, 1987.

T. Enevoldsen *et al.*, *A Political, Economic and Social Bibliography on Mozambique*, Copenhagen: Centre for Development Research, 1978.

T.L. Eriksen and A. Ofstad, *Bibliography on Mozambique and International Aid*, Bergen: Chr. Michelsen Institute, 1990.

Other books and articles

C. Beitz, 'Sovereignty and Morality in International Affairs' in D. Held (ed.), *Political Theory Today* Cambridge: Polity Press, 1991, pp. 236-54.

R. Bruce Douglas, G.M. Mara and Henry Richardson (eds), *Liberalism and the Good*, London: Routledge, 1990.

C. Clapham, 'The African State' in D. Rimmer (ed.), *Africa Thirty Years On*, pp. 91-104.

J. Clark, *Democratising Development*, London: Earthscan, 1991.

S. Diamond, *Spiritual Warfare: The Politics of the Christian Right*, New York: Black Rose Books, 1990.

S.E. Finer, *Five Constitutions*, Harmondsworth: Penguin, 1979.

Tom Gallagher, *Portugal: A twentieth-century interpretation*, Manchester University Press, 1983.

P. Gibbon, Kjell J. Havnenik and Kenneth Hermele, *A Blighted Harvest: The World Bank and African Agriculture in the 1980s*, London: James Currey, 1993.

P. Hollander, *Political Pilgrims*, New York: Oxford University Press, 1981.

R.D. Jeffries, 'The State, Structural Adjustment and Good Government in Africa', *Journal of Commonwealth and Comparative Politics*, 31, 1 (1993), pp. 20-35.

S. Kaviraj, 'On State, Society and Discourse in India' in J. Manor (ed.), *Rethinking Third World Politics*, Harlow, Longman, 1991, pp. 72-99.

C. Lawson, 'Socialist Relations with the Third World: A case study of the New International Economic Order', *Economics of Planning*, 16, 3 (1980), pp. 148-60.

A. Laroui, *The Crisis of the Arab Intellectual*, Berkeley: University of California Press, 1976.

M. Lewin, *Russian Peasants and Soviet Power*, London: Geo. Allen and Unwin, 1968.

G. Littlejohn, 'Central Planning and Market Relations in Socialist Societies', *Journal of Development Studies*, 24, 4 (1988), pp. 75-101.

J. Lonsdale, 'Political Accountability in African History' in P. Chabal (ed.), *Political Domination in Africa*, Cambridge University Press, 1986, pp. 126-57.

P. Paret, *Clausewitz and the State*, Oxford: Clarendon Press, 1976.

A.J. Polan, *Lenin and the End of Politics*, London: Methuen, 1984.

L. Sanneh, 'Religion and Politics in Africa. A Thematic Approach' in D. Rimmer (ed.), *Africa Thirty Years On*, pp. 105-14.

J. Rawls, 'Justice as Fairness: Political not Metaphysical', *Philosophy and Public Affairs*, 14, 3 (1985), pp. 223-51.

D. Riches (ed.), *The Anthropology of Violence*, Oxford: Basil Blackwell, 1986.

D. Rimmer (ed.), *Africa Thirty Years On*, London: James Currey, 1991.

M. Sandel, 'The Procedural Republic and the Unencumbered Self', *Political Theory*, 12 (1984), pp. 81-96.

I. Shapiro, *The Evolution of Rights in Liberal Theory*, Cambridge University Press, 1986.

C. Taylor, *Sources of the Self*, Cambridge University Press, 1989.

J. Tully, 'Governing Conduct' in E. Leites (ed.), *Conscience and Casuistry in early modern Europe*, Cambridge University Press, 1988, pp. 12-71.

M. Walzer, *Interpretation and Social Criticism*, Cambridge, MA: Harvard University Press, 1987.

S. White, 'What is a communist system?', *Studies in Comparative Communism*, 16, 4 (1983), pp. 247-63.

D. Williams, 'Liberalism and the Development Discourse', *Africa*, 63, 3 (1993), pp. 419-29.

D. Williams and Tom Young, 'Governance, the World Bank and Liberal Theory', *Political Studies*, 42, 1 (1994), pp. 84-100.

INDEX